™

Network

Operating

System for

Business

Computing

System Messages

NOVELL®

NetWare® 3.12

NETWORK COMPUTING PRODUCTS

disclaimer

Novell, Inc. makes no representations or warranties with respect to the contents or use of this manual, and specifically disclaims any express or implied warranties of merchantability or fitness for any particular purpos Further, Novell, Inc. reserves the right to revise this publication and to make changes to its content, at any time, without obligation to notify ar person or entity of such revisions or changes.

Further, Novell, Inc. makes no representations or warranties with respect any NetWare software, and specifically disclaims any express or implied warranties of merchantability or fitness for any particular purpose. Furth Novell, Inc. reserves the right to make changes to any and all parts of NetWare software, at any time, without any obligation to notify any person or entity of such changes.

trademarks

Novell, the N design, and NetWare are registered trademarks of Novell, Ir

For a complete list of all trademarks and their respective owners, see pag 452.

Novell, Inc.
122 East 1700 South
Provo, UT 84606
U.S.A.

NetWare 3.12 System Messages
July 1993
Part Number 100-001716-001

Contents

2 Server Abend Messages

3 Across-the-Wire Migration Error Messages

A Troubleshooting

B Error Codes

Trademarks

How to Use this Manual

Overview

This manual is a reference to system messages generated by the NetWare v3.12 operating system, NetWare utilities, shell software, LAN drivers, and DOS ODI drivers.

This manual is not intended to be used as a diagnostic or troubleshooting guide, but as a reference for understanding error conditions and the actions needed to correct them. It is written for experienced NetWare users. We recommend that any course of action to remedy error conditions be taken by experienced NetWare users only.

Arrangement of the Manual

Most of the messages contained in this book are listed alphabetically.

Messages beginning with numbers or variables are listed in a section before the regularly alphabetized messages. Within this section, the following conventions are used:

- Messages beginning with a number are listed alphabetically from the first alphabetic character in the message, as in the following examples:

  Example 1

  `16 Bit Multiply Failure`

  This message is alphabetized from the word "Bit."

Example 2

`<Filename> has an invalid size`

This message is alphabetized from the word "has."

- Many NetWare numbered error codes (decimal and hexadecimal) are described in Appendix A.

Format of Message Explanations

Each alphabetized message entry is composed of four sections:

- The actual message that you see on your file server console or workstation screen
- The source of the message: the name of the utility (if the message was generated by a utility) or a general entry such as OS (for operating system)
- The explanation of why the message probably occurred
- A recommended course of action to solve the problem that causes the message to appear (most status messages do not require any course of action)

Messages Not Included in This Manual

The majority of the system messages in NetWare v3.12 are documented in this manual. However, because of the complexity of this product, it was not possible to list all of them.

Messages may be generated by DOS (or another client operating system) or by applications running on your network. If you receive a message not listed in this manual, look in the following sources:

- Appendix A of your DOS manual (if you are using DOS)
- Appendixes G and H of Volume 1 of the OS/2 manual (if you are using OS/2)

- The appropriate section of the documentation for whatever operating system you are using
- The manual documenting error messages for the application you are running

Other Resources for Help

Besides this manual, you may want to use the following resources:

- **Context-sensitive help.** If you are using a NetWare menu utility and want more information about how to complete a task, press <F1> for help.

  If you are unsure how to use a command line utility, type the utility name and add the /? option for help. For instance, for help with using the RIGHTS utility, type RIGHTS /?.

- **Novell ElectoText.** The NetWare Communication Services™ viewer allows you to read NetWare manuals from your Windows or OS/2 workstation.

  All NetWare 3.12 manuals except the *Quick Access Guide* are available on the NetWare 3.12 CD-ROM.

- **Hardware manuals.** Many network problems occur because of malfunctioning hardware. If you can isolate a problem to a certain computer component or cable segment, check the manuals that came with the hardware involved.
- **Novell Network Management System (NMS).** This product helps you manage the cabling system, computers, software, and other components of the network. Contact your Novell Authorized Reseller for more information about using NMS on your network.
- **NetWare Application Notes and Research Reports.** These documents cover technical aspects of NetWare-based system design, implementation, and management. Application Notes are a collection of technical articles published monthly.

  Novell publishes *Research Reports* as the research becomes available.

You may purchase subscriptions and back issues of these publications from within the United States or Canada by calling the Novell Research Order Desk at (800) UPDATE1. From outside the United States or Canada, call (801) 429-5380.

- **Third-party books and periodicals.** A number of books on NetWare, including books published by Novell Press, are available at most bookstores. In addition, numerous networking periodicals give advice on configuring, managing, and troubleshooting your network.

- **NetWire on CompuServe.** A fairly inexpensive way to get up-to-date advice and patches is through NetWire on the CompuServe bulletin board. To open a CompuServe account, call one of the following numbers:

  - From within the United States or Canada, call (800) 524-3388.
  - From within the United Kingdom, call 0800-289-378.
  - From within Germany, call 0130-37-32.
  - From the rest of Europe, call 44-272-255-111.
  - From outside of the United States, Canada, and Europe, use the appropriate country code for the U.S. to call (614) 457-0802.

  Ask for "Representative 200." This key phrase simply lets the membership representative know that you are a Novell customer.

- **NetWare Support Encyclopedia.** The NSE program gives customers access to regularly-updated information from Novell and other vendors on products and services. In addition, an NSE Professional Volume is available that provides customers with all of the information in the NSE, plus patches, fixes, and more.

  Both versions of the NSE are distributed on CD-ROM on a subscription basis. Updates are sent out to subscribers several times each year.

  For more information on the NSE, contact your Novell Authorized Reseller.

- **Troubleshooting hardware and software.** Specialized hardware and software packages, such as Novell's LANalyzer, are available to help you isolate network problems.

- **NetWare training.** Many Novell courses are available to help you learn more about NetWare. In addition, you can pursue the title of Certified NetWare Engineer (CNE), Enterprise Certified NetWare Engineer (ECNE), Certified NetWare Administrator (CNA), or Certified NetWare Instructor (CNI) by taking classes and passing tests. For more information on the CNE, ECNE, CNA, and CNI programs, contact Novell's NetWare Technical Institute (NTI) at (512) 794-1795.

- **Customer service.** You may want to contact your Novell Authorized Reseller for technical assistance. Most Novell Authorized Resellers have Certified NetWare Engineers on their staffs ready to assist users with their networking problems.

User Comments

We are continually looking for ways to make our products and our manuals as easy to use as possible. You can help us by sharing your comments and suggestions about how our manuals could be made more useful to you and about any inaccuracies or information gaps they may currently contain.

You can submit your comments either by filling out the "User Comments" form at the end of this manual or by writing to us directly at the following address:

Novell, Inc.
Technical Publications
MS C-23-1
122 East 1700 South
Provo, UT 84606 USA

We sincerely appreciate your comments about our products.

chapter **1** *System Messages in NetWare 3.12*

Nonalphabetized Messages

16 Bit Multiply Failure NETWARE v3.12 CANNOT RUN CORRECTLY ON THIS MACHINE!!! (contact your PC supplier for a new revision 386 microprocessor)

Source OS

Explanation Since NetWare 3.12 uses 16-bit multiplications, it cannot run on machines that do not support this operation. Some early versions of the 80386 chip did not support 16-bit multiplication.

Action Use a 386 machine that will support 16-bit multiplications.

32 Bit Multiply Failure NETWARE v3.12 CANNOT RUN CORRECTLY ON THIS MACHINE!!! (contact your PC supplier for a new revision 386 microprocessor)

Source OS

Explanation Since NetWare 3.12 uses 32-bit multiplications, it cannot run on machines that do not support this operation. Some early versions of the 80386 chip did not support 32-bit multiplication.

Action Use a 386 machine that will support 32-bit multiplications.

<User> cannot be added to the notify list for printer *<printer>*, because the print server is not attached to that file server.

Source PSERVER (.EXE, .NLM, OR .VAP)

Explanation The print server was attached to the file server when the user was added to the notification list, but the print server is not currently attached to the file server.

Action Run PCONSOLE and attach the print server to the file server.

<*Drive name*> **deactivated by driver due to device failure.**

Source: OS Media Manager

Explanation: This is a hardware error that usually generates other messages.

Action: Look for other messages for additional information about the problem. See "Hardware Errors" on page 435 in Appendix A, "Troubleshooting."

<*Drive name*> **deactivated due to driver unload.**

Source: OS Media Manager

Explanation: The specified drive was deactivated because the driver was unloaded.

Action: None. This message is for information only.

<*Drive name*> **deactivated due to hot fix failure.**

Source: OS Media Manager

Explanation: The specified drive was deactivated because of a Hot Fix error.

Action: None. This message is for information only.

<*Drive name*> **deactivated due to media dismount.**

Source: OS Media Manager

Explanation: The specified drive was deactivated because of a media dismount.

Action: None. This message is for information only.

<*Drive name*> **deactivated due to media eject.**

Source: OS Media Manager

Explanation: The specified drive was deactivated because of a media eject.

Action: None. This message is for information only.

<*Drive name*> **deactivated due to server down.**

Source: OS Media Manager

Explanation: The specified drive was deactivated because the server went down.

Action: None. This message is for information only.

<Drive name> **deactivated due to server failure.**

Source OS Media Manager

Explanation The specified drive was deactivated because of a server failure.

Action None. This message is for information only.

<Drive name> **deactivated due to user request.**

Source OS Media Manager

Explanation The specified drive was deactivated at the user's request.

Action None. This message is for information only.

<Drive name> **deactivated for unknown reason.**

Source OS Media Manager

Explanation A hardware error probably occurred, which deactivated the drive.

Action See "Hardware Errors" on page 435 in Appendix A, "Troubleshooting."

<Server>/<volume> **directory size is getting too large for available memory. If the directory grows much larger, you may need to add more memory to the file server.**

Source OS

Explanation The size of the volume directory table has increased since the volume was mounted. The next time this volume is mounted, more memory will be used for the directory tables because a larger hash table will be created.

The system has determined that the amount of memory available in the server is very low, and there may not be enough memory available to mount this volume again

Action See "Insufficient Server Memory Errors" on page 440 in Appendix A, "Troubleshooting."

<Filename> has an invalid size.

Source OS

Explanation This message reports when and how many incomplete packets were received. This problem can result from a defective network board, a malfunctioning LAN driver, or a problem with some other LAN hardware component.

Action See "Hardware Errors" on page 435 in Appendix A, "Troubleshooting."

<Jobname> is not a valid PrintCon job definition.

Source CAPTURE

Explanation You either mistyped the print job name or specified a print job name that has not been defined with the PRINTCON utility for your account. The PRINTCON utility is used to define print job configurations for your account. Job configuration options are usually included in the CAPTURE command.

Action Use the PRINTCON utility to see the names of print jobs defined with your account. Type the name of the print job correctly. Use a different number.

<Servername> NetWare Copyright Violation! Call SUPERVISOR! Server at address *<network address>* also has my serial number.

Source OS

Explanation You have violated the NetWare copyright. It is illegal to use the copy of NetWare running on the specified file server because another file server on the network has the same serial number. All logged-in users will receive this message.

Action Bring down the file server using the illegal copy of NetWare and purchase a valid copy of NetWare to run on the server.

<Servername> TTS shut down because backout volume *<name>* was dismounted

Source OS

Explanation The SYS: volume was dismounted. Since TTS was on this volume, TTS is no longer effective.

Action None. This message is for information only.

<*Module1*>.VLM is not loaded. The <*module2*>.VLM file cannot be loaded before <*module1*>.VLM. Load the <*module1*>.VLM file first then try to load the <*module2*>.VLM file.

Source — VLMs (AUTO, BIND, CONN, FIO, GENERAL, IPXNCP, NDS, NETX, NMR, NWP, PRINT, REDIR, RSA, SECURITY, TRAN)

Explanation — The <*module2*>.VLM requires that the <*module1*>.VLM be loaded first. Either the current configuration has <*module1*>.VLM and <*module2*>.VLM loading out of order, or <*module1*>.VLM did not load successfully.

Action — Make sure that <*module1*>.VLM is configured to load before <*module2*>.VLM. To do this, change the load order of the "VLM=" parameter in the NET.CFG file. For more information about the NET.CFG file, see "Configuring Your DOS Workstation" in *Workstation for DOS and Windows*.

A data stream cannot be opened.

Source — TSA

Explanation — For some reason, the TSA cannot open the specified data stream.

Action — Make sure that you are using a valid data stream name and that the data stream exists. Also make sure that you have appropriate user access rights.

A directory entry with no parent exists in the Directory Entry Table. The Directory Entry Table translation process should proceed normally.

Source — 2XUPGRADE

Explanation — A directory was found without a complete path to it. The directory and its files cannot be accessed.

Action — Do one of the following:

- Reboot the server and run the NetWare v2.1*x* VREPAIR utility; then restart the upgrade. (You may need to run VREPAIR several times until the problem is fixed.)
- Complete the upgrade and run the NetWare v3.1*x* VREPAIR utility afterwards.

A duplicate VLM ID was found during VLM load test. The file will not be loaded. Check the VLM= and USE DEFAULTS= parameter specified in the NET.CFG file before continuing.

Source — VLM.EXE

Explanation — The VLMs for the DOS Requester have been improperly configured to include two VLMs with the same VLM ID. This can be caused by either including a VLM twice in the "VLM=" list, or by a VLM that has attempted to reuse a VLM ID assigned to a different VLM.

Action — Check the NET.CFG file for duplicates in the "VLM=" list. Make sure that the "USE DEFAULTS=" parameter is set to "OFF." See "Configuring Your DOS Workstation" in *Workstation for DOS and Windows* for more information about the NET.CFG file.

A FAT chain has an invalid next link.

Source OS

Explanation A File Allocation Table (FAT) chain is a list of directory block locations. This message indicates that the next link in a FAT chain is invalid. This error probably indicates file system corruption.

If this problem occurs during a volume mount, the operating system will attempt to load VREPAIR to correct the problem.

Action If VREPAIR does not fix the problem, make sure you have a backup of the volume. Delete the volume, re-create it using INSTALL, and restore the data from the backup.

A file cannot be opened.

Source TSA

Explanation For some reason, the TSA cannot open the specified file.

Action Make sure that you are using a valid file name and that the file exists. Also make sure that you have appropriate user access rights.

A file cannot be read.

Source TSA

Explanation The cause for this error is unknown. The file may be corrupted.

Action Try the operation again. If the problem persists, contact your Novell Authorized Reseller.

A file or directory cannot be restored. You are out of disk space.

Source TSA

Explanation Restore cannot continue until you add more disk space.

Action In addition to adding disk space, you may try one or both of the following:

- Restore to another volume with sufficient space.
- Remove unwanted files from the target volume; then try again.

A File Server could not be found.

Source — Shell

Explanation — The shell tried to build a connection with the network, but no file server responded to the request in the given timeout period.

Action — Check the cable connection. Make sure at least one active file server on the network is running. Use "IPX I" to verify that IPX and the network board have the same configuration.

A file server could not be found. Check the network cabling and the server's status before continuing.

Source — VLM.EXE

Explanation — No file server was found when attempting to build an initial connection. This could be caused by one of the following: an improperly configured network board, an improperly configured IPX, a disconnected network cable, or an attempt to load the DOS Requester before a file server has been initialized.

Action — Try one or more of the following:

- Make sure that the network board is properly configured by checking the network board's settings and the NET.CFG file settings. See "Configuring Your DOS Workstation" in *Workstation for DOS and Windows* for more information about the NET.CFG file.

- Make sure that IPX is configured properly to be bound to the correct LAN driver.

- Check the network cabling.

- Make sure a file server is up and running before attempting to load the DOS Requester.

Note: If the server has not been loaded properly, attempting to access an invalid drive from the workstation will attempt to build an initial connection again.

A file with a non-zero length doesn't have a FAT chain.

Source OS

Explanation A File Allocation Table (FAT) chain is a list of directory block locations. This error indicates an invalid file, probably due to corruption.

Action Run VREPAIR. If the problem persists, make sure you have a backup of the volume. Delete the volume, re-create it using INSTALL, and restore the data from the backup.

A file's FAT chain collides with another FAT chain.

Source OS

Explanation The File Allocation Table (FAT) chain is a list of directory block locations. The FAT tables for both files involved are invalid; updates to either file could cause damage to both of them.

Action Run VREPAIR. If the problem persists, make sure you have a backup of the volume. Delete the volume, re-create it using INSTALL, and restore the data from the backup.

A file's FAT chain contains entries out of order.

Source OS

Explanation A File Allocation Table (FAT) chain is a list of directory block locations. The data of the file may not be damaged, but the file is invalid due to the sequence of the data. This error probably indicates file system corruption.

Action Run VREPAIR. If the problem persists, make sure you have a backup of the volume. Delete the volume, re-create it using INSTALL, and restore the data from the backup.

A maximum of 8 volume segments can be created on a single NetWare partition.

Source INSTALL

Explanation You tried to add a ninth disk partition to a mirrored group.

Action Do not try to mirror more than eight disks.

A queue error occurred.

Source NPRINT

Explanation An operating system error involving the queue occurred. A string that was too long was passed to the output formatter.

Action Wait a few minutes and try the command again.

A particular NetWare v2.1*x* or v2.2 bindery value cannot be written to the NetWare v3.1*x* bindery.

Source 2XUPGRADE

Explanation A bindery value read from NetWare v2.1*x*'s NET$BVAL.SYS could not be written to NetWare v3.1*x*'s NET$VAL.SYS. The NetWare v2.1*x* bindery may have been corrupted.

Action At this point, the file system has been upgraded to NetWare v3.1*x*, but it has no bindery. Restore your server to NetWare v2.1*x*, and replace your two bindery files (NET$BIND.SYS and NET$BVAL.SYS) with an uncorrupted version of the bindery from your backups before restarting the upgrade.

A random password cannot be assigned to user *<username>*.

Source 2XUPGRADE

Explanation User passwords cannot be transferred from NetWare v2.1*x*'s bindery to NetWare v3.1*x*'s bindery. An attempt to assign a newly generated password to the user failed. No new password was given to this user.

Action Manually assign users new passwords after the upgrade is completed, using the SYSCON utility from a workstation.

A subdirectory is named PIPE.

Source OS

Explanation "PIPE" is a reserved DOS name. No subdirectories can have this name, or the volume will not mount. In most instances, NetWare will not allow this name to be used.

Action Rename the subdirectory to something else, or contact your Novell Authorized Reseller for suggestions on resolving this problem.

A task switcher has been detected in memory. The VLM.EXE file cannot be loaded under a task switcher. Exit the task switcher; then try again.

Source VLM.EXE

Explanation A task switcher has been loaded. The DOS Requester cannot function properly when loaded after a task switcher. (Task switchers include DR DOS TaskMax, MS DOS 5.0 DOSSHELL, and MS Windows 3.1 in standard mode.)

Action Exit the task switcher before attempting to load the DOS Requester.

A UINT64 value has overflowed.

Source TSA

Explanation A number overflow has occurred. The number is too large for the UINT64 type variable. This error is probably caused by invalid or corrupted data.

Action Contact your Novell Authorized Reseller.

Abort transaction attempted on station *<number>* and could not occur because transactions were disabled

Source OS

Explanation A station requested an "abort transaction" when TTS was not enabled.

Action Determine why TTS is disabled. A preceding message will indicate whether the operating system disabled TTS on its own. Otherwise, TTS may have been disabled at the system console.

Aborted remirror of partition # *<logical partition number>*.

Source OS Media Manager

Explanation The system found the remirroring process to be out of synchronization due to hardware failure. The designated partition cannot be mirrored. Data integrity may be lost for the volumes that reside on the designated partition.

The operating system supports the partition as an unmirrored device. This error may have been caused by a hard disk or channel failure. Another possibility is that the directory was corrupted.

Action — See "Hardware Errors" on page 435 in Appendix A, "Troubleshooting." Also see "Device numbering" in *Concepts* for more information.

Access denied to <*servername*>.

Source — SBACKUP

Explanation — A login attempt to the target server failed.

Action — Make sure that both the username and password for the target server are valid.

Access denied to <*servername*>/<*username*>, password not changed.

Source — SETPASS

Explanation — Access was denied for one of the following reasons:

- Your network supervisor or Workgroup Manager has restricted your account so that you cannot change your password.
- You mistyped your password when prompted to "Enter your old password."

Action — Ask the network supervisor or Workgroup Manager to use SYSCON to remove the account restriction for changing your password. Try the command again and type your old password correctly.

Access has been denied. An invalid user name or authentication was used.

Source — TSA312

Explanation — An invalid authentication has occurred.

Action — Repeat the process; make sure the username and password are correct.

Access to file server <*servername*> denied.

Source — PSERVER (.EXE, .NLM, or .VAP)

Explanation — The print server's name or password was entered incorrectly.

Action — Type the print server's name and password correctly.

Access to server *<servername>* denied.

Source — CAPTURE, MAP

Explanation — You entered your username, your password, or both incorrectly, or you tried to attach to a file server on which you are not defined as a user.

Action — When the utility prompts you for login information, make sure you type your username and password correctly. You can attach to most file servers as GUEST, since user GUEST seldom requires a password.

Access to the server *<servername>* denied.

Source — NPRINT

Explanation — You used NPRINT to print to a file server you were not attached to. You were denied access to the server because you do not have an account on the server, or because your password is invalid.

Action — Either specify a valid password or ask the network supervisor to make you a user on the server.

Account *<servername>*/*<username>* has been locked due to intruder detection.

Source — SETPASS

Explanation — You or someone else tried to log in to your account without supplying the correct password within the allowed number of login attempts. The network supervisor can limit any account on the file server to a specific number of login attempts to protect the account from intrusion by unauthorized persons.

You will not be able to access your account until it has been reopened by the network supervisor.

Action — If you have difficulty typing your password, change it using the SETPASS command.

Account Funds Exhausted

Source — OS

Explanation — The NetWare accounting function for charging user accounts based on credit limit is functional. This message indicates that the user has no balance or has exceeded the balance.

Action — Reset or increase the user's credit limit and balance.

Account has been locked because of intruder detection.

Source VOLINFO

Explanation You or someone else tried to log in to your account without supplying the correct password within the allowed number of login attempts. The network supervisor can limit any account on the file server to a specific number of login attempts to protect the account from intrusion by unauthorized persons.

You will not be able to access your account until it has been reopened by the network supervisor.

Action If you have difficulty typing your password, change it using the SETPASS command.

Account has expired or been disabled by the supervisor.

Source ATTACH, MAP, VOLINFO

Explanation This message could occur for one of the following reasons:

- Your account has expired. The network supervisor can limit your account to a specific period, after which the account will expire and will no longer be accessible.
- Your account has been disabled. The network supervisor can disable your account for any reason.
- You did not type your password correctly. The network supervisor can limit the number of failed attempts to log in to your account.

  In other words, if the maximum number of failed login attempts for your account is three and you type your password incorrectly during four consecutive login attempts, the operating system will consider you an intruder and will disable your account.

Action The network supervisor will have to enable your account before you will be able to access the account again.

Add name space aborted by the user.

Source OS

Explanation After starting installation of a name space, the user opted to discontinue the operation.

Action None. This message is for information only.

Add name space aborted by the user due to insufficient disk space.

Source OS

Explanation There is insufficient disk space to add the desired name space.

Action See "Locked Device Errors" on page 440 in Appendix A, "Troubleshooting."

Add name space aborted due to insufficient server RAM.

Source OS

Explanation There is insufficient memory to add the desired name space.

Action See "Insufficient Server Memory Errors" on page 440 in Appendix A, "Troubleshooting."

AddNameSpace error reading volume header...volume is left in a bad state. *<name>* name space support was NOT added to volume *<name>*

Source OS

Explanation An error occurred when an ADD NAME SPACE command was issued.

Action Run VREPAIR. If the problem persists, make sure you have a backup of the volume. Delete the volume, re-create it using INSTALL, and restore the data from the backup.

All IPX sockets on this machine are already in use by other applications.

Source RPRINTER

Explanation Other applications loaded in the workstation are using all of the defined IPX sockets.

Action Increase the IPX SOCKETS parameter in the NET.CFG file by 10; then reboot the workstation.

All SPX connections in this machine are in use. This application cannot be run, until an active connection has terminated or more SPX connections are allocated.

Source RPRINTER

Explanation Other applications loaded in the workstation are using all defined SPX connections.

Action Increase the SPX CONNECTIONS parameter in the NET.CFG file and reboot the workstation.

An error occurred while the program attempted to write to a file.

Source TSA

Explanation You may not have enough disk space, or the file may be corrupted.

Action Do one or more of the following:

- Check the contents of the file; it may be corrupted.
- Delete unnecessary files from the volume.
- See "Locked Device Errors" on page 440 in Appendix A, "Troubleshooting."

An error was detected in the baud rate, stop bits, parity, etc.

Source RPRINTER

Explanation RPRINTER was unable to initialize the serial port. Either an invalid value was entered in the printer's configuration file or the configuration file is corrupted.

Action Run PCONSOLE and correct the error in the printer's configuration file.

An external SMDR failed to respond to the connection request.

Source SMDR

Explanation You may have typed an invalid SMDR name, or one that is outside your SAP advertising scope and is therefore "invisible."

Visible SMDRs may remain visible somewhat longer than they are available. When you unload a SMDR, it takes a short amount of time before other servers stop "seeing" it.

Also, a loaded SMDR may fail to respond to a connection request if it does not get a time slice on the CPU within the allotted timeout interval.

Action — Make sure that the SMDR is properly loaded; then retry the operation. If the problem persists, contact your Novell Authorized Reseller.

An internal error has occurred. A handle is tagged invalid or the pointer to the handle is null.

Source — SMDR

Explanation — An internal error has occurred in the program. An SMS resource user (SBACKUP, for example) passed corrupted data to an SMS routine. There might be a bug in your software program.

Action — Report the error to the vendor of your SMS-compliant software.

An internal error has occurred. An external SMDR requested a connection that cannot be opened.

Source — SMDR

Explanation — An internal error has occurred in the program. The underlying transport was unable to complete the connection transaction due to a network disruption or failure in the protocol driver (SPXS.NLM, for example).

Action — Retry the operation. If the problem persists, contact your Novell Authorized Reseller.

An internal error has occurred. An invalid parameter was passed.

Source — SMDR

Explanation — An internal error has occurred in the program. An SMS resource user (SBACKUP, for example) passed corrupted data to an SMS routine. There may be a bug in your program.

Action — Report the error to the vendor of your SMS-compliant software.

An internal error has occurred. Either the list has no more entries or the specified name space type does not exist.

Source SMDR

Explanation This error indicates to a developer that all of the name spaces in the data set have been represented and processed to completion by SMS.

Action Report the error to the vendor of your SMS-compliant software.

An internal error has occurred. Insufficient memory is available for SMDR tables. The SMDR will unload.

Source SMDR

Explanation This error may be caused by insufficient memory. When SMS resources (such as TSAs) are loaded on the server, they register with a SMDR. If the SMDR cannot allocate a table to record these registrations, other SMS modules (local or remote) will not be able to access SMS resources.

Action See "Insufficient Server Memory Errors" on page 440 in Appendix A, "Troubleshooting."

An internal error has occurred. No sockets are available for remote communication. The SMDR will unload.

Source SMDR

Explanation This error may be caused by insufficient memory. The SMDR "listens" for remote SMDRs requesting local access, and uses a listening socket in conjunction with the underlying transport. If no sockets are available, the SMDR cannot recognize connection requests.

Action See "Insufficient Server Memory Errors" on page 440 in Appendix A, "Troubleshooting."

An internal error has occurred. One or more of the parameters is null or invalid.

Source SMDR

Explanation An internal error has occurred in the program. An SMS resource user (SBACKUP, for example) passed corrupted data to an SMS routine. There may be a bug in your program.

Action Report the error to the vendor of your SMS-compliant software.

An internal error has occurred. The connection number to a module is invalid.

Source SMDR

Explanation An internal error has occurred in the program. An SMS resource user (SBACKUP, for example) is using an obsolete or damaged connection number. No resources (TSAs, for example) can be accessed through the connection number given.

Action Report the error to the vendor of your SMS-compliant software.

An internal error has occurred. The protocol selected by the redirector is not available.

Source SMDR

Explanation SMS uses proxy TSAs, loaded on the server, to represent workstations to the SMS architecture. When a workstation (Macintosh, DOS, Windows, UNIX, etc.) registers with the appropriate proxy TSA on the server, it gives its name and address and then names the underlying protocol.

When a backup engine connects to the proxy TSA, it assumes it has connected to the actual workstation. However, the proxy TSA informs the backup engine that it is only a proxy, and broadcasts the real workstation address and protocol. At an underlying level, the SMDR disconnects the proxy TSA, and uses the information it has received to attempt to connect to the real workstation.

This error message indicates that the workstation is available only on a protocol not supported by that SMDR, causing the redirection attempt to fail.

Action Replace the SMDR with one that supports the needed protocols; then retry the operation. If the problem persists, contact your Novell Authorized Reseller.

An internal error has occurred. The requested function is not supported.

Source SMDR

Explanation An internal error has occurred. You may have a bad connection. Many SMS routines have a call gate that traps the call if the proper connect routine has not been called first. If this error message appears, it indicates a bug.

Action Report the error to the vendor of your SMS-compliant software.

An internal error has occurred. The SIDF data type is corrupted on overflow.

Source SMDR

Explanation This error indicates corrupted data in the file or in the tape format.

Action Retry the operation. If the problem persists, contact your Novell Authorized Reseller.

An internal error has occurred. The SIDF data type is corrupted on underflow.

Source SMDR

Explanation This error indicates corrupted data in the file or in the tape format.

Action Retry the operation. If the problem persists, contact your Novell Authorized Reseller.

An internal error has occurred. The SMDR encountered an invalid field identifier.

Source SMDR

Explanation This error indicates corrupted data in the file or in the tape format.

Action Retry the operation. If the problem persists, contact your Novell Authorized Reseller.

An internal error has occurred. The SMDR was unable to allocate a listening socket. The SMDR will unload.

Source SMDR

Explanation This error may be caused by insufficient memory. The SMDR "listens" for remote SMDRs requesting local access, and uses a listening socket in conjunction with the underlying transport. If no sockets are available, the SMDR cannot recognize connection requests.

Action See "Insufficient Server Memory Errors" on page 440 in Appendix A, "Troubleshooting."

An internal error has occurred. The SMDR was unable to broadcast a SAP. The SMDR will unload.

Source SMDR

Explanation An internal error has occurred in the program. The SAP protocol failed.

Action Reload the SMDR. Try bringing down the server, then rebooting it. If the problem persists, contact your Novell Authorized Reseller.

An internal error has occurred. The SMDR was unable to provide a thread to service the connection.

Source SMDR

Explanation The SMDR attempts to spin a thread for a new service process for each connection. In this case, the server did not have enough memory.

Action See "Insufficient Server Memory Errors" on page 440 in Appendix A, "Troubleshooting."

An internal error has occurred. The TLI transport underlying SMS has failed.

Source SMDR

Explanation An internal error has occurred in the TLI transport for the SMDR. The likelihood of this error occurring increases as the number of hops between servers increases. The reason for the failure is internal to the supported protocol (SPX, TCP/IP, or ADSP). Heavy traffic can also contribute to the difficulty.

Action Run the backup or restore on a server closer to the target, during off hours. If the problem persists, contact your Novell Authorized Reseller.

An invalid command line parameter was encountered.

Source 2XUPGRADE

Explanation An unrecognized command line parameter was entered. Valid command line parameters include /B, /H, /?, /P, and /R. Parameters are not case sensitive.

Action Check for typographical errors and try again.

An invalid command line parameter was specified.

Source VLM.EXE

Explanation The VLM.EXE file was loaded with an invalid command line parameter.

Action Run the VLM.EXE file with the /? parameter (type "VLM /?") to display the valid parameters; then load the VLM.EXE file with a valid command line parameter.

An invalid connection handle was passed.

Source TSA

Explanation Your connection may no longer be valid.

Action Check your connection, then restart.

An invalid data stream was found for *<data set name>*, data set type *<type>*.

Source TSA

Explanation A data stream is invalid for the indicated data set and type.

Action Specify a valid data stream type. Also make sure the requested name space is supported on this volume.

An invalid file type was used.

Source SBACKUP

Explanation SBACKUP has an invalid filename.

Action Check the syntax of the filename for the specified name space. The filename must be complete and contain no "wildcard" characters (for example, * and ?).

An invalid or inactive TSA was specified.

Source TSA

Explanation A TSA was specified that cannot be found.

Action Make sure the TSA you want is valid and active. If it is not loaded, load it and try again.

An invalid path was used.

Source TSA

Explanation The path is invalid for the specified name space.

Action Make sure the path is valid for the specified name space. Also make sure that you have appropriate user access rights.

An older version of the shell is loaded. The NetWare Requester for DOS cannot be loaded. Unload the shell; then load the NetWare Requester for DOS files.

Source CONN.VLM

Explanation The DOS Requester cannot be loaded with the NetWare shell. The NetWare shell has been loaded in your machine. For NetWare shell compatibility, use NETX.VLM rather than loading the NetWare shell.

Action Type NETX /U to unload the NetWare shell. If the version of the NetWare shell in use does not support the /U parameter, reboot the machine without loading the NetWare shell.

See "Configuring Your DOS Workstation" in *Workstation for DOS and Windows* for more information.

An unknown flag <*flag*> was encountered.

Source CAPTURE

Explanation You either mistyped the flag or specified an invalid flag (option) in your command.

Action Type the flag (option) correctly in your command.

An unknown queue error occurred.

Source NPRINT

Explanation The file server encountered a condition that NPRINT has not accounted for. This is not necessarily a fatal error.

Action Wait a few minutes, then try the command again.

An unknown switch (<*option*>) was found on the command line.

Source NCOPY

Explanation You used an invalid option in your command.

Action Specify a valid option in the command. See "NCOPY" in *Utilities Reference* for a list of valid options.

Attempt to access FAT entry <*number*> and the highest FAT entry is <*number*>.

Source INSTALL

Explanation An internal system error has occurred. The installation process has terminated prematurely, and INSTALL will be unloaded.

Action Try again. If the problem persists, contact your Novell Authorized Reseller.

Attempt to allocate memory to hold NetWare partition information failed.

Source OS

Explanation The file server does not have enough memory to hold partition information.

Action See "Insufficient Server Memory Errors" on page 440 in Appendix A, "Troubleshooting."

Attempt to allocate memory to read volume definition tables failed.

Source OS

Explanation The file server does not have enough memory to mount the volume.

Action See "Insufficient Server Memory Errors" on page 440 in Appendix A, "Troubleshooting."

Attempt to assign a FAT block to an unreachable block.

Source INSTALL

Explanation An internal system error has occurred. The installation process has terminated prematurely, and INSTALL will be unloaded.

Action Try again. If the problem persists, contact your Novell Authorized Reseller.

Attempt to bind (or unbind) *<name>* LAN protocol to *<name>* failed. (error=*<number>*)

Source OS

Explanation A text string should appear before this error, indicating what went wrong during the BIND (or UNBIND) process.

Action Look up the message that appeared before this message for additional help.

Attempt to expand the mounted volume tables returned error *<number>*.

Source INSTALL

Explanation INSTALL could not write to the disk or allocate memory to expand the volume FAT and directory tables.

Action See "General Disk I/O Errors" on page 438 and "Insufficient Server Memory Errors" on page 440 in Appendix A, "Troubleshooting."

Attempt to reinitialize re-entrant module FAILED

Source OS

Explanation The LOAD command was used to load an NLM that has already been loaded. As a result, the existing code image was used reentrantly. An error occurred while the operating system was reinitializing the module.

Action Complete one or more of the following:

- Check the configuration information given on the command line. The hardware configuration information specified for the second LOAD command may have been invalid.
- Check the hardware. Make sure that the board is properly seated. The hardware may not be responding. See "Hardware Errors" on page 435 in Appendix A, "Troubleshooting."

Attempting to attach to server *<servername>* during an unauthorized time period. The supervisor has limited the time that this user account can be accessed.

Source CAPTURE, NPRINT

Explanation The network supervisor of the specified file server has set specific time periods when you can use the file server. You cannot use the file server until the next authorized time period.

Action Ask the network supervisor for a list of authorized time periods.

Attempting to login during an unauthorized time period.

Source ATTACH, MAP

Explanation The network supervisor has set specific time periods when you can use the file server. You cannot use the file server until the next authorized time period.

Action Ask the network supervisor for a list of authorized time periods.

Attempting to login from an unapproved station.

Source ATTACH, MAP

Explanation You tried to access an account from an unauthorized workstation. A network supervisor can restrict an account to one or more particular workstations from which users can access the account.

Action Use only authorized workstations to access the account.

Attempting to simultaneously login from too many workstations.

Source ATTACH, LOGIN, MAP

Explanation You could not log in for one of the following reasons:

- You could not log in to the file server because you are already logged in to the file server from the maximum allowable number of workstations.

  The network supervisor can limit the maximum number of workstations from which you can log in to your account. In this case, you have used the maximum number of workstations from which you can log in to your account. You will have to log out of a workstation before you can log in from another workstation.

- You could not log in to the user account because the account is currently being used by the maximum allowable number of users. You will have to wait for a user to log out from this account before you can log in.

  The network supervisor can limit the number of users who can be concurrently logged in to any particular user account. For example, the supervisor can limit the GUEST account to a maximum of five concurrent connections.

Action — In either case, the account you are trying to log in to is already being accessed by the maximum number of workstations or users. A user will have to log out from the account before you can log in.

Audit file write error, volume: *<name>*.

Source — OS

Explanation — The operating system encountered an error when attempting to write to the audit file. The file system may be failing.

Action — See "General Disk I/O Errors" on page 438 and "Hardware Errors" on page 435 in Appendix A, "Troubleshooting."

Auditing disabled, cannot open valid audit configuration file, volume: *<name>*.

Source — OS

Explanation — The operating system disabled auditing for the indicated volume because the configuration file is an old version or is corrupted.

Action — Delete the old audit files.

B

Bad local network address.

Source — Shell

Explanation — The 6-byte network address in the request header was invalid. The server may be down, or the bridge's routers may be corrupted.

Action — Check the file server status and bridge connections. Run RESET ROUTER on each file server to build new routing tables. Run SLIST to view a list of currently broadcasting file servers and bridges.

Bad session ID encountered on the backup media cartridge. The session ID in the data field didn't match the expected session ID. Either the data is corrupt or the data file was renamed.

Source — SBACKUP

Explanation — The session ID on the media does not match the session log filename.

Action — Use the "Restore without session files" option.

Batch file missing

Source — DOS

Explanation — This is a DOS error message. If you are using remote boot, DOS could not find a copy of the AUTOEXEC.BAT file. DOS needs a copy of the AUTOEXEC.BAT file in the SYS:LOGIN directory and in the default directory listed in the login script.

Action — Copy the AUTOEXEC.BAT file to the SYS:LOGIN directory of all file servers on the network and to the default directory listed in the login script.

Battery discharge time has almost expired. The file server will be shut down in one minute unless commercial power is restored.

Source — UPS

Explanation — The server has been running on battery power too long; it will be brought down in one minute unless line power is restored.

Action Have all users save open files and log out from the server immediately; otherwise, the users will be logged out automatically. Then bring down the file server.

Note: Be sure to turn off the power switches on the file server and its monitor, disks, and any other electronic equipment on the affected electrical circuits to avoid damage from voltage transients when the line power comes back on. Files that were not saved properly may be lost or damaged.

Bindery open requested by the SERVER failed. The bindery volume is not mounted

Source OS

Explanation If volume SYS: does not mount, this informational message is displayed at the server console.

Action Try to mount volume SYS: again. If it doesn't mount, run VREPAIR and try again.

Bindery open requested by user *<name>* on station *<number>* failed. The bindery volume is not mounted

Source OS

Explanation If volume SYS: does not mount and the station number is not equal to zero, this informational message is displayed at the server console.

Action Try to mount volume SYS: again. If it doesn't mount, run VREPAIR and try again.

Block *<number>* is an invalid block number for volume *<name>*.

Source INSTALL

Explanation An internal system error has occurred. The installation process has terminated prematurely, and INSTALL will be unloaded.

Action Try again. If the problem persists, contact your Novell Authorized Reseller.

Block allocation size does not match

Source OS

Explanation Two segments of the volume claim different block allocation sizes. This error could be caused by one of the following:

- Two volumes on the file server have identical names, and a segment from each volume is causing the error.
- The volume is corrupted.

Action If you have two volumes with the same name, unload the disk driver for the volume that you do not want to rename. Rename the other volume (the volume that is on the hard disk that still has its disk driver loaded). Then load the disk driver that you just unloaded. Mount both volumes.

If the volume is corrupted, run VREPAIR. If the volume cannot be fixed, run INSTALL, delete the volume, and re-create it.

Note: If you delete the volume, all data will be destroyed. You will have to restore the data from a backup.

Btrieve error *<number>* while executing function *<number>*.

Source INSTALL

Explanation INSTALL received an error from Btrieve.

Action Look up the error in a Btrieve manual and take appropriate action, or contact your Novell Authorized Reseller.

Cache memory allocator exceeded minimum cache buffer left limit.

Source OS

Explanation The SET server utility's "Minimum File Cache Buffers" and "Minimum Directory Cache Buffers" parameters limit the minimum number of cache buffers for the system. The default minimum for both parameters is 20 buffers.

This error occurs when other areas of the server attempt to allocate more memory and only the minimum number of cache buffers is left. System performance may be degraded. The subsystem that requested additional memory will not be able to perform the requested action because the required memory was not available.

Action See "Insufficient Server Memory Errors" on page 440 in Appendix A, "Troubleshooting."

Cache memory allocator out of available memory.

Source OS

Explanation All cache memory has been used. System performance is severely degraded. This error occurs when the NetWare operating system tries to allocate a cache buffer and the remaining number of buffers is less than the System Cache Limit. The default value is 20 buffers.

Action See "Insufficient Server Memory Errors" on page 440 in Appendix A, "Troubleshooting."

Cannot append to empty media, will create new media set.

Source SBACKUP

Explanation An append was requested on media having no label or a label that cannot be read. If the media has been used previously, an error has occurred reading the media header, indicating that the media could be damaged.

Action If the media has not been used previously, restart without the append option. If the media has been used, service the device and inspect the media for damage.

Cannot concatenate a data set name *<name>* and *<name>*!

Source SBACKUP

Explanation SBACKUP cannot concatenate the specified names. The names may have invalid lengths, or you may not have enough server memory.

Action Make sure that the names are within valid length range. If you suspect insufficient memory, see "Insufficient Server Memory Errors" on page 440 in Appendix A, "Troubleshooting."

If the problem persists, try adding more memory to the server. You should have a minimum of 8 MB of RAM on the server.

Cannot connect to the print server *<print server>*.

Source PSC

Explanation The print server did not respond to the request.

Action If the print server is a nondedicated print server, unload it and then reload it. If it is a dedicated print server, try rebooting. Check all connections and cabling.

Cannot create the path *<path>*.

Source SBACKUP

Explanation SBACKUP cannot create the specified directory path.

Action Make sure that the volume and directories specified in the path exist, and that you have rights to create the specified directory path.

Cannot get connection numbers for user *<servername>/<username>*.

Source SEND

Explanation An error occurred when SEND tried to obtain the connection number for the server or user.

Action Try again.

Cannot get connection status (<*number*>)

Source ATTACH

Explanation The ATTACH utility was unable to get the connection status from the file server.

Action Try again.

Cannot get name space type information. <*name space type*>.

Source SBACKUP

Explanation SBACKUP could not get the name space information for the specified name space.

Action Make sure that name spaces are supported on the volume, and that name space driver NLMs are loaded.

Cannot get the information about the specified form.

Source NPRINT

Explanation The form definition that you specified in your command exists, but a network error prevented NPRINT from obtaining the form information.

Action Wait a few minutes, then try again.

Cannot open audit data file. Enter volume audit password to mount with auditing disabled. Enter password:

Source OS

Explanation The auditing system could not open the audit data file because the audit file has been corrupted or accidently deleted.

Action Follow the directions after the message. In most instances, the system can continue operation if the auditor's password is entered. This will result in the system working with auditing disabled.

If the system does not continue, reboot the server. If all troubleshooting remedies fail, contact your Novell Authorized Reseller.

Cannot read mirror Directory entry.

Source INSTALL

Explanation An error occurred when the program attempted to read a volume.

Action See of "Volume I/O Errors" on page 441 in Appendix A, "Troubleshooting."

Cannot read mirror FAT entry.

Source INSTALL

Explanation INSTALL could not read from the volume.

Action See "Volume I/O Errors" on page 441 in Appendix A, "Troubleshooting."

Cannot read primary Directory entry.

Source INSTALL

Explanation INSTALL could not read from the volume.

Action See "Volume I/O Errors" on page 441 in Appendix A, "Troubleshooting."

Cannot read primary FAT entry.

Source INSTALL

Explanation INSTALL could not read from the volume.

Action See "Volume I/O Errors" on page 441 in Appendix A, "Troubleshooting."

Cannot separate a data set name <*name*>!

Source SBACKUP

Explanation SBACKUP cannot recognize a data set name (probably a file or directory) in the specified path.

Action Make sure that the specified path conforms to syntax requirements for the specified name space.

Can't get status, error *<value>* returned.

Source PSC

Explanation The print server was unable to determine the status of the printer.

Action Try again. If the error reoccurs repeatedly, record the error value and contact your Novell Authorized Reseller.

Capture requires a 2.10 or later shell in order to work.

Source CAPTURE

Explanation You tried to use the CAPTURE command on a workstation using a NetWare shell earlier than v2.1.

Action Ask your network supervisor to generate a NetWare shell (v2.1 or later) for your workstation.

CheckAndAddHardware could not allocate a resource tag

Source OS

Explanation The loadable module made a call to a NetWare v3.0 API. The operating system tried to allocate memory for the resource, but it does not have enough memory.

Action See "Insufficient Server Memory Errors" on page 440 in Appendix A, "Troubleshooting."

Commercial power has failed. Server *<servername>* is running on battery power. Server *<servername>* will stay up for *<n>* minutes. Prepare users to logout.

Source UPS

Explanation Commercial power has failed, and the server is running off the battery.

Action Have users save open files and log out within the next *<n>* minutes, or the users will be logged out automatically.

Note: Be sure to turn off the power switches on the file server and its monitor, disks, and any other electronic equipment on the affected electrical circuits to avoid damage from voltage transients when the line power comes on. Files that were not saved properly may be lost or damaged.

Connector is BNC.

Source 3C503.COM

Explanation The connector selected for the board is for thin Ethernet cabling.

Action None. This message is for information only.

Connector is DIX.

Source 3C503.COM

Explanation The connector selected for the board is for thick Ethernet cabling.

Action None. This message is for information only.

Control characters found in command line.

Source NPRINT

Explanation You may have accidentally typed a character while you were pressing the Control key. This will produce a "control character." Control characters such as ^C and ^E are special characters used for formatting text in word processors, controlling printers, transmitting data, etc. These characters should not be included in commands.

Action Retype your command.

Control characters not allowed in command.

Source ATTACH, FLAGDIR, LOGIN, MAP, PAUDIT, SETPASS, SLIST, WHOAMI

Explanation You may have accidentally typed a character while you were pressing the Control key. This will produce a "control character." Control characters such as ^C and ^E are special characters used for formatting text in word processors, controlling printers, transmitting data, etc. These characters should not be included in commands.

Action Retype your command.

Could not allocate enough memory for internal tables.

Source SEND

Explanation Your workstation does not have enough free memory to execute the SEND command.

Action Reboot your workstation to clear out any memory-resident programs, and then log in again. If this does not work, you will have to install more memory in your workstation.

Could not execute external program "<*name*>", not enough memory.

Source LOGIN

Explanation Your workstation does not have enough memory to run a transient command contained in your login script. A transient command is one that is external to the login script. See the explanation for the "# (Execute External Program)" command in *Installation and Upgrade.*

Action See "Insufficient Workstation Memory Errors" on page 442 in Appendix A, "Troubleshooting."

Could not parse specified path. (Error <*number*>)

Source GRANT

Explanation A network error prevented GRANT from obtaining information about the path.

Action Make sure the file server is still running, and try again. If the problem persists, record the error number and contact your Novell Authorized Reseller.

Could not parse specified path. (Error: "<*number*>")

Source RIGHTS

Explanation You specified a network drive that has not been defined.

Action Use the MAP command to check your drive mappings; then try the command again using a defined drive.

Could not redirect block *<number>* on partition *<number>*.

Source OS Media Manager

Explanation This is an alert message indicating a potential device failure and data loss caused by one of the following:

- An I/O error occurred that could not be corrected by Hot Fix. Either no redirection blocks are left or the hard disk is no longer operational.
- Due to insufficient space, the system was unable to redirect data during a Hot Fix operation.

Action Use the messages that follow this message to determine why Hot Fix has failed. See "General Disk I/O Errors" on page 438 and "Locked Device Errors" on page 440 in Appendix A, "Troubleshooting."

Could not route to File Server.

Source Shell

Explanation The 12-byte address in the request header was invalid. The server may be down, or the bridge's routers may be corrupted.

Action Check file server status and bridge connections. Run RESET ROUTER on each file server to build new routing tables. Run SLIST to view a list of currently broadcasting file servers and bridges.

CreateProcess called with stack size too small.

Source OS

Explanation The system tried to load an NLM that allocated an inadequate amount of stack space for itself. The NLM is either outdated or corrupted.

Action Try reloading the NLM from its original media and try again. If the problem persists, contact the vendor for an updated version of the NLM.

CreateProcess could not allocate a process control block.

Source OS

Explanation The system does not have enough memory to start a new process. The request to create a new process may have been internal to the server or generated by an NLM. If this error occurs while the system is attempting to load an NLM, the NLM will not be able to load and run properly.

Action See "Insufficient Server Memory Errors" on page 440 in Appendix A, "Troubleshooting."

D

DCB Message: Found Devices during Scan, but could not get them to respond

Source DCB

Explanation Either of the following has occurred:

- The DCB has been used with different hard disks, and the EEPROM table does not match the hard disks that are now attached to the DCB.
- You have more than one subsystem attached to the DCB. The driver was able to locate the hard disks on one subsystem, but failed to locate the hard disks on the other system.

Action Complete one of the following:

- If you have attached different hard disks to the DCB, run DISKSET and reconfigure the EEPROM to match the attached disks.
- If you have more than one subsystem, check the subsystems' power supplies. Make sure the power is turned on and that all hard drives are connected to a power supply.

Definition for sync *<number>* of volume *<name>* removed.

Source OS, INSTALL

Explanation While checking a volume definition during mounting of the volume, the operating system discarded an unneeded synchronization value.

Action None. This message is for information only.

Definition for volume *<name>* is invalid.

Source OS, INSTALL

Explanation While mounting one or more volumes, the operating system found an invalid definition for the specified volume.

Action None. This message is for information only.

Delete Inhibit is valid only on NetWare 386.

Source FLAGDIR

Explanation The Delete Inhibit attribute is supported in NetWare v3.*x* and later.

Action Use the Delete Inhibit attribute on file servers running NetWare v3.*x* and later.

DeleteFileToLimbo failed, unable to save migrated file (<*path*>).

Source OS

Explanation This is probably an internal program error.

Action Retry the operation. If the problem persists, contact your Novell Authorized Reseller.

Directory <*dir*> not found.

Source FLAGDIR

Explanation The directory specified on the command line was not found.

Action Retype the command, specifying a valid directory.

Directory block is inconsistent...has several Subdirectory numbers.

Source OS

Explanation The volume's directory tables have been corrupted. Upon initialization, the subdirectory number vector table should contain a value of -1 (which is then changed to a 0).

If the value residing in the table is not equal to -1 or 0, the volume mount is aborted and all resources are returned to the system. In this case, the table contained a different value.

Action Run VREPAIR and restart system. If the problem persists, make sure you have a backup of the volume. Delete the volume, re-create it using INSTALL, and restore the data from the backup.

Directory FAT chain has a hole.

Source OS

Explanation A File Allocation Table (FAT) chain is a list of directory block locations. If the FAT chain skips a block, a hole appears in the chain.

(A hole is a section that is not sequential.) A hole indicates that the location was never allocated.

This message indicates that while a volume was being initialized, a directory volume structure initialization routine found that the FAT was not sequential. The FAT value did not match the directory length. The volume mount was aborted and all resources were returned. This error probably indicates corruption.

Action — Run VREPAIR and restart the system. If the problem persists, make sure you have a backup of the volume. Delete the volume, re-create it using INSTALL, and restore the data from the backup.

Directory is not locatable.

Source — MAP

Explanation — You used an invalid directory name with either an INCLUDE command or a MAP command. If this error occurs when you log in, the incorrect INCLUDE or MAP command is located in your login script.

Action — Do one or both of the following:

- If the error occurs at your network prompt, use the LISTDIR command or the FILER utility to examine the directory structure. Then make sure all directory names in the INCLUDE or MAP command are typed correctly.
- If the message appears when you log in, use the SYSCON utility to access your login script and modify the INCLUDE or MAP command.

Directory rights are not associated with Local drives

Source — LISTDIR

Explanation — You used the Rights flag (option) with the LISTDIR command for a local drive. However, directory rights do not exist for local drives. You can use the LISTDIR command to view the directory structure of local drives, but you cannot use the Rights flag (option).

Action — Use the Rights flag for network drives only.

Directory table 0's first block does not match

Source OS, INSTALL

Explanation Two segments of the volume claim a different first block for Directory table 0. This error could be caused by one of the following:

- Two volumes mounted on the file server have identical names, and a segment from each volume is causing the error.
- The volume is corrupted.

Action If you have two volumes with the same name, unload the disk driver for the volume that you do not want to rename. Rename the other volume (the volume that is on the hard disk that still has its disk driver loaded). Then load the disk driver that you just unloaded. Mount both volumes.

If the volume is corrupted, run VREPAIR. If the volume cannot be fixed, backu up the volume. Then run INSTALL, delete the volume, and re-create it.

Directory table 1's first block does not match

Source OS, INSTALL

Explanation Two segments of the volume claim a different first block for Directory table 1. This error could be caused by one of the following:

- Two volumes mounted on the file server have identical names, and a segment from each volume is causing the error.
- The volume is corrupted.

Action If you have two volumes with the same name, unload the disk driver for the volume that you do not want to rename. Rename the other volume (the volume that is on the hard disk that still has its disk driver loaded). Then load the disk driver that you just unloaded. Mount both volumes.

If the volume is corrupted, run VREPAIR. If the volume cannot be fixed, back up the volume. Then run INSTALL, delete the volume, and re-create it.

Directory tree is circularly linked.

Source OS

Explanation A directory contains a subdirectory that is also its parent.

Action Run VREPAIR and restart the system. If the problem persists, make sure you have a backup of the volume. Delete the volume, re-create it using INSTALL, and restore the data from the backup.

Directory tree is too deep.

Source OS

Explanation The maximum subdirectory tree depth of 25 levels has been exceeded.

Action Change the SET server utility's "Maximum Subdirectory Tree Depth" parameter to be able to go beyond the default limit of 25. This SET parameter can be set to a maximum of 100 levels. See "SET" in *Utilities Reference* for more information.

Disk #<*disk number*> cannot be opened. Ensure that its disk driver is properly loaded.

Source 2XUPGRADE

Explanation The disk cannot be opened for reads and writes.

Action Make sure that the correct disk drivers have been loaded properly.

Disk Coprocessor Initialization Error: *Could not Detected the DCB Card selected.

Source DCB

Explanation As you were loading the DCB, you selected an I/O port that did not match the I/O port on the DCB that is installed in the file server.

Action Check the configuration of the DCB in the file server, and select the configured I/O port when loading the driver.

Disk Coprocessor Initialization Error: *Hardware Diagnostics have failed.

Source DCB

Explanation The DCB detects no power coming from the drives attached to it. Either the power is not turned on or the power supply has failed.

Action Check the power supply.

Disk I/O read error.

Source NPRINT

Explanation The file server is having hardware problems with disk drives, memory, controller boards, etc.

Action Load MONITOR and check the status of the hard disks.

DisMount timed out waiting for the last buffer to be transferred.

Source SBACKUP

Explanation The last data buffer from SBACKUP could not be read before the dismount function's timeout period expired. You may not have enough server memory, or the device may not be operating properly.

Action Check SBACKUP's error message screen. Make sure that the storage device is operating correctly. If you suspect insufficient memory, see "Insufficient Server Memory Errors" on page 440 in Appendix A, "Troubleshooting." You should have a minimum of 8 MB of RAM on the server.

Does not exist.

Source SBACKUP

Explanation SBACKUP has received a volume name that does not exist on the specified target.

Action Make sure that you have specified an existing volume, and that you have typed the volume name correctly.

DOS is only configured for <*number*> drives, NETX.VLM requires 26 drives for full functionality. The NETX.VLM file will load with partial support. Add LASTDRIVE=Z to the CONFIG.SYS file and reboot the workstation; then load the NETX.VLM file.

Source NETX.VLM

Explanation This message is only a warning. For full NetWare shell compatibility, the LASTDRIVE parameter in the CONFIG.SYS file must be set to Z. Otherwise problems will occur when mapping drives, etc.

Action Add "LASTDRIVE=Z" to the CONFIG.SYS file; then reboot the workstation before loading the DOS Requester.

DOS version is not 3.1 or later. The NetWare Requester for DOS cannot be loaded. Reboot your computer with DOS v3.1 or later; then load the NetWare Requester for DOS files.

Source CONN.VLM

Explanation The DOS Requester requires DOS version 3.1 or later to operate. The current DOS version is not 3.1 or later, so the DOS Requester cannot be loaded.

Action Upgrade the DOS version on your machine to 3.1 or later.

Drive <*drive*> is unusable.

Source INSTALL

Explanation Four attempts were made to read information on the drive, and all failed.

Action See "General Disk I/O Errors" on page 438 in Appendix A, "Troubleshooting."

Drive failed while reading in volume information tables.

Source OS

Explanation The drive containing the volume had a physical failure while the volume information tables were being read.

Action See "Hardware Errors" on page 435 in Appendix A, "Troubleshooting."

Drive is not mapped to network.

Source GRANT

Explanation You entered an invalid drive letter.

Action Use MAP to check your drive mappings, and select a network drive.

Duplicate file names in the same directory.

Source OS

Explanation The operating system encountered a problem while mounting a volume because the directory contains two files with identical names.

Action Complete one or more of the following:

- Check the version of the operating system. Do not run an earlier version of NetWare on a server that has been running a later version. If you need to return the server to an earlier version, run the earlier version's VREPAIR on all volumes, or purge all deleted files.
- Run VREPAIR.
- If the problem persists, make sure you have a backup of the volume. Delete the volume, re-create it using INSTALL, and restore the data from the backup.

Either no more entries are in the list or the name space type does not exist.

Source TSA

Explanation This message is recorded in the error log file.

Action None. This message is for information only.

Either no resource name can be found or all resource names have been found.

Source TSA

Explanation The Scan Target Service Resource function has found all resources, or no resources were found.

Action If you are expecting a resource list, make sure the data set sequence is correct. Then try again.

Either the server is out of memory or memory allocation failed.

Source TSA

Explanation You are out of server memory.

Action See "Insufficient Server Memory Errors" on page 440 in Appendix A, "Troubleshooting."

EMM Error during DEALLOCATE PAGES

Source Expanded memory shell

Explanation Any of the following could cause this error:

- The handle used to deallocate EMM was corrupted.
- The Expanded Memory Manager cannot release the memory.
- You are using a different copy of the shell to unload the shell than was used to load the shell.

Action Do one of the following:

- Check the Expanded Memory Manager state to ensure that it is working properly. (See the vendor's documentation.)
- Make sure the copy of the shell being used to unload the shell is the same copy that was used to load the shell.

EMM Shell Error: <*number*>h during EMM function <*number*>h

Source Expanded memory shell

Explanation The expanded memory shell relies on an Expanded Memory Manager (EMM) driver to handle expanded memory input/output. This messages appears when the EMM driver returns an error during one of the shell requests.

Action Check the Expanded Memory Manager state to ensure that it is working properly. (See the vendor's documentation.) If the problem persists, record the error numbers and contact your Novell Authorized Reseller.

Endcap requires NetWare 2.10 or higher in order to work.

Source ENDCAP

Explanation You tried to use the ENDCAP command on a workstation using a NetWare shell earlier than v2.1.

Action Ask your network supervisor to generate a NetWare shell (v2.1 or later) for your workstation.

ENTRY STACK SIZE too small.

Source Shell

Explanation The shell attempted to preserve a page mapping on its internal stack, but the shell has run out of room. This may occur when other programs that are using expanded memory place a heavy load on the shell for interrupt requests. Such a load causes the shell to be reentered.

Action Increase the "ENTRY STACK SIZE" parameter in the NET.CFG file. The default is 10; the maximum is 255.

Error *<code>* **closing** *<file>*. **An error occurred attempting to close a file. Processing will continue.**

Source	SBACKUP
Explanation	The indicated file could not be closed, but the backup session is continuing. The file or volume may be corrupted.
Action	After the backup finishes, check the session and error files. Repeat the backup procedure on any files that were not backed up.

Error *<code>* **deleting** *<file>*. **An error occurred while attempting to delete the error file. Most likely, you have insufficient rights or file attributes are set that don't allow file deletion.**

Source	SBACKUP
Explanation	You may have specified an invalid filename, the file may not exist, or you may not have rights to delete the file.
Action	Make sure you have specified a valid filename, that the file exists, and that you have user access rights.

Error *<code>* **dismounting media.** *<media label>*.

Source	SBACKUP
Explanation	SBACKUP cannot dismount the media.
Action	Check for media already in the device. If none is present, make sure that the device is operating properly.

Error *<code>* **mounting media.** *<media label>*.

Source	SBACKUP
Explanation	SBACKUP is unable to mount a media in the selected device. Another media may already be in the device.
Action	Check for media in the device. Insert media if none are found, or select another device.

Error #*<code>* occurred during an attempt to get information about server "*<servername>*".

Source CAPTURE

Explanation A network error prevented CAPTURE from getting information about the file server.

Action Make sure the file server is still running, and try again. If the problem persists, contact your Novell Authorized Reseller.

Error *<code>* occurred while creating a portal.

Source SBACKUP

Explanation SBACKUP cannot create the requested portion of the user screen. The backup process cannot continue.

Action See "Insufficient Server Memory Errors" on page 440 in Appendix A, "Troubleshooting." You should have a minimum of 8 MB of RAM on the server.

Error *<code>* opening *<filename>*. An error occurred attempting to open a file. SBACKUP will try to recover from this error.

Source SBACKUP

Explanation You may have specified an invalid filename, or you may not have access rights to the file.

Action Make sure that the file exists, that you have user access rights, and that appropriate file access flags have been set.

Error *<code>* opening directory *<name>*.

Source SBACKUP

Explanation The specified directory in the directory selection list could not be opened. The directory may not exist, or you may not have rights to the directory.

Action Verify that the specified directory exists and that you have access rights.

Error *<code>* reading from a file.

Source SBACKUP

Explanation The program could not completely read the file. The file may be corrupted.

Action Check the integrity of the file and volume.

Error *<code>* reading from media, *<number>* sectors requested, *<number>* sectors not read.

Source SBACKUP

Explanation The media could not be read, possibly due to a media defect or device failure.

Action Make sure that the device is functioning properly and that the media is not corrupted.

Error *<value>* returned.

Source PSC

Explanation An error occurred that PSC could not correct.

Action Try again. If this fails, reboot the print server. If the problem persists, record the *<value>* and contact your Novell Authorized Reseller.

Error *<code>* returned from GetServerInformation.

Source SBACKUP

Explanation The program was unable to read the file server configuration information, including the list of mounted volumes.

Action Exit SBACKUP and restart the backup process. If the error occurs again, test the server for correct operation and configuration. If the problem persists, contact your Novell Authorized Reseller.

Error *<code>* seeking in *<filename>*. An attempt was made to seek within a file and the attempt failed.

Source SBACKUP

Explanation An error prevented the program from completing the seek process within the indicated file.

Action Make sure that the file exists and that it is not corrupted.

Error (*<code>*) was returned from "*<function>*", while attempting to initialize the remote printer.

Source RPRINTER

Explanation The print server returned an error that RPRINTER has not accounted for. This error prevented the remote printer from initializing.

Action Try again. If the problem persists, record the error number and the function, and contact your Novell Authorized Reseller.

Error *<code>* writing to media, *<number>* sectors requested, *<number>* sectors not written. An attempt was made to write to the specified media, but the attempt failed.

Source SBACKUP

Explanation This is a media write error, or a possible media or device failure.

Action Make sure that the device is functioning properly and that the media is not corrupted.

Error allocating a directory entry to add a name space root.

Source OS

Explanation The system tried to add a name space root and failed. The AllocateDirectoryEntry routine found there were no available directory entries in the subdirectory, so the system tried to extend it.

This attempt failed because there were either too many directory blocks, or because there was not enough memory for the volume's directory tables.

Action See "Insufficient Server Memory Errors" on page 440 in Appendix A, "Troubleshooting."

Error allocating Hi Memory Area (HMA): HMA already in use

Source: Extended Memory Shell

Explanation: The extended memory driver (XMS driver) has already allocated the high memory area (HMA) to another program.

Action: If you want to use the extended memory shell, unload the other program.

Error allocating Hi Memory Area (HMA): unknown error code

Source: Extended Memory Shell

Explanation: The extended memory driver (XMS driver) returned an invalid error code.

Action: Check the installation of the XMS driver. Consult the reference guide for the XMS driver. If the problem persists, contact the vendor of the XMS driver.

Error allocating Hi Memory Area (HMA):VDisk detected

Source: Extended Memory Shell

Explanation: The extended memory driver (XMS driver) detected a virtual disk driver (VDISK.SYS) in use; the XMS driver is not compatible with the VDISK.SYS driver. The VDISK.SYS currently distributed by IBM is not compatible with Microsoft's HIMEM.SYS (XMS v2.0 driver).

Action: Use a VDISK.SYS driver and an XMS v2.0 driver that are compatible.

Error allocating Hi Memory Area (HMA): XMS driver /HMAMIN= parameter too high

Source: Extended Memory Shell

Explanation: The minimum usage parameter in the extended memory driver (XMS driver) has been set too high for the high memory area.

Action: Reduce the minimum usage parameter in the XMS driver.

Error allocating memory for disk initialization.

Source: OS

Explanation: Upon initialization of the disk, the allocation of permanent memory for the disk was checked and found to be null.

Action See “Insufficient Server Memory Errors” on page 440 in Appendix A, “Troubleshooting.”

Error allocating memory for Directory Table.

Source INSTALL

Explanation The server does not have enough memory.

Action See “Insufficient Server Memory Errors” on page 440 in Appendix A, “Troubleshooting.”

Error allocating memory for FAT Table.

Source INSTALL

Explanation The server does not have enough memory.

Action See “Insufficient Server Memory Errors” on page 440 in Appendix A, “Troubleshooting.”

Error allocating new entry on NameSpace upgrade...volume is left in a bad state. *<name>* name space support was NOT added to volume *<name>*

Source OS

Explanation An error occurred when an ADD NAME SPACE command was issued.

Action Run VREPAIR. You may need to use the “Remove All Name Space Entries” option.

Error: Control characters not allowed in the command line.

Source TLIST

Explanation You may have accidentally typed a character while you were pressing the Control key. This will produce a “control character.” Control characters such as ^C and ^E are special characters used for formatting text in word processors, controlling printers, transmitting data, etc. These characters should not be included in commands.

Action Retype your command.

Error copying file.

Source NCOPY

Explanation A network error prevented NCOPY from copying the file.

Action Make sure the source and destination filenames are valid, and try again. If the problem persists, contact your Novell Authorized Reseller.

Error creating TTS backout file.

Source OS

Explanation You may not have enough space on the volume to create the Transaction Tracking System (TTS) backout file.

Action Try adding another drive to the backout volume, deleting or compressing existing files on the backout volume, or moving files from the backout volume to another volume. (Increasing disk space on volumes other than the backout volume probably will not help.)

Error deleting trustee.

Source REMOVE

Explanation This message indicates a shortage of dynamic memory or problems with the system bindery. The system bindery contains the names of users, their rights, file servers to which they are attached, etc.

Action Notify the network supervisor. The network supervisor may have to increase the file server's memory or run BINDFIX to repair the system bindery.

Error: Drive not mapped to Network.

Source REMOVE, REVOKE

Explanation The drive specified in your command is not mapped to a network directory.

Action Use the MAP command to display your network drives. Then try the command again.

Error during ALLOCATE PAGES.
**** EMM Error:** *<number>* **during EMM function** *<number>*.

Source: Expanded Memory Shell

Explanation: During the initialization of the expanded memory shell, the shell must allocate expanded memory pages for the expanded memory portion of the shell. This message indicates that the Expanded Memory Manager responded with an error when the shell made a request for memory pages.

Action: Check the Expanded Memory Manager state to ensure that it is working properly. If the problem persists, record the error numbers in the message and contact your Novell Authorized Reseller.

Error during GET SIZE OF PARTIAL PAGE.
**** EMM Error:** *<number>* **during EMM function** *<number>*.

Source: Expanded Memory Shell

Explanation: During initialization of the expanded memory shell, the shell must determine how much memory to allocate for the page mapping array. This message indicates that the Expanded Memory Manager responded with an error when the shell asked for memory information.

Action: Check the Expanded Memory Manager state to ensure that it is working properly. If the problem persists, record the error numbers in the message and contact your Novell Authorized Reseller.

Error during MAP MULTIPLE PAGES.
**** EMM Error:** *<number>* **during EMM function** *<number>*.

Source: Expanded Memory Shell

Explanation: During the initialization of the expanded memory shell, the shell must map its allocated expanded memory pages into the expanded memory page frame. This message indicates that the Expanded Memory Manager responded with an error when the shell tried to map its memory pages.

Action: Check the Expanded Memory Manager state to ensure that it is working properly. If the problem persists, record the error numbers in the message and contact your Novell Authorized Reseller.

Error during MOVE MEMORY REGION.
EMM Error: *<number>* **during EMM function** *<number>*.

Source: Expanded Memory Shell

Explanation: During the initialization of the expanded memory shell, the shell must move its code and data from conventional memory to expanded memory. This message indicates that the Expanded Memory Manager responded with an error when the shell requested that the code and data be moved to expanded memory.

Action: Check the Expanded Memory Manager state to ensure that it is working properly. If the problem persists, record the error numbers in the message and contact your Novell Authorized Reseller.

Error expanding *<server\volume>* **directory because directory size limit was exceeded.**

Source: OS

Explanation: The system needs to allocate another directory block on the volume, but the maximum number of directory blocks has been reached.

The server limits the amount of disk space used for the directory table to between 5% and 50% of the total space on a volume. This is controlled by the SET server utility's "Maximum Percent Of Volume Used By Directory" parameter; its default is 13% of the disk space.

The system allocates new directory blocks when a new directory is created, or when a new file is added to an existing directory; the system did not have any entries left to track the new file.

Action: See "Locked Device Errors" on page 440 in Appendix A, "Troubleshooting."

Error expanding *<server>\<volume>* **directory because no more disk space is available.**

Source: OS

Explanation: The system needs to allocate another directory block on the volume, but the volume is out of disk space. The system attempts to allocate new directory blocks when a new directory is created or when a new file is added to an existing directory, but in this instance it did not have any entries left to track the new file.

Action See “Locked Device Errors” on page 440 in Appendix A, “Troubleshooting.”

Error expanding *<server>**<volume>* directory because no more memory available for tables.

Source OS

Explanation The system needs to allocate another directory block on the volume, and it needs to expand the tables that it uses to track the directory within memory. When the system attempted to expand the memory directory tables, there was not enough memory available to allocate the additional directory block. The station making the request will not be able to create the new file or directory.

Action See “Locked Device Errors” on page 440 in Appendix A, “Troubleshooting.”

Error expanding *<server>*/*<volume>* directory due to disk write errors.

Source OS

Explanation The system encountered a disk error while it was attempting to allocate a block on the disk. The station making the request will not be able to create the new file or directory.

This error may have been caused by a hard disk or channel failure. The disk may have other data integrity problems.

Action See “Hardware Errors” on page 435 in Appendix A, “Troubleshooting.”

Error getting effective directory rights

Source GRANT, REMOVE, REVOKE

Explanation This message indicates a shortage of dynamic memory or problems with the system bindery. The system bindery contains the names of users, their rights, file servers to which they are attached, etc.

Action Notify the network supervisor. The supervisor may need to increase the file server's memory or use the BINDFIX command to repair the system bindery.

Error getting file server name.

Source NCOPY

Explanation A network error prevented NCOPY from getting the file server name.

Action Check the syntax of the command, and try again. If the problem persists, contact your Novell Authorized Reseller.

Error getting log information from server *<servername>*. Error code = *<value>*.

Source SEND

Explanation The SEND command could not read the log information from the file server because of a shortage of Alloc Short Term memory or problems with the system bindery.

The system bindery contains the names of users, their rights, file servers to which they are attached, etc. Log information tells the file server which users have logged in, at what times, etc.

Action Wait a few minutes; then resend your message. If you still have problems, notify your network supervisor. The network supervisor may have to add more memory to the file server or use the BINDFIX command to repair the system bindery.

Make sure that your boot diskette is formatted with the latest version of DOS and that you are using the correct version of the shell.

Error getting object number.

Source GRANT

Explanation The file server was unable to get the ID number of the object to which the user was granting rights.

Action Make sure the file server is still running, and try again. If the problem persists, contact your Novell Authorized Reseller.

Error getting server name.

Source SEND

Explanation A memory error in your workstation destroyed the shell's drive table. The drive table keeps track of which drives are mapped to which file server directories.

Action: Save your work and reboot your workstation. If the problem persists, turn off your workstation, wait approximately 15 seconds, turn it on, and log in again.

Error hiding TTS backout file.

Source: OS

Explanation: This is a hardware error that occurred before the volume was mounted.

Action: See "Hardware Errors" on page 435 in Appendix A, "Troubleshooting."

Error in FAT entry sequence of last primary FAT block.

Source: INSTALL

Explanation: An internal system error has occurred. The installation process has terminated prematurely, and INSTALL will be unloaded.

Action: Try again. If the problem persists, contact your Novell Authorized Reseller.

Error in FAT entry sequence of last mirror FAT block.

Source: INSTALL

Explanation: An internal system error has occurred. The installation process has terminated prematurely, and INSTALL will be unloaded.

Action: Try again. If the problem persists, contact your Novell Authorized Reseller.

Error installing Hot Fix on drive.

Source: INSTALL

Explanation: INSTALL made a request to the operating system to create Hot Fix on the drive, but the request failed.

Action: See "General Disk I/O Errors" on page 438 in Appendix A, "Troubleshooting."

Error manipulating the TTS backout file.

Source OS

Explanation This is a hardware error.

Action See "Hardware Errors" on page 435 in Appendix A, "Troubleshooting."

Error mapping drive <*d*>:.

Source CHKVOL

Explanation The file server is having difficulty keeping track of workstation drive mappings because of heavy file server use.

Each drive mapping from a workstation to the file server requires a portion of the file server's memory. If the file server does not have adequate memory, it can lose drive mappings when a large number of users are logged in or when users are mapping a large number of drives to the file server.

Action Remap the drive. If you are still unable to map the drive, save your work and reboot your workstation. If the problem persists, turn off your workstation, wait approximately 15 seconds, turn it on, and log in again.

If your network experiences this problem continually during peak use, the network supervisor should consider installing additional memory in the file server.

Error obtaining file server information.

Source CHKVOL

Explanation The system could not access the bindery. The system bindery contains the names of users, their rights, file servers to which they are attached, etc.

This message may also indicate that you tried to use the SMODE command on a workstation using a NetWare shell earlier than v2.1.

Action The bindery is usually locked only momentarily. Wait a few minutes and retry the command.

Ask your network supervisor to generate a NetWare shell (v2.1 or later) for your workstation.

Error occurred in changing password.

Source ATTACH

Explanation An error has occurred that the operating system cannot identify.

Action Try again. If the problem persists, contact your Novell Authorized Reseller.

Error opening backout file.

Source OS

Explanation This error could indicate a hardware failure, or a corrupted Transaction Tracking System (TTS) backout file.

Action See "Hardware Errors" on page 435 in Appendix A, "Troubleshooting." If you suspect file corruption, delete the corrupted file and replace it with a backup.

Error opening boot disk image file

Source Remote Boot

Explanation When a remote boot workstation is on an internetwork and the default file server is busy, the workstation's "get-nearest-server" call can be answered by another file server. If this file server does not have a copy of the NET$DOS.SYS or BOOTCONF.SYS file (for multiple remote boot image files) in its SYS:LOGIN directory, this message is returned.

Action Copy the NET$DOS.SYS or BOOTCONF.SYS file to all SYS:LOGIN directories on all file servers on the internetwork.

Error opening file referenced by the backout file on volume *<name>*; file was deleted.

Source OS

Explanation The referenced file has been deleted before the Transaction Tracking System (TTS) could open it to back it out.

Action None. This message is for information only.

Error opening or creating TTS$LOG.ERR file.

Source OS

Explanation The Transaction Tracking System (TTS) could not open or create the TTS$LOG.ERR file, which is a file containing a history of what TTS has done. The volume may be running out of disk or directory space.

Action Erase or purge unnecessary files, or add more disk space to the volume containing the TTS files. See "Locked Device Errors" on page 440 in Appendix A, "Troubleshooting."

Error opening the file.

Source NPRINT

Explanation The file you are trying to print cannot be opened.

Action Check the file to make sure that it is not corrupted; then try again.

Error Parsing File *<name>*, Line *<number>*.

Source INSTALL

Explanation A syntax error occurred in a script or description file.

Action If you are writing the script or description file, refer to the documentation. If not, try again. If the problem persists, contact your Novell Authorized Reseller.

Error parsing path.

Source FLAGDIR

Explanation The path on the command line could not be read because the path was mistyped.

Action Retype the command with the correct path.

Error prevented preservation of file *<volume>*:*<filename>* during file erase.

Source OS

Explanation The operating system was unable to retain the specified deleted file in a salvageable state.

Action — This message should be preceded by a message stating the actual error condition (such as a disk write error). Use the preceding message to determine the actual cause and solution of the problem.

Error reading *<filename>*.

Source — OS

Explanation — The size or type of the NLM being loaded could not be read. This error probably indicates a bad NLM file.

Action — Recopy the NLM from the original disk and try again. If the problem persists, contact the vendor of the NLM.

Error reading directory on NameSpace upgrade...volume is left in a bad state. *<name>* **name space support was NOT added to volume** *<name>*

Source — OS

Explanation — This error occurred when an ADD NAME SPACE command was issued. The error could indicate file system corruption.

Action — Try running VREPAIR with the "Remove Name Space Support from the Volume" option. If the problem persists, make sure you have a backup of the volume. Delete the volume, re-create it using INSTALL, and restore the data from the backup.

Error reading file *<filename>*
Offset *<number>* **data stream** *<number>*
Read was requested by the SERVER
File path *<volume>*:*<path>*

Source — OS

Explanation — The operating system was processing a request to read data from a file, and it encountered an error while reading the data. The file read request will fail, possibly causing the applications that were requesting the read to fail.

The data stream number indicates the name space stream (0=DOS or Macintosh data fork, 1=Macintosh resource fork).

This error may have been caused by a hard disk or channel failure. The disk may have other data integrity problems.

Action — See "Hardware Errors" on page 435 in Appendix A, "Troubleshooting."

Error reading file *<name>*.
Offset *<offset>* **data stream** *<number>*.
Read was requested by user *<name>* **on station** *<number>*.
File path *<path>*.

Source OS

Explanation When the operating system attempted to read existing data from disk, it got a disk read error. The operating system was unable to determine the name of the file where the read error occurred because it got additional errors when it attempted to read directory blocks to generate the filename.

This error may have been caused by a hard disk or channel failure. The disk may have other data integrity problems.

Action See "Hardware Errors" on page 435 in Appendix A, "Troubleshooting."

Error reading from file.

Source VERSION

Explanation A disk error occurred while VERSION was trying to read the file.

Action The medium (hard drive or diskette) containing the file is bad, or the copy of the utility is corrupted. Replace the faulty component.

Error reading in the FAT.

Source OS

Explanation A File Allocation Table (FAT) is an index to one or more disk allocation blocks in which a file is located. This error probably indicates file system corruption.

Action Run VREPAIR. If the problem persists, make sure you have a backup of the volume. Delete the volume, re-create it using INSTALL, and restore the data from the backup.

Error reading in volume directory.

Source OS

Explanation The current directory entry being examined did not have the correct root subdirectory code number. This error probably indicates corruption.

Action Run VREPAIR and restart the system. If the problem persists, make sure you have a backup of the volume. Delete the volume, re-create it using INSTALL, and restore the data from the backup.

Error reading load file

Source OS

Explanation The operating system attempted to load an NLM, but the process failed. This error is caused by internal errors relating to the NLM or to physical disk errors in the loading process.

Action This is a warning error. Either the NLM is bad or the disk system is faulty. Load a new copy of the NLM from the master disk. If the NLM is not at fault, check the disk system (cables, disk drive, and controller) for potential problems.

If you are still unable to load the NLM, contact the manufacturer of the NLM for any fixes or updates.

Error reading one copy of the directory on *<server>/<volume>*.

Source OS

Explanation The server maintains two copies of the directory on each volume. An error occurred while the server was reading from one copy of the directory. The server was able to read the other copy, and it found the needed information.

This error may have been caused by a hard disk or channel failure. The disk may have other data integrity problems.

Action Run VREPAIR when this error first appears. If both directory copies become corrupted, VREPAIR cannot fix the problem. The possibility of losing data increases significantly when the system uses only one of the mirrored directories. See "Hardware Errors" on page 435 in Appendix A, "Troubleshooting."

Error reading original data.

Source OS

Explanation This error may indicate hardware failure or a corrupted Transaction Tracking System (TTS) backout file.

Action See "Hardware Errors" on page 435 in Appendix A, "Troubleshooting." If you suspect file corruption, delete the corrupted file and replace it with a backup.

Error reading source file.

Source OS

Explanation The operating system attempted to load an NLM, but the process failed. This error is caused by internal errors relating to the NLM or to physical disk errors in the loading process.

Action This is a warning error. Either the NLM is bad or the disk system is faulty. Load a new copy of the NLM from the master disk. If the NLM is not at fault, check the disk system (cables, disk drive, and controller) for potential problems. See "Hardware Errors" on page 435 in Appendix A, "Troubleshooting."

If you are still unable to load the NLM, contact the vendor of the NLM for any fixes or updates.

Error reading the destination server.

Source NPRINT

Explanation The file server returned a condition that NPRINT cannot account for. This condition prevented NPRINT from reading the file server connection number.

Action Make sure the destination file server is running, and try again. If the problem persists, contact your Novell Authorized Reseller.

Error reading volume information; unable to lock disk *<disk label>*.

Source INSTALL

Explanation The disk is probably being used by another process. A mounted volume may be using it.

Action See "Locked Device Errors" on page 440 in Appendix A, "Troubleshooting."

Error renaming old TTS backout file.

Source OS

Explanation This could be a hardware error.

Action See "Hardware Errors" on page 435 in Appendix A, "Troubleshooting."

Error re-reading a directory entry.

Source OS

Explanation The operating system encountered a problem while mounting a volume because the second time a directory entry was read, the read failed. This error probably indicates file system corruption.

Action Run VREPAIR. If the problem persists, make sure you have a backup of the volume. Delete the volume, re-create it using INSTALL, and restore the data from the backup.

Error scanning file information on the <*filename*> file.

Source NCOPY

Explanation An operating system error prevented NCOPY from obtaining file information for the specified file.

Action Try the command again, using a valid filename. If the problem persists, contact your Novell Authorized Reseller.

Error scanning trustee list.

Source REMOVE, REVOKE

Explanation This error indicates either a shortage of Alloc Short Term memory, or system bindery problems. The system bindery contains the names of users, their rights, file servers to which they are attached, etc.

Action Notify the network supervisor. The network supervisor may need to increase the file server's memory or use the BINDFIX command to repair the system bindery.

Error setting file information.

Source NCOPY

Explanation NCOPY was unable to transfer the date and time from the original file to the new file.

Action This is not a serious error. Try copying the file again.

Error setting workstation's date and time.

Source LOGIN

Explanation The LOGIN command could not synchronize your workstation's date and time with the file server's date and time, probably because of an internal memory error in your workstation.

Action Save your work and reboot your workstation.

Error trying to add trustee.

Source GRANT

Explanation The file server could not add the specified trustee.

Action Make sure the file server is still running, and try again. If the problem persists, contact your Novell Authorized Reseller.

ERROR: Two volume segments with same sync value have mismatched data

Source OS

Explanation The values specified by two segments on the volume do not match. Another message should follow this message indicating which values do not match.

Action Run VREPAIR. If the problem persists, make sure you have a backup of the volume. Delete the volume, re-create it using INSTALL, and restore the data from the backup.

Error: Unable to obtain connection information.

Source CHKDIR, CHKVOL

Explanation A network error prevented CHKVOL from obtaining your connection information.

Action Try again. If the problem persists, contact your Novell Authorized Reseller.

Error: Unable to read volume restriction information.

Source CHKDIR, CHKVOL

Explanation A network error prevented CHKVOL from obtaining volume restriction information.

Action Try again. If the problem persists, contact your Novell Authorized Reseller.

Error unloading killed loadable module

Source OS

Explanation An error occurred while an NLM was being unloaded. The NLM is still loaded. A preceding message should explain why the module could not be unloaded.

The error may have occurred because another module is still referencing public symbols or resources exported by this module. An NLM can be unloaded only when all other NLMs that use its global variables are unloaded.

Action Check the preceding message to see why the NLM was not unloaded. If necessary, unload the NLM that is using this module's public symbols or resources; then unload this NLM.

Error unloading NETBIOS: Different NETBIOS emulator/version, or interrupt was shelled.

Source NETBIOS.COM

Explanation One of the following occurred:

- An attempt was made to unload a version of NetBIOS other than the version that was loaded.
- An attempt was made to unload another vendor's emulator, but the attempt to unload NetBIOS failed.
- Another program has control over an interrupt used by NetBIOS; therefore, NetBIOS cannot be unloaded.

Action Complete one or more of the following.

- Use the U parameter to unload NetWare's v3.01 NetBIOS.
- Unload the program that is using a NetBIOS's interrupt before unloading NetBIOS.
- Make sure that the NetBIOS that is loaded is the same as the version that is used to unload NetBIOS.

Error unloading NETBIOS: Novell NETBIOS not loaded.

Source NETBIOS.COM

Explanation An attempt was made to unload NetBIOS when it had not been previously loaded.

Action None. This message is for information only.

Error unloading NETBIOS: TSR loaded after NETBIOS.

Source NETBIOS.COM

Explanation An attempt was made to unload NetBIOS, but another TSR (terminate-and-stay-resident) program was loaded afterwards. The memory used by NetBIOS cannot be safely released.

Action Unload the TSR before unloading NetBIOS.

Error unloading NetWare shell—CRITICAL—error freeing shell memory.

Source Shell

Explanation DOS indicated an error in freeing the memory belonging to the resident shell. The shell cannot be unloaded because DOS is in an unpredictable state.

Action Try again. If the problem persists, reboot the workstation.

Error unloading NetWare shell: Different NetWare shell or a NetWare shell interrupt has been hooked.

Source Shell

Explanation This error is caused by one of the following:

- You are using a different copy of the shell to unload the shell than was used to load the shell initially. The version, revision, or size is different.
- A TSR (terminate-and-stay-resident) program has been loaded that uses one of the interrupts also used by the NetWare shell. As a result, the NetWare shell no longer has the interrupt hooked.

Action Try again. If the problem persists, complete one of the following:

- Make sure the copy of the shell being used to unload the shell is the same copy that was used to load the shell.
- Unload the TSR that is hooking the interrupt used by the shell.

Error unloading NetWare shell: NetWare shell not loaded.

Source Shell

Explanation The shell cannot be unloaded because it was not found in memory.

Action None. This message is for information only.

Error unloading NetWare shell: The shell indicates it cannot be unloaded.

Source Shell

Explanation A program has hooked itself to the NetWare shell. As a result, the shell cannot be unloaded. A program cannot be unhooked from the NetWare shell once it is hooked.

Action None. This message is for information only.

Error unloading NetWare shell: There is a problem with the Memory Control Block for the shell.

Source	Shell
Explanation	The Memory Control Block chain that DOS maintains has become corrupted. The shell cannot be unloaded because DOS is in an unpredictable state.
Action	Try again. If the problem persists, reboot the workstation.

Error unloading NetWare shell: There is a TSR loaded above the load shell.

Source	Shell
Explanation	A TSR (terminate-and-stay-resident) program has been loaded after the shell. This TSR may be relying on the NetWare shell's functions or on NetWare files. It is unsafe to unload the NetWare shell under this condition.
Action	Unload the TSR first. Then try to unload the shell.

Error: Version string *<string>* not terminated.

Source	VERSION
Explanation	The copy of the utility is corrupted.
Action	Recopy the utility to the network; then try again.

Error writing *<name>* Directory block sequence <number>.

Source	INSTALL
Explanation	INSTALL could not write to the volume. This could indicate an internal system error.
Action	See "Volume I/O Errors" on page 441 in Appendix A, "Troubleshooting."

Error writing *<volume name>* FAT block sequence *<number>*.

Source	INSTALL
Explanation	INSTALL could not write to the volume.
Action	See "Volume I/O Errors" on page 441 in Appendix A, "Troubleshooting."

Error writing FAT table for volume *<server>/<volume>*

Source OS

Explanation A write error has prevented the operating system from recording changes made to the File Allocation Table (FAT). The FAT tracks what disk blocks are allocated and free; it also records what disk blocks are grouped together to store a file's data.

The server will still have the correct FAT information in memory, and it still can access the volume correctly. However, when you attempt to mount this volume the next time, the FAT information on disk will be incorrect, and the volume probably will not mount.

This error may have been caused by a hard disk or channel failure. The disk may have other data integrity problems.

Action See "Hardware Errors" on page 435 in Appendix A, "Troubleshooting."

Error writing header information to TTS backout file.

Source OS

Explanation This is a hardware error.

Action See "Hardware Errors" on page 435 in Appendix A, "Troubleshooting."

Error writing out file to network.

Source NPRINT

Explanation NPRINT was prevented from writing the print file into the print queue.

Action Check the file server to make sure it is still running, and try again. If the problem persists, contact your Novell Authorized Reseller.

Error writing to a newly allocated directory block on *<server>/<volume>*.

Source OS

Explanation A write error prevented the server from allocating a new directory block and writing the directory information to the disk. When this directory block is flushed from the directory cache, the server will not be able to read the data from disk when it is needed again.

This error may have been caused by a hard disk or channel failure. The disk may have other data integrity problems.

Action — See "Hardware Errors" on page 435 in Appendix A, "Troubleshooting."

Error writing to file *<name>* data stream *<number>*. Write was requested by the SERVER. File path *<name>*:*<name>*.

Source — OS

Explanation — A write error occurred on the system while writing data to disk. Hot Fix was not able to redirect the data to a new block. The data stream number indicates the name space stream (0=DOS or Macintosh data fork, 1=Macintosh resource fork).

This error may have been caused by a hard disk or channel failure. The disk may have other data integrity problems.

Action — See "General Disk I/O Errors" on page 438 in Appendix A, "Troubleshooting."

Error writing to file *<name>* data stream *<number>*. Write was requested by user *<name>* on station *<number>*. File path *<name>*:*<name>*.

Source — OS

Explanation — A write error occurred on the system, while writing file data to disk. Hot Fix was not able to redirect the data to another block on the disk. The data stream number indicates the name space stream (0=DOS or Macintosh data fork, 1=Macintosh resource fork). The data was not written to disk and will be lost.

This error may have been caused by a hard disk or channel failure. The disk may have other data integrity problems. Another possibility is that the designated file was lost or corrupted.

Action — See "Hardware Errors" on page 435 in Appendix A, "Troubleshooting."

Error writing to file (filename not accessible) data stream *<number>*. Write was requested by the SERVER.

Source OS

Explanation A write error has prevented the operating system from correctly writing file data to the disk. Hot Fix was not able to redirect the data to a new block. The data stream number indicates the name space stream (0=DOS or Macintosh data fork, 1=Macintosh resource fork). The data was not written to disk and will be lost.

This error may be due to a hard disk or channel failure. The disk may have other problems with data integrity.

Action See "Hardware Errors" on page 435 in Appendix A, "Troubleshooting."

Error writing to file (filename not accessible) data stream *<number>*. Write was requested by user *<name>* on station *<number>*.

Source OS

Explanation A write error has prevented the operating system from correctly writing file data to the disk. Hot Fix was not able to redirect the data to a new block. The data stream number indicates the name space stream (0=DOS or Macintosh data fork, 1=Macintosh resource fork). The data was not written to disk and will be lost.

This error may be due to a hard disk or channel failure. The disk may have other problems with data integrity.

Action See "General Disk I/O Errors" on page 438 in Appendix A, "Troubleshooting."

Error writing to the directory on *<server>*/*<volume>*.

Source OS

Explanation A write error prevented the server from writing updated directory table information to a directory block. The updated directory information was not recorded on the disk. When the directory block is flushed from the directory cache, the server will not be able to read the information from the disk.

This error may have been caused by a hard disk or channel failure. The disk may have other data integrity problems.

Action See "Hardware Errors" on page 435 in Appendix A, "Troubleshooting."

Error writing to the extended directory space

Source OS

Explanation The operating system was attempting to write extended directory information to disk. When it attempted to write the information, it got a disk error. The information was not written to the disk and will be lost. The information which was lost may have been extended attribute data.

This error may have been caused by a hard disk or channel failure. The disk may have other data integrity problems.

Action Use the warning message that preceded this message to determine the actual cause and solution of the problem. See "Hardware Errors" on page 435 in Appendix A, "Troubleshooting."

Error writing to TTS$LOG.ERR file

Source OS

Explanation A Transaction Tracking System (TTS) error could not be logged in the TTS error log file. The volume is probably out of space.

Action Add more disk space to the volume containing the TTS files. See "Locked Device Errors" on page 440 in Appendix A, "Troubleshooting."

Error writing volume name information to TTS backout file.

Source OS

Explanation This is a hardware error.

Action See "Hardware Errors" on page 435 in Appendix A, "Troubleshooting."

Error writing volume information; unable to lock disk <*disk label*>.

Source INSTALL

Explanation The disk is probably being used by another process. A mounted volume may be using it.

Action See "Locked Device Errors" on page 440 in Appendix A, "Troubleshooting."

Expanded Memory Manager is not v4.0 or better. Cannot continue initialization.

Source Shell

Explanation The Expanded Memory Manager (EMM) driver must support LIM EMS v4.0 or later. This EMM driver does not support LIM EMS v4.0.

Action Contact the vendor for an EMM driver that supports LIM EMS v4.0. Install the driver according to the vendor's documentation. Then load the shell.

Expanded memory used has been released.

Source Shell

Explanation The expanded memory used by the resident shell has been released successfully.

Action None. This message is for information only.

Expected board name missing or invalid

Source OS

Explanation As the LAN driver was loaded, a NAME parameter was used. Either the equal sign (=) or a name was not entered in the command.

Action To enter a name, unload the LAN driver and reload it with a name using 17 characters or less. For example, to name the board "Backbone," you would use the following command for the NE1000 driver:

```
LOAD NE1000 NAME=BACKBONE
```

Expected cache buffer size missing

Source OS

Explanation While executing the operating system file SERVER.EXE with the [-c <*number*>k] parameter, the <*number*> portion of the parameter was not entered.

Action Execute SERVER.EXE again and include the appropriate cache buffer size number. The cache buffer sizes are; 4 KB, 8 KB, and 16 KB. If you execute SERVER.EXE without any parameters, the default cache size is 4 KB.

Expected DMA number missing or invalid

Source OS

Explanation The "DMA=" option was specified in the hardware configuration for a BIND or LOAD command, but the DMA number was missing or invalid.

Action Specify a valid DMA number (use the hexadecimal value).

Expected frame type missing or invalid

Source OS

Explanation The LOAD command was used to load a LAN driver. The "FRAME=" option was specified in the command, but the frame type name was missing or invalid.

Action Specify the frame type name with the "FRAME=" option.

Expected interrupt number missing or invalid

Source OS

Explanation The "INT=" option was specified in the hardware configuration for a BIND or LOAD command, but the interrupt number was either missing or invalid.

Action Specify a valid interrupt number.

Expected I/O port address missing or invalid

Source OS

Explanation The "PORT=" option was specified in the hardware configuration for a BIND or LOAD command, but the I/O port address was missing or invalid.

Action Specify a valid I/O port address.

Expected I/O port length missing or invalid

Source OS

Explanation The "PORT=*address*:*length*" option was specified in a LOAD command, but the length value was missing or invalid.

Severity Specify a valid length value.

Expected memory address missing or invalid

Source OS

Explanation The "MEM=" option was specified in the hardware configuration of a BIND or LOAD command, but the memory address was either missing or invalid.

Action Specify a valid memory address.

Expected memory length missing or invalid

Source OS

Explanation The "MEM=*address*:*length*" option was specified in the hardware configuration for a BIND or LOAD command, but the length value was missing or invalid.

Action Specify a valid length value.

Expected network number missing

Source OS

Explanation The "NET=" option was used with the BIND command when binding a protocol module to a driver, but the network number was not specified.

Action Specify a valid network number with the "NET=" option.

Expected node number missing or invalid

Source OS

Explanation The LOAD command was used to load a LAN driver. The "NODE=" option was specified, but the node number was missing or invalid.

Action Specify a valid node number.

Expected number of retries missing or invalid

Source OS

Explanation The LOAD command was used to load a LAN driver. The "RETRIES=" option was specified in the command, but the number of retries was missing or invalid.

Action Specify the number of retries.

Expected slot number missing or invalid

Source OS

Explanation "SLOT" was specified in the hardware configuration for a BIND or LOAD command, but the slot number was either missing or invalid.

Action Specify a valid slot number.

Extended directory entry duplicate chains lengths don't match.

Source OS

Explanation While attempting to validate extended directory structures, the system compared directory 0's length against the length of directory 1 and found they did not match. One of the duplicate directories has become corrupted.

Action Run VREPAIR and restart the system. If the problem persists, make sure you have a backup of the volume. Delete the volume, re-create it using INSTALL, and restore the data from the backup.

Extended directory entry mirrored copies don't match.

Source OS

Explanation The volume mount was aborted when an attempt to compare mirrored directories failed. This error could indicate file system corruption.

Action Run VREPAIR and restart the system. If the problem persists, make sure you have a backup of the volume. Delete the volume, re-create it using INSTALL, and restore the data from the backup.

Extended Memory Manager is not v2.0 or better. Cannot continue initialization.

Source Extended memory shell

Explanation The shell found an XMS driver, but the XMS driver does not support v2.0 or later specifications.

Action Obtain an XMS driver that supports v2.0 specifications. Load the updated XMS driver; then load the extended memory shell.

Failed to attach the server *<servername>*

Source NPRINT

Explanation You used NPRINT to print to a file server that you are not attached to. The file server returned a condition that NPRINT cannot account for.

Action Wait a few moments; then try again. Make sure the file server is still running. If the problem persists, contact your Novell Authorized Reseller.

Failed to create destination directory.

Source NCOPY

Explanation NCOPY could not create a directory when it tried to copy a subdirectory.

Action Use the RIGHTS command to verify that you have the Create right in the destination directory. If you do, try again. If you don't, have a user with the Create right copy the files for you, or have the network supervisor grant you the Create right in the destination directory.

Failed to create file.

Source NCOPY

Explanation You tried to copy a file to either a file that is currently opened for use or a file that is flagged as Read-Only.

Action If you have Supervisory or Modify rights in this directory, flag the file as Read/Write; then try your command again. If the file is being used by another application or user, you will have to wait until the file is no longer in use.

Failed to get AFP entry ID.

Source NCOPY

Explanation A network error prevented NCOPY from obtaining the MAC entry ID for a Macintosh file.

Action Verify that the file is a Macintosh file, and try again. If the problem persists, contact your Novell Authorized Reseller.

Failed to open the <*filename*> file.

Source NCOPY

Explanation You tried to copy a file that is currently in use or flagged as Read-Only.

Action If you have Supervisory or Modify rights in this directory, flag the file as Read/Write and try the command again. If the file is in use, you will have to wait until the file is no longer being accessed.

Failure occurred while reading the file.

Source NCOPY

Explanation A network error prevented NCOPY from reading the source file.

Action Use NDIR or FLAG to verify the flags on the file. If the file is flagged Execute Only, you can neither copy the file nor remove the flag.

Failure setting destination file date and time.

Source NCOPY

Explanation A file that you tried to restore was restored, even though the time and date information of the file could not be set to the destination disk's directory. This condition indicates serious problems with the destination disk.

Action Although the time and date information of the restored file will not be correct, you can still use the data in the file. If the file is corrupted, however, you will have to restore it from another backup.

FAT table 0's first block does not match.

Source OS, INSTALL

Explanation Two segments of the volume claim a different first block for File Allocation Table (FAT) 0. This error could be caused by one of the following:

- Two volumes mounted on the file server have identical names and a segment from each volume is causing the error.
- The volume is corrupted.

Action If you have two volumes with the same name, dismount the volume you do not want to rename and unload the disk driver for that volume. Use INSTALL to rename the other volume (the volume that is on the hard disk that still has its disk driver loaded). Then load the disk driver that you just unloaded. Mount both volumes.

If the volume is corrupted, run VREPAIR. If the volume cannot be fixed, run INSTALL, delete the volume, and re-create it.

Note: If you delete the volume, all data will be destroyed. You will have to restore the data from a backup.

FAT table 1's first block does not match.

Source OS, INSTALL

Explanation Two segments of the volume claim a different first block for File Allocation Table (FAT) 1. This error could be caused by one of the following:

- Two volumes mounted on the file server have identical names and a segment from each volume is causing the error.
- The volume is corrupted.

Action If you have two volumes with the same name, dismount the volume you do not want to rename and unload the disk driver for that volume. Use INSTALL to rename the other volume (the volume that is on the hard disk that still has its disk driver loaded). Then load the disk driver that you just unloaded. Mount both volumes.

If the volume is corrupted, run VREPAIR. If the volume cannot be fixed, run INSTALL, delete the volume, and re-create it.

Note: If you delete the volume, all data will be destroyed. You will have to restore the data from a backup.

FAT table length error on volume *<name>*. There should be *<number>* FAT blocks, but the FAT table length is *<number>* blocks.

Source INSTALL

Explanation Errors have occurred in the volume structure.

Action See "Volume I/O Errors" on page 441 in Appendix A, "Troubleshooting."

FATAL: 3C503—Card not found.

Source 3C503.COM

Explanation The 3C503.COM driver could not locate a 3C503 board at the specified hardware settings.

Action Make sure that a 3C503 board is installed. Verify the hardware jumper settings. If the settings do not match the defaults, specify the settings in the NET.CFG file.

FATAL: 3C503—Card will not initialize.

Source 3C503.COM

Explanation A hardware failure occurred.

Action Check for possible hardware settings that conflict with other installed boards.

FATAL: 3C503—Interrupt is invalid (2,3,4,5,9 valid).

Source 3C503.COM

Explanation An invalid interrupt value was specified in the NET.CFG file.

Action Correct the "INT *number*" entry in the NET.CFG file; then try again.

FATAL: 3C503—I/O port does not match NICs jumper.

Source 3C503.COM

Explanation The specified base I/O port address (the driver default or the value specified in the NET.CFG file) is different from the address setting on the 3C503 board.

Action Make sure that the value for the driver matches the value set on the board; then try again.

FATAL: 3C503—Memory does not match NICs jumper.

Source 3C503.COM

Explanation The specified base memory address (the driver default or the value specified in the NET.CFG file) is different from the address setting on the 3C503 board.

Action Make sure that the value for the driver matches the value set on the board; then try again.

FATAL: Board # *<number>* doesn't provide enough look ahead, IPX needs 18 or more bytes.

Source IPXODI

Explanation IPX requires at least the first 18 bytes of incoming packets for it to preview the packets properly.

Action Increase the MLID look ahead size by specifying "LOOK AHEAD SIZE 18" in the NET.CFG file under the MLID main section heading, as in the following example:

```
LINK DRIVER NE1000
  LOOK AHEAD SIZE 18
```

FATAL: Board failed to initialize correctly.

Source MLID

Explanation The MLID was unable to initialize its board correctly; this is usually due to hardware failure.

Action Refer to the MLID documentation for a description of the error.

FATAL: Could not find a board that supports IPX (See PROTOCOL keyword).

Source IPXODI

Explanation IPX could not find a board to bind with. For IPX to bind, it must have a protocol ID registered with the Link Support Layer.

Most MLIDs will register an IPX Protocol ID by default. However, if you have specified the PROTOCOL keyword under an MLID's section heading in the NET.CFG file, this error may be generated.

When a protocol ID has been specified for another protocol stack, the MLID will *not* register a default protocol ID for IPX.

Action — If you want to use IPX, register a protocol ID for IPX along with the other Protocol IDs you are registering.

FATAL: Could not find an enabled 3C523 adapter in any slot.

Source — 3C523.COM

Explanation — By default, the 3C523.COM driver scans the PS/2 slots to find the 3C523 board it should use. The driver starts scanning at slot 1. The driver was unable to find a 3C523 board in any slot.

Action — Make sure that the 3C523 board is firmly seated in the slot.

FATAL: Could not find an NE2 adapter in any slot.

Source — NE2.COM

Explanation — By default, the NE2.COM driver will scan the PS/2 slots to find the NE/2 board it should use. The driver starts scanning at slot 1. The driver was unable to find an NE/2 board in any slot.

Action — Make sure that the NE/2 board is firmly seated in the slot.

FATAL: Could not find an NE2-32 adapter in any slot.

Source — NE2-32.COM

Explanation — By default, the NE2-32.COM driver will scan the PS/2 slots to find the NE/2-32 board it should use. The driver starts scanning at slot 1. The driver was unable to find an NE/2-32 board in any slot.

Action — Make sure that the NE/2-32 board is firmly seated in the slot.

FATAL: Could not find <*name*> MLID to unload.

Source — MLID

Explanation — A request was made to unload the MLID, but the MLID is not loaded.

Action — None. This message is for information only.

FATAL: Different IPX or a IPX interrupt has been hooked.

Source: IPXODI

Explanation: You attempted to unload the LSL from memory, but the LSL detected a condition that would not allow IPX to be removed from memory safely. This can occur for two reasons:

- The resident IPXODI and the IPXODI used to unload the resident IPXODI are not the same version.
- Another program has been loaded that has hooked one of IPXODI's interrupt vectors. IPXODI uses the following interrupt vectors: INT 08h, INT 2Fh, INT 64h, and INT 7Ah.

Action: Complete one of the following:

- Use the same version of IPXODI to unload IPX that you used to load IPXODI.
- Unload the program that has hooked to one or more IPX interrupt vectors, and then unload IPXODI.

FATAL: Different LSL or a LSL interrupt has been hooked.

Source: LSL

Explanation: You attempted to unload the LSL from memory, but the LSL detected a condition that would not allow it to be safely removed from memory. This can occur for two reasons:

- The resident LSL and the LSL used to unload the resident LSL are not the same version.
- Another program has been loaded that has hooked one of the LSL's interrupt vectors. The LSL uses the following interrupt vectors: INT 08h and INT 2Fh.

Action: Complete one of the following:

- Use the same version of LSL to unload LSL that you used to load LSL.
- Unload the program that has hooked to the LSL's interrupt vectors, and then unload the LSL.

FATAL: Direct Station 0 already in use by another application.

Source LANSUP.COM

Explanation The LANSUP.COM driver uses Direct Station 0. Only one application running on the IBM LAN Support program can use Direct Station 0.

Action Unload the other application.

Fatal error granting access rights.

Source GRANT

Explanation Either the system bindery is locked or you lack sufficient trustee rights to execute this command. The system bindery contains the names of users, their rights, file servers to which they are attached, etc. The network supervisor may have locked the bindery for maintenance.

Action If the bindery is not locked and you have sufficient rights, contact your Novell Authorized Reseller.

FATAL: Error initializing board.

Source LANSUP.COM

Explanation The LAN Support program could not initialize the network board.

Action Check the installation of the LAN Support software.

FATAL: Error opening board.

Source LANSUP.COM

Explanation The LAN Support program could not open the network board.

Action Check the installation of the LAN Support software.

FATAL: Error shutting down *<name>* MLID, unload operation aborted.

Source MLID

Explanation The MLID was attempting to remove the resident MLID from memory. The MLID was unable to successfully shut down the resident MLID. A hardware failure has probably occurred.

Action See "Hardware Errors" on page 435 in Appendix A, "Troubleshooting.".

FATAL: Failed to locate MLID Section Heading in NET.CFG file.

Source MLID

Explanation You tried to load the MLID again. Normally you would do this so that you could use two or more boards in the workstation. When two or more of the same type of network boards are installed in the workstation, an associated MLID section heading must be specified in the NET.CFG file.

An entry in the NET.CFG file for two boards should look similar to the following:

```
#Allow the first one to use default values.

  LINK DRIVER NE1000

#This section is for the second board

  LINK DRIVER NE1000
  INT 4
  PORT 320
```

Action Add the commands for both MLID boards to the NET.CFG file. Then try again.

FATAL: IBM LAN Support Program has not been loaded.

Source LANSUP.COM

Explanation The LANSUP.COM driver requires that the IBM LAN Support program be loaded.

Action Load the LAN Support software and retry the operation. Add lines similar to the following to the CONFIG.SYS file:

```
DEVICE=DXMA0MOD.SYS
DEVICE=DXMC0MOD.SYS
```

FATAL: Init586: Configure command failed.

Source 3C523.COM

Explanation A hardware failure has occurred.

Action Install the 3C523 board in a different slot. If the driver still fails to load, the 3C523 board is probably bad and should be replaced.

FATAL: Init586: IA_Setup command failed.

Source 3C523.COM

Explanation A hardware failure has occurred.

Action Install the 3C523 board in a different slot. If the driver still fails to load, the 3C523 board is probably bad and should be replaced.

FATAL: Init586: Initial communication with 82586 failed.

Source 3C523.COM

Explanation A hardware failure has occurred.

Action Install the 3C523 board in a different slot. If the driver still fails to load, the 3C523 board is probably bad and should be replaced.

FATAL: Invalid base memory address—Must be C0000 or D0000.

Source NE2-32.COM

Explanation Because the NE/2-32 board is a true 32-bit board, the board can have its base memory located above the 1MB real mode memory limit. Since DOS ODI is executing in real mode, the NE2-32.COM driver cannot access the board's RAM when it is located above the 1MB address range.

Action Use the Reference program to change the board's base memory setting to either C0000 or D0000.

FATAL: Invalid Ethernet node address specified.

Source MLID

Explanation You used the "NODE ADDRESS" option in the NET.CFG file to override the node address on the network board. The number specified was not a valid address. An Ethernet address is 6 bytes in length. This error occurs if Bit 0 of the first address byte is a 1. This bit must always be 0.

Action Change the NET.CFG file so that a valid node address is specified.

FATAL: Invalid parameter.

Source
: IPXODI

Explanation
: When you attempted to load IPXODI, you specified an invalid parameter on the command line. IPXODI was not loaded. The only valid parameters are ? (for information), D (to prevent the remote diagnostic responder from loading), A (to prevent SPX and the remote diagnostic responder from loading), and U (to unload).

Action
: Specify a valid parameter.

FATAL: Invalid parameter.

Source
: LSL

Explanation
: When you attempted to load the LSL, you specified an invalid parameter on the command line. The LSL was not loaded. The only valid parameters are ? (for information) and U (to unload).

Action
: Specify a valid parameter.

FATAL: Invalid parameter.

Source
: MLID

Explanation
: When you attempted to load the MLID, you specified an invalid parameter on the command line. The MLID was not loaded. The only valid parameters for MLID are ? (for information) and U (to unload).

Action
: Specify a valid parameter.

FATAL: Invalid Token-Ring node address specified.

Source
: MLID

Explanation
: You used the "NODE" option in the NET.CFG file to override the node address on the network board. The number specified was not a valid Token-Ring node address. A Token-Ring address is 6 bytes in length.

: This error will occur if Bit 7 of the first address byte is a 1. This bit should always be a 0. The error also occurs if Bit 7 of the third address byte is 1.

Action
: This bit should always be 0. Change the NET.CFG file so that a valid node address is specified.

FATAL: IPX already loaded.

Source IPXODI

Explanation IPX has already been loaded. IPX needs to be loaded only once.

Action None. This message is for information only.

FATAL: IPX is already registered with the LSL.

Source IPXODI

Explanation IPX was not removed from the LSL's register when it was unloaded. The system may be corrupted.

Action Reboot the workstation.

FATAL: IPX is not loaded.

Source IPXODI

Explanation You tried to unload IPX, but IPX has not been loaded.

Action None. This message is for information only.

FATAL: Loading MLID again requires configuration information in NET.CFG.

Source MLID

Explanation You tried to load the MLID again. Normally you would do this so that you could use two or more network boards in the workstation. When two or more network boards of the same type are installed in the workstation, an associated MLID section heading must be specified in the NET.CFG file.

An entry in the NET.CFG file for two boards should look similar to the following:

```
#Allow the first one to use default values.

  LINK DRIVER NE1000

#This section is for the second board.

  LINK DRIVER NE1000
  INT 4
  PORT 320
```

Action — Create a NET.CFG file and add the commands for both MLID boards to the file. Then try again.

FATAL: LSL already loaded.

Source — LSL

Explanation — The Link Support Layer has already been loaded. The LSL can only be loaded once.

Action — None. This message is for information only.

FATAL: LSL is not loaded.

Source — LSL

Explanation — You attempted to unload the LSL, but the LSL is not loaded.

Action — None. This message is for information only.

FATAL: Multiplex interrupt 2Fh has no free slots.

Source — LSL

Explanation — LSL could not find a free slot for use with INT 2Fh. When your computer is first booted, approximately 63 multiplex slots are available. All available slots are already being used by applications.

Action — Unload an application that is using the INT 2Fh multiplex interrupt; then load the LSL.

FATAL: NE2 NIC command port failed to respond.

Source — NE2.COM

Explanation — The installed NE/2 board has malfunctioned.

Action — Replace the board.

FATAL: NE2 NIC RAM failure.

Source — NE2.COM

Explanation — The installed NE/2 board's onboard memory has malfunctioned.

Action — Replace the board.

FATAL: NE2-32 NIC command port failed to respond.

Source NE2-32.COM

Explanation The installed NE/2-32 board has malfunctioned.

Action Replace the board.

FATAL: NE2-32 NIC RAM failure.

Source NE2-32.COM

Explanation The installed NE/2-32 board's onboard memory has malfunctioned.

Action Replace the board.

FATAL: NE1000 NIC command port failed to respond.

Source NE1000.COM

Explanation The NE1000 board has malfunctioned, is not installed, or is not configured to the same port selected for the driver.

Action Complete one or more of the following:

- Make sure that an NE1000 board has been installed and configured.
- Make sure that the configuration for the NE1000 board matches the configuration for the NE1000 driver. (Any configuration options other than the defaults must be entered in the NET.CFG file.)
- Replace the board.

FATAL: NE1000 NIC RAM failure.

Source NE1000.COM

Explanation The installed NE1000 board's onboard memory has malfunctioned.

Action Replace the board.

FATAL: NE2000 NIC command port failed to respond.

Source NE2000.COM

Explanation The NE2000 board has malfunctioned, is not installed, or is not configured to the same port as selected for the driver.

Action Complete one or more of the following:

- Make sure that an NE2000 board has been installed and configured.
- Make sure that the configuration for the NE2000 board matches the configuration for the NE2000 driver. (Any configuration options other than the defaults must be entered in the NET.CFG file.)
- Replace the board.

FATAL: NE2000 NIC is NOT supported in a 8-bit slot.

Source NE2000.COM

Explanation The NE2000 board is located in an 8-bit slot in the machine. The NE2000.COM driver only supports the NE2000 in a 16-bit AT bus slot.

Action Place the NE2000 board in a 16-bit slot, and try again.

FATAL: NE2000 NIC RAM failure.

Source NE2000.COM

Explanation The installed NE2000 board's onboard memory has malfunctioned.

Action Replace the board.

FATAL: NE2000 NIC was not found at specified hardware settings.

Source NE2000.COM

Explanation The NE2000.COM driver found a board at the specified hardware settings, but the board is not an NE2000 board.

Action Check the installed hardware.

FATAL: No more room in the LSL for another protocol stack.

Source IPXODI

Explanation The maximum number of protocol stacks have been registered with the Link Support Layer. The DOS ODI LSL can support up to eight protocol stacks.

Action Remove an existing protocol stack.

FATAL: RXNet command port failed to respond.

Source TRXNET.COM

Explanation The TRXNET.COM driver could not find an RX-Net board in the workstation.

Action Make sure that an RX-Net board is installed in the workstation and that it is firmly seated. Make sure that the values for the hardware settings in the driver (the default or the values set in the NET.CFG file) match the values set on the board.

FATAL: RXNet RAM failure.

Source TRXNET.COM

Explanation The installed RX-Net board's RAM has failed the RAM test.

Action Replace the board.

FATAL: Specified PS/2 slot contains an NE2 but it is not enabled.

Source NE2.COM

Explanation The located NE/2 board was not enabled. The NE/2 board has probably malfunctioned.

Action Replace the board.

FATAL: Specified PS/2 slot contains an NE2-32 but it is not enabled.

Source NE2-32.COM

Explanation The located NE/2-32 board was not enabled. The NE/2-32 board has probably malfunctioned.

Action Replace the board.

FATAL: Specified PS/2 slot does not contain an enabled 3C523 adapter.

Source 3C523.COM

Explanation A "PS/2 SLOT *number*" option was specified in the NET.CFG file. The specified slot does not contain a 3C523 board. Slot numbers are 1 based and correspond to the slot numbers on the back of the computer.

Action Modify the NET.CFG so that the specified slot number matches the slot that the board is installed in.

FATAL: Specified PS/2 slot does not contain an NE2 adapter.

Source NE2.COM

Explanation A "PS/2 SLOT *number*" option was specified in the NET.CFG file. The specified slot does not contain an NE/2 board. Slot numbers are 1 based and correspond to the slot numbers on the back of the computer.

Action Modify the NET.CFG file to specify the correct slot number.

FATAL: Specified PS/2 slot does not contain an NE2-32 adapter.

Source NE2-32.COM

Explanation A "PS/2 SLOT *number*" option was specified in the NET.CFG file, but the specified slot does not contain an NE/2-32 board. Slot numbers are 1 based and correspond to the slot numbers on the back of the computer.

Action Modify the NET.CFG file to specify the correct slot number.

FATAL: The LSL is not loaded.

Source IPXODI

Explanation IPX requires that the LSL be loaded first.

Action Load LSL.COM; then load IPXODI.COM.

FATAL: The LSL is not loaded.

Source MLID

Explanation LSL must be loaded before an MLID can be loaded.

Action Load LSL.COM; then load the MLID.

FATAL: There is a TSR above the loaded IPX.

Source IPXODI

Explanation You attempted to unload IPX from memory, but IPX detected another TSR (terminate-and-stay-resident) program loaded above IPX. For IPX to *safely* unload, TSRs that have been loaded after IPX was loaded must be unloaded before IPX is unloaded.

Action Either load the TSR before loading IPX, or unload the TSR before attempting this operation.

FATAL: There is a TSR above the loaded LSL.

Source LSL

Explanation You attempted to unload the LSL from memory, but the LSL detected another TSR (terminate-and-stay-resident) program loaded above the LSL. For the LSL to *safely* unload, TSRs that have been loaded after LSL was loaded must be unloaded before LSL is unloaded.

Action Either load the other TSR before loading the LSL, or unload the TSR before attempting this operation.

FATAL: There is a TSR above the loaded *<name>* MLID.

Source MLID

Explanation You attempted to unload the MLID from memory, but the MLID detected another TSR (terminate-and-stay-resident) program loaded above the MLID. For the MLID to *safely* unload, TSRs that have been loaded after the MLID was loaded must be unloaded before the MLID is unloaded.

Action Either load the other TSR before loading the MLID, or unload the TSR before attempting this operation.

FATAL: This old LSL is not supported.

Source IPXODI

Explanation IPXODI is unable to run correctly using this version of the LSL.

Action Update your LSL.COM to a newer version.

FATAL: This old LSL is not supported.

Source MLID

Explanation The MLID is unable to run correctly using this version of the LSL.

Action Update your LSL.COM to a newer version.

FATAL: Work Area Exceeded, reduce number of SAPs and/or Link Stations.

Source LANSUP.COM

Explanation The number of SAPs or Link Stations specified in the NET.CFG file exceeded the maximum number of SAPs or Link Stations that the network board can handle.

Action Modify the number of SAPs or Link Stations specified in the NET.CFG file.

File block sequence *<number>* not found in FAT chain starting at entry *<number>*.

Source INSTALL

Explanation An internal system error has occurred. The installation process has terminated prematurely, and INSTALL will be unloaded.

Action Try again. If the problem persists, contact your Novell Authorized Reseller.

File in use

Source FLAG, SMODE

Explanation A file was locked by another user or application when the archiving program tried to archive the file.

Action Wait until the file is unlocked; then archive the file again.

File server *<servername>* cannot support any more connections.

Source PSERVER.EXE

Explanation The print server needs one connection slot to run. All 250 connection slots are in use.

Action Wait until a connection slot becomes available. You can also load MONITOR or use the FCONSOLE utility to clear a connection.

File server *<servername>* is unknown.

Source LISTDIR

Explanation You mistyped the name of the file server, specified a file server that is not on the network, or specified a file server that has been brought down for system maintenance.

Action Use the SLIST command to list all the file servers that your station can recognize. Type the name of the file server correctly. If the file server has been brought down for maintenance, try the command when the file server has been brought back up. If you still have problems, ask your network supervisor for help.

File server *<servername>* is unknown at this time.

Source PSERVER

Explanation You mistyped the name of the file server, specified a file server that is not on the network, or specified a file server that has been brought down for system maintenance.

Action Use the SLIST command to list all the file servers that your station can recognize. Type the name of the file server correctly. If the file server has been brought down for maintenance, try the command when the file server has been brought back up. If you still have problems, ask your network supervisor for help.

File Server has no free connection slots.

Source Shell

Explanation The shell tried to attach the workstation to the nearest file server, but the maximum number of connections on that file server has been reached.

Action Complete one or more of the following:

- Try loading the shell after a user has logged out from the file server.
- If you are on an internetwork, add a "Preferred Server" command to the workstation's NET.CFG file.

File server not serialized

Source OS

Explanation The serial number initialization process failed.

Action Reinstall a new copy of SERVER.EXE from the master disk. Make sure the copy of NetWare you are attempting to use is a correct and legal (nonpirated) original. If the problem persists and the disks are original (and have not been tampered with), contact your Novell Authorized Reseller.

File without trustee definitions had a trustee node.

Source OS

Explanation The information about a given file indicated that the file had specific trustee assignments, but no trustee assignments could be found. This is a warning error, but in most cases it will not cause serious problems

Action Run VREPAIR. If the problem persists, make sure you have a backup of the volume. Delete the volume, re-create it using INSTALL, and restore the data from the backup.

File write pre-read error
Offset *<number>* data stream *<number>*
Error getting file name
Read was requested by the SERVER

Source OS

Explanation When the operating system attempted to write data to an existing file, it got an error in trying to read existing data from the disk. The new data could not be written to the disk and will be lost.

The operating system was unable to determine the name of the file where the read error occurred, because it got additional errors when it attempted to read directory blocks to generate the filename.

This error may have been caused by a hard disk or channel failure. The disk may have other data integrity problems.

Action See "Hardware Errors" on page 435 in Appendix A, "Troubleshooting."

File write pre-read error
Offset *<number>* data stream *<number>*
Error getting file name
Read was requested by user *<username>* on station *<number>*

Source OS

Explanation When the operating system attempted to write data to an existing file, it got an error in trying to read existing data from the disk. The new data could not be written to the disk and will be lost.

The operating system was unable to determine the name of the file where the read error occurred, because it got additional errors when it attempted to read directory blocks to generate the filename.

This error may have been caused by a hard disk or channel failure. The disk may have other data integrity problems.

Action See "Hardware Errors" on page 435 in Appendix A, "Troubleshooting."

Files could not be found with pattern "*<pattern>*"

Source FLAG

Explanation One of the following occurred:

- You specified a file *<pattern>*, but the system could not find any files that match your file specification.
- You specified a file in your command that cannot be found in the directory
- You mistyped the directory name or the last subdirectory name in a directory path.

Action Do one or both of the following:

- Use the NDIR command to list the files in the directory; then retry the command using a wildcard designation that matches a set of files in the directory.
- Type the entire directory path correctly. If you are unsure about the structure of the directory path, use the LISTDIR command or the FILER utility to examine the directory structure.

Files not found.

Source FLAG, NCOPY

Explanation One of the following occurred:

- You specified a file <*pattern*>, but the system could not find any files that match your file specification.
- You specified a file in your command that cannot be found in the directory.
- You mistyped the directory name or the last subdirectory name in a directory path.

Action Do one or both of the following:

- Use the NDIR command to list the files in the directory; then retry the command using a wildcard designation that matches a set of files in the directory.
- Type the entire directory path correctly. If you are unsure about the structure of the directory path, use the LISTDIR command or the FILER utility to examine the directory structure.

FlagDir only works on network directories.

Source FLAGDIR

Explanation FLAGDIR does not work on local drives (workstation floppy disk drives and hard disks).

Action If you need to alter the flags of a directory on a local drive, use another utility.

Form name <*name*> does not exist.

Source CAPTURE

Explanation You either specified a form name that is not defined on your file server or mistyped the name of the form.

Action Use the PRINTDEF utility to see which forms are currently defined on your file server. Type the name of the form correctly.

Form number must between 0 and 255.

Source CAPTURE, NPRINT

Explanation A form number greater than 255 was entered with the "Form" option.

Action Enter a valid form number (0 through 255).

Form number or name expected.

Source CAPTURE

Explanation You used the Form flag (option) in your command, but either you omitted the form name or form number, or you specified a form name or number that is not defined and configured on the file server.

Action Include a valid form name or number with the Form flag (option) in your command. If you are unsure which forms are available to you, ask your network supervisor.

Forms type ID number expected with the FORM flag.

Source CAPTURE, NPRINT

Explanation You used the Form flag (option) in a CAPTURE or NPRINT command, but you did not specify a form name or a form identification number.

Action Specify a form name or form number (0 to 255) with the Form flag.

FreeFATTable was called when no FAT table was allocated.

Source OS

Explanation An internal system error has probably occurred.

Action Try again. If the problem persists, contact your Novell Authorized Reseller.

G

General failure on device NETWORK

Source VLM.EXE

Explanation This is a critical communications error between the workstation and the file server. A communications error can be caused by a hardware or software failure.

Action See "Hardware Errors" on page 435 in Appendix A, "Troubleshooting." If the problem persists, contact your Novell Authorized Reseller.

GetVolumeNumber called with unmounted volume.

Source INSTALL

Explanation An internal system error has occurred. The installation process has terminated prematurely, and INSTALL will be unloaded.

Action Try again. If the problem persists, contact your Novell Authorized Reseller.

Group *<servername>*/*<groupname>* does not exist.

Source SEND

Explanation You either specified a group that does not exist on the network or mistyped the name of the group.

Action Use the SYSCON utility to see the names of groups (or trustees) on the network.

Group "*<groupname>*" not found.

Source GRANT, REMOVE, REVOKE

Explanation You either specified a group that does not exist on the network or mistyped the name of the group.

Action Use the SYSCON utility to see the names of groups (or trustees) on the network.

Group *<servername>/<groupname>* **not logged in.**

Source SEND

Explanation You sent a message to one or more users who belong to the specified group, but no members of the group are currently logged in.

Action None. This message is for information only.

Hardware Error: *<LAN driver>* DMA not complete in write

Source: NE1000.COM, NE2000.COM

Explanation: The network board's DMA did not complete a write after data was sent to it. The driver will send the data to the board again.

Action: None. If the problem persists, replace the faulty board.

Hardware Error: Ethernet buffer memory failure.

Source: 3C503.COM, NE1000.COM, NE2000.COM

Explanation: The network board failed the memory test during initialization of the driver. Either the memory parameter did not match the setting on the board or the board has a bad memory chip.

Action: Complete one or more of the following:

- Check the memory address setting on the board. Make sure that the driver is loaded with the correct setting.
- Check the memory chip(s) on the board. Replace any faulty chips.

Hardware Error: Ethernet hardware failure.

Source: 3C503.COM, NE1000.COM, NE2000.COM

Explanation: The LAN driver was able to reset the network board, but the board did not return a confirming response.

Action: Replace or repair the network board.

Hardware Error: NE2000 is in an 8-bit slot. Place in 16-bit slot before loading.

Source: NE2000.COM

Explanation: The NE2000.COM LAN driver has been written to use a 16-bit bus. The NE2000 board must be installed in a 16-bit slot for the NE2000.COM LAN driver to load.

Action: Install the NE2000 board in a 16-bit slot.

Hardware Error: Node entered matches a multicast address.

Source 3C503.COM, NE1000.COM, NE2000.COM

Explanation The LAN driver aborted loading because the node address entered is a multicast address.

Action Reload the driver. Use a unique 12-digit hexadecimal node address.

Hardware Error: The IO Base configuration didn't match the hardware configuration of the Etherlink II board.

Source 3C503.COM

Explanation The network board has been set to one I/O port address, but the driver was loaded with another I/O port address.

Action Load the driver with the I/O port address that the board has been configured to.

Hardware Error: The RAM configuration didn't match the hardware configuration of the Etherlink II.

Source 3C503.COM

Explanation The network board has been set to one memory address, but the driver was loaded with another memory address.

Action Load the driver with the memory address that the board has been configured to.

Hardware Error: This card thinks its an NE1000

Source NE2000.COM

Explanation An NE1000 network board has been installed in the file server, but you tried to load the NE2000.COM LAN driver.

Action Use the NE1000.COM LAN driver for the NE1000 network board.

Hardware Error: Unable to find NE2000 hardware.

Source NE2000.COM

Explanation The driver was unable to locate an NE2000 network board in the file server.

Action — Check the network boards in the file server. The NE2000 board has part number ASSY 810-149. Make sure the boards are properly seated.

Hi Memory Area (HMA) does not exist. Cannot continue initialization.

Source — Extended memory shell

Explanation — The XMS driver was unable to locate extended memory starting at the 1MB boundary.

Action — Verify the existence of the extended memory. Consult the workstation's hardware reference manual for information about extended memory.

Hidden is valid on NetWare 2.15 and above, including NetWare 386.

Source — FLAGDIR

Explanation — The Hidden flag is supported in NetWare v2.15 and later and in NetWare v3.*x*.

Action — Use the Hidden flag on file servers running the appropriate version of the software.

High Memory Area (HMA) has been released.

Source — Shell

Explanation — The extended memory used by the resident shell has been released successfully.

Action — None. This message is for information only.

I

Illegal banner specification. (length 1–12)

Source NPRINT

Explanation You either used the banner flag (option) without specifying a banner or specified a banner longer than 12 characters. (A banner cannot exceed 12 characters in length.)

Action None. This message is for information only.

Illegal character found in the specified password.

Source CAPTURE, NPRINT, VOLINFO

Explanation You may have accidentally typed a character while you were pressing the Control key. This will produce a "control character." Control characters such as ^C and ^E are special characters used for formatting text in word processors, controlling printers, transmitting data, etc. These characters should not be included in passwords.

Action Retype your password.

Illegal control character encountered in command line.

Source CHKVOL, RIGHTS, SEND, SETTTS

Explanation You may have accidentally typed a character while you were pressing the Control key. This will produce a "control character." Control characters such as ^C and ^E are special characters used for formatting text in word processors, controlling printers, transmitting data, etc. These characters should not be included in commands.

Action Retype the command.

Illegal drive <*d*>: specified.

Source CHKVOL

Explanation You specified a drive (<*d*>:) that is neither a local drive nor a network drive.

Action Specify only local drives or network drives that have been defined with the MAP command.

Illegal name specification. (length 1–12)

Source NPRINT

Explanation You either used the Banner flag (option) without specifying a banner name or specified a banner name longer than 12 characters. A banner name cannot exceed 12 characters in length.

Action None. This message is for information only.

Illegal path specification.

Source NPRINT

Explanation You specified a path that does not exist.

Action Specify a valid path in the command.

Illegal print server account name. Unable to attach to file server *<servername>*.

Source PSERVER (.EXE, .NLM, or .VAP)

Explanation The name specified for the print server is not a valid bindery name. The name you typed contains an invalid DOS character, a typographical error, or too many characters.

Action Use a valid print server name. Run PCONSOLE on the specified file server; then select "Print Server Information" for a list of defined print servers.

Illegal queue name specification.

Source NPRINT

Explanation You either specified a queue name that is not defined on the file server or mistyped the name of the queue.

Action Use the PCONSOLE utility to see which queues are currently defined on the file server. Type the queue name correctly in your command.

Illegal server name specification.

Source NPRINT

Explanation You used an invalid DOS character in the file server's name.

Action Use the SLIST command to list the file servers on your network. Type the file server name correctly in your command.

Illegal syntax in the flag list.

Source NPRINT

Explanation You used a valid flag (option) in your command, but you used the flag improperly.

Action For the correct syntax, see the explanation for NPRINT in *Print Server.*

In order to load the *<module3>*.VLM, one of the following VLMs must be loaded: *<module1>*.VLM, *<module2>*.VLM.

Source VLMs (AUTO, BIND, CONN, FIO, GENERAL, IPXNCP, NDS, NETX, NMR, NWP, PRINT, REDIR, RSA, SECURITY, TRAN)

Explanation The *<module3>*.VLM requires that *<module1>*.VLM or *<module2>*.VLM be loaded first. Either the current configuration has *<module3>*.VLM loading before the modules in the *<module1>*.VLM or *<module2>*.VLM list, or *<module1>*.VLM or *<module2>*.VLM did not load successfully.

Action Make sure that *<module1>*.VLM or *<module2>*.VLM load successfully before loading *<module3>*.VLM.

Incomplete Transactions Referencing UnMounted Volumes Were Preserved.

Source OS

Explanation Not all of the volumes are mounted yet, so the Transaction Tracking System (TTS) backout file is being saved. An incomplete transaction occurred on one of these unmounted volumes.

Action None. This message is for information only.

Information applicable to a specific name space cannot be scanned.

Source TSA

Explanation Information applicable to a specific name space cannot be scanned.

Action Make sure that you have specified a valid name space and that name space support is loaded on the selected volume.

InsertInPortalList returned error *<code>*.

Source SBACKUP

Explanation This is an SBACKUP screen interface error; the program could not process the menu list correctly. You may not have sufficient memory. You should have a minimum of 8 MB of RAM on the server.

Action See "Insufficient Server Memory Errors" on page 440 in Appendix A, "Troubleshooting."

Insufficient directory space (or memory) to preserve *<volume>*:*<filename>* during file erase.

Source OS

Explanation While attempting to delete a file, the server was unable to obtain the needed directory table space or memory to retain the deleted file in a state in which it could be salvaged. The file was deleted and purged. A preceding message on the screen should indicate the cause of this error.

Action Use the message displayed before this one to determine the actual cause of and solution for the problem.

Insufficient disk space to create a print file.

Source NPRINT

Explanation The SYS: volume is full.

Action Delete unused files from the SYS: volume; then try again.

Insufficient memory.

Source NCOPY, NPRINT, RPRINTER

Explanation Your workstation has insufficient memory. If the problem occurs while you are using RPRINTER, keep in mind that the workstation needs to have 128 KB of available memory during the initialization of RPRINTER. After RPRINTER is initialized, RPRINTER needs only 8 KB of memory to run.

Action See "Insufficient Workstation Memory Errors" on page 442 in Appendix A, "Troubleshooting."

Insufficient memory available for user restriction nodes.

Source OS

Explanation The server does not have enough memory. A call for memory from within the set_user_restriction routine failed. This memory would have been used to create user restriction node IDs.

Action See "Insufficient Server Memory Errors" on page 440 in Appendix A, "Troubleshooting."

Insufficient memory for directory tables.

Source OS

Explanation One of the steps in volume directory initialization is to request resource tags and memory for directory tables, directory hash tables, and extended directory tables. The volume did not mount because the server does not have enough memory available.

Action See "Insufficient Server Memory Errors" on page 440 in Appendix A, "Troubleshooting."

Insufficient memory to add search path

Source OS

Explanation The SEARCH ADD command was used, but the server cannot allocate memory to expand the search path mapping.

Action See"Insufficient Server Memory Errors" on page 440 in Appendix A, "Troubleshooting."

Insufficient memory to create the copy buffer.

Source NPRINT

Explanation The print job configuration used to print the file used the Mode option. The workstation does not have enough available RAM to copy in the escape sequences defined in the Mode option.

Action See "Insufficient Workstation Memory Errors" on page 442 in Appendix A, "Troubleshooting."

Insufficient memory to initialize communications.

Source PSERVER

Explanation The file server or workstation that is running PSERVER does not have enough memory to run the print server.

Action Add more memory to the file server or workstation, or free memory by doing one of the following:

- To free memory in the file server, see "Insufficient Server Memory Errors" on page 440 in Appendix A, "Troubleshooting."
- To free memory in the workstation, see "Insufficient Workstation Memory Errors" on page 442 in Appendix A, "Troubleshooting."

Insufficient memory to load file.

Source OS

Explanation The file server does not have enough memory to load a given file.

Action See "Insufficient Server Memory Errors" on page 440 in Appendix A, "Troubleshooting."

Insufficient memory to load module.

Source OS

Explanation An attempt to load an NLM failed because the file server does not have enough memory currently available to load it.

Insufficient memory to load NLM.

Source OS

Explanation The file server does not have enough memory to load a given NLM.

Action See "Insufficient Server Memory Errors" on page 440 in Appendix A, "Troubleshooting."

Insufficient memory to load OS.

Source OS

Explanation The file server does not have enough memory to load the NetWare operating system.

Action See "Insufficient Server Memory Errors" on page 440 in Appendix A, "Troubleshooting."

Insufficient memory to run NetWare v3.12 (requires at least 1 megabyte of extended memory)

Source OS

Explanation The NetWare v3.12 operating system requires a minimum of 1 MB of extended RAM. Most systems require more than 1 MB of extended RAM. The recommended minimum is 4 MB.

Action Install more memory and reload NetWare.

Insufficient rights.

Source RPRINTER

Explanation You do not have enough rights to execute the RPRINT$$.EXE file. In NetWare v3.*x*, you need Read and File Scan rights to the file. In NetWare v2.*x*, you need Search, Read, and Open rights to the file.

Action Check your rights to the file and have the network supervisor or your Workgroup Manager grant you the necessary rights.

Insufficient Rights to create the file "*<filename>*".

Source CAPTURE

Explanation You tried to create a file in a directory in which you do not have sufficient trustee rights. To create a file in a directory, you must have at least Write and Create rights in that directory.

Action If you need to create a file in this directory, ask your network supervisor to give you the necessary rights in the directory.

Internal error: message buffer overflow. *<code>*.

Source SBACKUP

Explanation An error message exceeds the maximum allowable length, possibly due to message expansion during translation.

Action Refer to the error message that preceded this error message. If the problem persists, contact your Novell Authorized Reseller.

Internal error: StatusMediaID was called with an invalid environment. SBACKUP will try to recover from this error.

Source SBACKUP

Explanation A nonfatal error occurred during the program's attempt to read the media ID. SBACKUP can continue.

Action None. This message is for information only.

Intruder detection lockout has disabled this account.

Source ATTACH, CAPTURE, LOGIN, MAP, NPRINT

Explanation You or someone else has tried to log in to your account without supplying the correct password within the allowed number of login attempts.

The network supervisor can limit any account on the file server to a specific number of login attempts to protect the account from intrusion by unauthorized persons. You will not be able to access your account until it is reopened by the network supervisor.

Action If you have difficulty typing your password, you can change it using the SETPASS command.

Intruder lock-out on account *<username>* [*<number>*:*<number>*]

Source OS

Explanation This notice appears on the console and in the error log that can be viewed in SYSCON.

A user repeatedly entered an invalid password while attempting to log in to the file server. The number of invalid passwords exceeded

volume has an invalid table zero starting block. The table is probably corrupted.

Action: Run VREPAIR. If the problem persists, make sure you have a backup of the volume. Delete the volume, re-create it using INSTALL, and restore the data from the backup.

Invalid FAT table 1 starting block of <*number*> on volume of size <*number*>.

Source: OS, INSTALL

Explanation: A File Allocation Table (FAT) is an index to one or more disk allocation blocks in which a file is located. The FAT table on this volume has an invalid table one starting block. The table is probably corrupted.

Action: Run VREPAIR. If the problem persists, make sure you have a backup of the volume. Delete the volume, re-create it using INSTALL, and restore the data from the backup.

Invalid file name being loaded

Source: OS

Explanation: This is a warning. The portion of the header that contains the name of the NLM has become corrupted. The NLM tried to pass (to the system) a filename that was either zero characters or greater than 12 characters long. The NLM may have been damaged by the manufacturer, or the disk drive may be malfunctioning.

Action: Reload the NLM from the master disks, or fix any faulty hardware. See "Hardware Errors" on page 435 in Appendix A, "Troubleshooting." If the problem persists, contact the vendor of the NLM for updates or fixes.

Invalid line in command file

Source: OS

Explanation: A command line in the STARTUP.NCF file was too long.

Action: Edit the STARTUP.NCF file and shorten the line.

Invalid line in command file—line length exceeds 511 characters

Source OS

Explanation A line in the command file exceeds 512 bytes.

Action Make sure no trailing information comes after the commands in .NCF files. The file being processed should be a command (DOS) text file.

Invalid load file format

Source OS

Explanation The description text field of an NLM was invalid. This field should contain text (about the NLM) that is greater than zero and less than 128 characters long. The NLM in this case did not meet these criteria. This problem is due to manufacturer error, NLM corruption, or disk malfunction.

Action Reload the NLM from the master CD-ROM or diskette. If the problem persists, check your disk drive for proper operation. See "Hardware Errors" on page 435 in Appendix A, "Troubleshooting." If the drive functions correctly, contact the vendor for the NLM for updates or fixes.

Invalid load file version. Module *<name>* NOT loaded

Source OS

Explanation The version number of the file to be loaded is incorrect.

Action Specify the name of a valid NetWare loadable file (probably an NLM), or check whether the file has been corrupted. If the file is corrupted, get a new copy of the file.

Invalid logical level "*<value>*", level must be between 0 and 255.

Source SETTTS

Explanation SETTTS allows values from 0 to 255.

Action Retype the command with a valid value.

Invalid Maximum Space defined in Subdirectory.

Source OS

Explanation The operating system encountered a problem while mounting a volume. This error probably indicates corruption.

Action Run VREPAIR. If the problem persists, make sure you have a backup of the volume. Delete the volume, re-create it using INSTALL, and restore the data from the backup.

Invalid name space list.

Source OS

Explanation While scanning subdirectory name space list entries, the system found that the next name space list entry was greater than or equal to the number of defined name spaces for the volume.

Another reason for this error might be the next entry scanned was greater than the maximum directory entries. In either case, this error probably indicates corruption.

Action Run VREPAIR and restart the system. If the problem persists, make sure you have a backup of the volume. Delete the volume, re-create it using INSTALL, and restore the data from the backup.

Invalid name space list order.

Source OS

Explanation While scanning subdirectory name space list entries, the system found that the next name space list entries are not in the correct sequence. This error probably indicates corruption.

Action Run VREPAIR and restart the system. If the problem persists, make sure you have a backup of the volume. Delete the volume, re-create it using INSTALL, and restore the data from the backup.

Invalid name space value.

Source OS

Explanation One of the following probably occurred:

- While scanning volume directories, the system found that the defined name space was greater than the maximum number of name space entries available.
- You tried to mount a volume that had a particular name space supported on the volume, but you did not load the name space support before you mounted the volume.

Action Load the name space support before you mount the volume. If this doesn't correct the problem, run VREPAIR on the volume.

Invalid NetWare File Path.

Source INSTALL

Explanation NetWare paths cannot be used for this operation.

Action Specify a drive path for a floppy or fixed disk.

Invalid number of volume segments *<number>*.

Source OS, INSTALL

Explanation During an attempt to mount a volume, the operating system determined that the volume contained too many segments (the limit is eight segments).

Action Run VREPAIR. If the problem persists, make sure you have a backup of the volume. Delete the volume, re-create it using INSTALL, and restore the data from the backup.

Invalid or local drives are not supported by ALLOW

Source ALLOW

Explanation ALLOW does not work with local drives, because local drives do not use inherited rights. Invalid drives have no rights.

Action Specify only valid network drives, directories, or files.

Invalid or missing Protocol ID number

Source OS

Explanation The PROTOCOLS REGISTER command was used to register a new protocol ID number, but the number is either missing or invalid.

Action Specify a valid protocol ID number in the command.

Invalid or wrong number of parameters

Source RPRINTER

Explanation You incorrectly entered the print server name, the printer number, or the "-r" (remove) parameter. Each parameter should be separated from the preceding parameter by a space.

Action Enter the command again with the proper parameters.

Invalid packed NLM <*filename*>.

Source OS

Explanation An NLM that is not a File System Engine NLM is too large to be loaded. The maximum size allowed is 4 MB.

Action Do not attempt to load that NLM.

Invalid Parameter. Use "I" option to query shell type.

Source Shell

Explanation I and U are the only parameters allowed after the shell name in the command.

Action Use the I parameter to display the shell type without loading the shell in the machine. Use the U parameter to unload the shell from memory. Use the shell name without a parameter to load the shell.

Invalid Parameter. Use "I" option to query shell type, or use the "U" option to unload the shell from memory.

Source Shell

Explanation I and U are the only parameters allowed after the shell name in the command.

Action — Use the I parameter to display the shell type without loading the shell in the machine. Use the U parameter to unload the shell from memory. Use the shell name without a parameter to load the shell.

Invalid Path.

Source — NCOPY

Explanation — You either specified a path that does not exist or mistyped the directory path.

Action — Use the LISTDIR command or the FILER utility to examine the directory structure you want to use. Type the directory path correctly. If you have mapped a network drive to the directory path, you can use the drive letter in your command instead of the directory path.

Invalid path specification.

Source — LOGIN, MAP

Explanation — Your login script has a command that contains an invalid path specification.

Action — Use the MAP command or the SESSION utility to display your current drive mappings or to establish new drive mappings. If the error occurs when you log in, use the SYSCON utility to access your login script; then correct the error.

Invalid path specified.

Source — OS

Explanation — The specified path length value is less than two characters long.

Action — Check the spelling of the path name; make sure the path begins with a volume name or a DOS drive letter.

Invalid physical level "*<value>*", level must be between 0 and 255.

Source — SETTTS

Explanation — SETTTS allows values from 0 to 255.

Action — Retype the command with a valid value.

Invalid print server name specified in DOS environment.

Source PSC

Explanation The print server name specified in the SET PSC command is not a valid print server name.

Action Retype the SET PSC command with a valid print server name.

Invalid printer number specified in DOS environment.

Source PSC

Explanation The printer number specified in the SET PSC command is not a valid printer number.

Action Retype the SET PSC command with a valid printer number (a "P" followed by digits).

Invalid procedure offsets within load file

Source OS

Explanation Values within the load file header for a particular NLM were not what the system expected. The items in question include the initialization offset, code image length, exit procedure offset, and check unload procedure offset.

Action This error indicates a corrupted NLM or a faulty disk system. Reload the NLM from the master CD-ROM or diskette, and check the disk system for potential problems. See "Hardware Errors" on page 435 in Appendix A, "Troubleshooting."

Invalid public record offset in load file

Source OS

Explanation This error indicates a corrupted NLM or a faulty disk system.

Action Reload the NLM from the master CD-ROM or diskette, and check the disk system for potential problems. See "Hardware Errors" on page 435 in Appendix A, "Troubleshooting."

Invalid record in load file.

Source: OS

Explanation: The operating system attempted to load an NLM whose code or data segments are invalid.

Action: Relink the NLM. If the problem persists, contact the vendor of the NLM or your Novell Authorized Reseller.

Invalid resource tag passed to AllocateConnectionNumber

Source: OS

Explanation: The server was processing a request to create a new connection, but the resource tag that was passed in as a parameter to create a connection call was invalid. The server will not allocate the connection, and it will return an error to the NLM that requested the connection.

This may be an internal program error in the NLM, or it may be associated with a lack of available memory.

Action: This problem may have been caused by a previous out-of-memory error when the NLM attempted to get the connection resource tag. If the preceding message indicates that the system is out of memory, make more memory available. See "Insufficient Server Memory Errors" on page 440 in Appendix A, "Troubleshooting."

If the problem does not appear to be memory-related, contact your Novell Authorized Reseller and provide an accurate account of the circumstances that led to the error, so that the reseller can re-create the problem and find a solution.

Invalid resource tag passed to CreateProcess.

Source: OS

Explanation: While processing a request to create a new process, the server passed an invalid resource tag to the create process routine. The server returned an error to the NLM that was attempting to create the new process. The process was not created.

The NLM may have had a problem when it attempted to get the resource tag prior to calling a create process. If the server is low on memory, a preceding error message should indicate the out-of-memory problem. There also could be a bug in the NLM, or the NLM may be corrupted.

In either case, the NLM will not be able to complete the operation for which the process was needed. If the NLM is in the process of loading, it may fail to load.

Action See "Insufficient Server Memory Errors" on page 440 in Appendix A, "Troubleshooting." If there is no memory problem, try reloading the NLM from the manufacturer's original media. If the problem persists, contact the vendor for an updated version of the NLM.

Invalid resource tag passed to ParseDriverParameters.

Source OS

Explanation An NLM tried to register a driver parameter, but the module did not create a resource tag for the process.

Action Contact the vendor for an updated version of the NLM.

Invalid resource tag passed to RegisterHardwareOptions

Source OS

Explanation An NLM was attempting to register hardware that it needed to use. The server detected that the resource tag passed as a parameter to the RegisterHardwareOptions routine was not valid. The hardware was not registered, and the server returned an error to the NLM. The NLM will not be able to perform properly.

The NLM may have had a problem when it attempted to get the resource tag prior to calling RegisterHardwareOptions. If the server is low on memory, the NLM's request to create the resource tag may have failed. In this case a preceding error message should indicate the out-of-memory problem.

There could also be a bug in the NLM that is calling RegisterHardwareOptions with an invalid resource tag.

Action First try adding more memory to the server or freeing up memory. See "Insufficient Server Memory Errors" on page 440 in Appendix A, "Troubleshooting." If memory is not the problem and the problem persists, contact the vendor for an updated version of the NLM.

Invalid right specified.

Source REVOKE

Explanation You specified an invalid right in your command.

Action Use a valid right in your command.

Invalid segment length of *<number>* starting at *<number>* on a drive of size *<number>*.

Source OS, INSTALL

Explanation A segment of a partition either has too many sectors or has sectors that exceed the allowable size. The segment is probably corrupted.

Action Run VREPAIR. If the problem persists, make sure you have a backup of the volume. Delete the volume, re-create it using INSTALL, and restore the data from the backup.

Invalid serial number

Source OS

Explanation When the operating system is initializing, the system checks its serial number to determine whether the number falls within a valid range. This message indicates that the number does not fit within a valid range.

Action Reinstall SERVER.EXE using a new copy from the master disk. Make sure the copy of NetWare you are attempting to use is a correct, legal (nonpirated) original. If the problem persists and the disks are original (and have not been tampered with), contact your Novell Authorized Reseller.

Invalid serial printer configuration data for printer *<number>* *<printer name>*. Printer not initialized.

Source PSERVER (.EXE, .NLM, or .VAP)

Explanation The configuration file for the specified printer is corrupted.

Action Run PCONSOLE and reconfigure the printer.

Invalid Shannon-Fano Tree.

Source OS

Explanation While a packed NLM was being unloaded, an error was found in the Shannon-Fano tree used to pack and unpack the NLM.

Action None. This message is for information only.

Invalid starting sector offset of <*number*>.

Source OS, INSTALL

Explanation The offset of the starting sector is invalid. The sector is probably corrupted.

Action Run VREPAIR. If the problem persists, make sure you have a backup of the volume. Delete the volume, re-create it using INSTALL, and restore the data from the backup.

Invalid starting sector offset of <*number*> on a drive of size <*number*>.

Source OS, INSTALL

Explanation The offset of the starting sector of a partition is greater than the size of the partition.

Action Run VREPAIR. If the problem persists, make sure you have a backup of the volume. Delete the volume, re-create it using INSTALL, and restore the data from the backup.

Invalid startup command: <*string*>

Source OS

Explanation A command other than LOAD or SET was issued from within a STARTUP.NCF file.

Action Edit the STARTUP.NCF file and delete any commands other than LOAD or SET.

Invalid Subdirectory number in file directory entry.

Source OS

Explanation While attempting an I/O control request, the operating system found that the device mapping table pointers were corrupted.

Action
: Run VREPAIR and restart the system. If the problem persists, make sure you have a backup of the volume. Delete the volume, re-create it using INSTALL, and restore the data from the backup.

Invalid Subdirectory number in trustee directory entry.

Source
: OS

Explanation
: While the system was scanning subdirectory entries, the trustee subdirectory number was greater than or equal to the number of directory entries. The trustee subdirectory number is less than zero. This error probably indicates corruption.

Action
: Run VREPAIR and restart the system. If the problem persists, make sure you have a backup of the volume. Delete the volume, re-create it using INSTALL, and restore the data from the backup.

Invalid Subdirectory number in user restriction directory entry.

Source
: OS

Explanation
: While scanning subdirectories on a volume to be mounted, the system found a subdirectory with a restriction subdirectory number not equal to zero. This number should always equal zero because it is predefined. This error probably indicates file system corruption.

Action
: Run VREPAIR and restart the system. If the problem persists, make sure you have a backup of the volume. Delete the volume, re-create it using INSTALL, and restore the data from the backup.

Invalid Time Format.

Source
: SBACKUP

Explanation
: An invalid time format was typed.

Action
: Press <F1> to see the correct format.

Invalid trustee directory entry.

Source OS

Explanation While scanning directories in the current volume for trustees, the system found one of the following problems:

- The trustee count was greater than the number of trustee entries.
- The trustee count equaled zero.

In either case, this error indicates file system corruption.

Action Run VREPAIR and restart the system. If the problem persists, make sure you have a backup of the volume. Delete the volume, re-create it using INSTALL, and restore the data from the backup.

Invalid value <*name*>. Parameter setting NOT changed

Source OS

Explanation A SET command was issued with a parameter that needed a number, but an invalid number was specified.

Action Type SET without a parameter to view the acceptable values for the parameter. Retype the SET command with a valid number.

Invalid volume block size of <*number*>K.

Source INSTALL

Explanation An invalid volume has been found. This volume has in some way become corrupted.

Action Delete the volume. If the data is required, restore it from backups. If this fails, contact your Novell Authorized Reseller.

Invalid volume header/root directory entry.

Source OS

Explanation The current directory entry being examined did not have the correct root subdirectory code number. This error probably indicates corruption.

Action Run VREPAIR and restart the system. If the problem persists, make sure you have a backup of the volume. Delete the volume, re-create it using INSTALL, and restore the data from the backup.

Invalid volume segment not found in disk segment list.

Source INSTALL

Explanation Either part of a volume is missing or the volume segment is corrupted. The remainder of the volume may be offline.

Action See "Volume I/O Errors" on page 441 in Appendix A, "Troubleshooting."

Invalid volume segment position of *<position number>* of *<number>* segments.

Source OS, INSTALL

Explanation The segment position is greater than the number of segments.

Action Run VREPAIR. If the problem persists, make sure you have a backup of the volume. Delete the volume, re-create it using INSTALL, and restore the data from the backup.

IPX has not been loaded. Please load and then run the shell.

Source Shell

Explanation The shell uses IPX to communicate with the network. IPX must be loaded before the shell can be run.

Action Run IPX first; then run the shell again.

IPX is not active on this machine. This application can't proceed without IPX.

Source RPRINTER

Explanation IPX has not been loaded in this workstation. RPRINTER requires IPX in order to execute.

Action Load IPX.

IPX protocol bound to *<name>* MLID Board # *<number>*.

Source IPXODI

Explanation This message is displayed after IPX has successfully loaded. It is not a error message, but simply informs you which logical MLID IPX is using.

- *<name>*The MLID's short name (NE1000, for example).
- *<number>*The logical board number of the MLID. This number is one-based (that is, the first MLID is assigned board #1).

Action None. This message is for information only.

IPX protocol successfully removed.

Source IPXODI

Explanation A request was made to unload IPXODI, and IPXODI was removed (unloaded) from memory.

Action None. This message is for information only.

IPX received an incomplete packet from *<network number>*:*<node number>*.

Source OS

Explanation The LAN driver from the specified node sent a valid IPX packet, but the data field was empty or incomplete. The operating system has discarded the packet to prevent data corruption. Users on the affected network node will experience interrupted network service and shell timeouts.

Action Update the LAN driver for the specified node.

L

LAN Driver loopback error detected. Driver for network <*number*> **received its own send packet**

Source OS

Explanation Packets have been transmitted incorrectly. The installed LAN driver is sending packets to itself. This error indicates a potential software problem in the LAN driver.

Action Unload the driver; then contact the vendor of the LAN driver for assistance.

LAN frame type name missing

Source OS

Explanation The PROTOCOL REGISTER command was used to register a new protocol ID number. The name of the frame type was not specified.

Action Specify a valid frame type.

LAN Protocol name missing

Source OS

Explanation The BIND command was not executed because the protocol name was not specified.

Action Specify a protocol name.

LAN receive buffer limit reached. All buffers are in use. Possible causes: disk channel bottleneck or buffers have been lost.

Source OS

Explanation A SET parameter limits the number of packet receive buffers that the operating system can allocate for itself. That limit has been reached.

Action Use SET to view the current maximum setting. (Select "Communications" and view the "Maximum Packet Receive Buffers" parameter.) You should have at least one packet receive buffer for each workstation attached to your server.

- If you do not have one buffer per workstation, increase the parameter and enter the command in the server's AUTOEXEC.NCF file.
- If you have one buffer per workstation, your server is too slow in responding to disk I/O requests. Add more memory to the server to help reduce the need for disk I/Os. See "Insufficient Server Memory Errors" on page 440 in Appendix A, "Troubleshooting."

Length differences on mirror directory chains could not be resolved.

Source OS

Explanation The operating system encountered a problem while mounting a volume. The amount of directory blocks of directory 0 didn't match the number of directory 1. The volume mount was aborted because the directory integrity was disrupted.

Action Run VREPAIR. If the problem persists, make sure you have a backup of the volume. Delete the volume, re-create it using INSTALL, and restore the data from the backup.

Line contains no end quote.

Source LOGIN

Explanation Your login script contains a WRITE command that has syntax errors. You used an invalid character or word, or you left out a quotation mark.

You must use quotation marks in pairs. You cannot use quotation marks within a pair of quotation marks (unless you use single quotation marks within a pair of double quotation marks).

Action Use the SYSCON utility to access your login script; then correct the error.

Load file contains invalid public variable name

Source OS

Explanation The public variable name in the NLM file header had a zero-character length. The name field can store up to 256 characters. This message indicates either a corrupted or outdated NLM.

Action Make sure you have a current version of the NLM. Reload the NLM from the master disk. If this does not correct the problem, contact the vendor of your NLM.

Load file defines a public variable that has already been defined. Symbol already defined: *<string>*

Source OS

Explanation While the system was loading an NLM, it found that one or more of the module's public variables had been defined previously. An NLM cannot use a previously defined public variable, because system integrity could be compromised.

This error is not fatal. The NLM will continue to load until all previously defined symbols have been listed to screen. The NLM will then be unloaded and all resources will be returned to the operating system.

Action Contact the vendor of the NLM for updates or patches.

Load file referenced undefined public variable.

Source OS

Explanation The loader could not find the module's public symbol *<name>* in the Public Symbol table.

Action Complete one of the following:

- If you are a user, check the documentation for the NLM. You must load another module before you can load this one.
- If you are a developer, check the spelling of the symbol. Make sure the module that defined this symbol made it public. Implement auto-loading so that the module that defines the public symbol is automatically loaded before other modules that need access to this symbol.

Loader cannot find public symbol: *<string>*

Source OS

Explanation When an NLM is loaded, it links itself to the operating system. One reason it does this is to share common variables with the system and with other linked NLMs. If the NLM is outdated, this message appears and lists all unresolved external public variables.

Action Obtain an updated version of the NLM; then try again.

Local printer number expected.

Source ENDCAP

Explanation The Printer flag (option) was used in the command, but the printer number was either missing or invalid.

Action Specify a printer number (1 through 3) with the Printer flag (option) in your command.

Local printer number (1, 2, or 3) expected.

Source CAPTURE

Explanation The Printer flag (option) was used in the command, but the printer number was either missing or invalid.

Action Specify a printer number (1 through 3) with the Printer flag (option) in your command.

Local printer number is invalid. It should be 1, 2, or 3.

Source ENDCAP

Explanation The Printer flag (option) was used in the command, but the printer number was either missing or invalid.

Action Specify a printer number (1 through 3) with the Printer flag (option) in your command.

Logical Partition <*number*> has mirror inconsistencies.

Source OS Media Manager

Explanation The indicated logical partition contains inconsistent data across the physical partitions that it spans; disk mirroring and duplexing are no longer active for this partition. Data integrity after remirroring cannot be guaranteed.

Synchronization probably failed because of a Hot Fix failure (all the redirection blocks on one of the disks are full), hardware failure, or device deactivation.

Action See "Insufficient Server Memory Errors" on page 440 in Appendix A, "Troubleshooting."

Macintosh files were found, but the Macintosh name space module was not loaded. Load MAC.NAM then restart the upgrade process. The In-Place Upgrade process is now being aborted.

Source 2XUPGRADE

Explanation During the System Analysis phase, Macintosh files and folders were found on the disks. The Macintosh name space module, MAC.NAM, was not loaded before the upgrade was started. Without this module loaded, the volumes with the Macintosh files will not mount.

If the SYS: volume has any Macintosh files, then the SYS: volume will not mount during the Bindery phase and the bindery will not be upgraded.

Action Exit the In-Place upgrade, load MAC.NAM, then restart the upgrade. MAC.NAM is usually found on the *NetWare v3.12 Operating System_2* diskette.

Memory for resident shell has been released.

Source Shell

Explanation The resident shell has been successfully unloaded, and the memory has been released.

Action None. This message is for information only.

Message NOT sent to *<servername>*/CONSOLE.

Source SEND

Explanation One of the following occurred:

- The message was not sent to the user or group because the user or group used the CASTOFF utility.
- A number of messages have been sent and not cleared, and the workstation's buffer for incoming messages is full.

Action Send the message later, or try another method of communication.

Message number is invalid.

Source TSA

Explanation An invalid message number was detected.

Action None. This message is for information only.

Mirror copies of the volume directory don't match.

Source OS

Explanation The contents of directory 0 were compared with those of directory 1. The compare routine found they did not match. This error probably indicates corruption.

Action Run VREPAIR. If the problem persists, make sure you have a backup of the volume. Delete the volume, re-create it using INSTALL, and restore the data from the backup.

Mirror Mismatch detected for directory block sequence *<number>*.

Source INSTALL

Explanation Errors have occurred in the file system.

Action See "Volume I/O Errors" on page 441 in Appendix A, "Troubleshooting."

Mirror Mismatch detected for FAT block sequence *<number>*.

Source INSTALL

Explanation Errors have occurred in the volume structure.

Action See "Volume I/O Errors" on page 441 in Appendix A, "Troubleshooting."

Mirrored partition *<number>* can not be remirrored.

Source OS Media Manager

Explanation A mirrored group cannot be remirrored because a redirected block with missing data could not be replicated on the out-of-sync partition. You may have a faulty drive.

Action If possible, try replacing the drive that has the bad redirection area. See "Hardware Errors" on page 435 in Appendix A, "Troubleshooting."

Missing path/file specification in the file list.

Source NPRINT

Explanation You omitted the directory path or the filename (or both) in your command. If the error occurs when you log in, the command in question is located in your login script.

Action Specify the directory path and the filename correctly. If the error occurs when you log in, use the SYSCON utility to access your login script; then correct the problem.

Module did not release *<number>* resources. Module: *<module>*. Resource: *<resource>*. Description: *<description>*

Source OS

Explanation An NLM failed to release an allocated resource when it was unloaded. In many cases, the NLM reclaims the resource. Unreleased resources are not available for system use if the operating system cannot recover them. This can cause memory allocation errors.

Action Contact the vendor of the NLM to determine whether the NLM should have released the resource. The vendor may have a newer NLM that corrects the problem.

Module did not release 1 resource. Module: *<module>*. Resource: *<resource>*. Description: *<description>*.

Source OS

Explanation An NLM failed to release an allocated resource when it was unloaded. In many cases, the NLM reclaims the resource. Unreleased resources are not available for system use if the operating system cannot recover them. This can cause memory allocation errors.

Action Contact the vendor of the NLM to determine whether the NLM should have released the resource. The vendor may have a newer NLM that corrects the problem.

Module initialization failed.

Source OS

Explanation The module you loaded could not be initialized. You will probably receive a message from the module that explains why the initialization failed.

Action Refer to the module's message.

N

Needed support modules are not present.

Source OS

Explanation You are attempting to load an NLM before loading a number of support modules that must be loaded previously. The load attempt aborted because these modules were required for the current NLM to operate properly.

Action Make sure that the required modules are loaded before loading the current NLM.

NetWare shell not loaded.

Source LOGIN, MAP

Explanation You tried to log in to a file server from your workstation without loading the NetWare shell into your workstation's memory.

When your workstation is booted, DOS is loaded into your workstation's memory. The NetWare shell is then loaded on top of DOS. The shell allows your workstation to communicate with the file server.

You cannot log in to any file server on your network unless the NetWare shell has been loaded into your workstation's memory.

Action Your network supervisor should have prepared a boot diskette for you that contains both DOS and the NetWare shell. Try rebooting your workstation and logging in again. If you still have problems, you may have a bad boot diskette. In this case, the network supervisor will need to provide a new boot diskette.

NetWare Workstation Shell has already been loaded.

Source Shell

Explanation This is just a notice. The shell is already in memory.

Action None. If you want to check the shell type, specify "-I" after the shell name on the command line.

Network Error: bad directory handle during *<operation>*. **File =** *<drive>:<filename>*. **Abort, Retry, Fail? or Abort, Retry?**

Source: Shell

Explanation: An invalid directory handle was passed to the file server. This error may occur because of a bug in the application program you are running on your workstation, or because of an internetwork address conflict.

Action: Make sure the directory handle is created and used properly. If the problem persists, contact the vendor of the application.

Network Error: file detached during *<operation>*. **File =** *<drive>:<filename>*. **Abort, Retry, Fail? or Abort, Retry?**

Source: Shell

Explanation: Your application program accessed a file without locking it. If an application program locks and unlocks a file in one routine, it must continue to lock that file whenever the file is accessed.

Action: Contact the vendor of the application. One portion of the application is neglecting to lock a file that another portion of the program previously accessed and locked.

Network Error: file in use during *<operation>*. **File =** *<drive>:<filename>*. **Abort, Retry, Fail? or Abort, Retry?**

Source: Shell

Explanation: Another workstation has opened the file.

Action: Use MONITOR to view which user has the file open. Access the file when that workstation has released the file.

Network Error: File Server went down during *<operation>*. **File =** *<drive>:<filename>*. **Abort, Retry, Fail? or Abort, Retry?**

Source: Shell

Explanation: The file server went down while your application program was in operation.

Action: Abort the operation (application) and try to connect to the file server again.

Network Error: illegal completion code during *<operation>*. **File =** *<drive>:<filename>*. **Abort, Retry, Fail? or Abort, Retry?**

Source — Shell

Explanation — A completion code was received that does not match the request. This error occurs if a internal consistency check in your workstation fails. The error may also occur if you are using different versions of the NetWare operating system and shell, or if you are using corrupted copies of the NetWare files.

Action — Copy SERVER.EXE from the *NetWare v3.12 Operating System_1* diskette to the file server's boot directory. Reboot the file server. Use the INSTALL program to reinstall the NetWare utilities. Boot the workstation with a newly-generated NetWare shell.

Network Error: invalid file handle during *<operation>*. **File =** *<drive>:<filename>*. **Abort, Retry, Fail? or Abort, Retry?**

Source — Shell

Explanation — The file handle used in a function is invalid. This error may result from a bug in the application program that you are running on your workstation.

Action — Make sure the handle is created successfully and used before being deleted. If the problem persists, contact the vendor of the application.

Network Error: IO attempted to physically locked area during *<operation>*. **File =** *<drive>:<filename>*. **Abort, Retry, Fail? or Abort, Retry?**

Source — Shell

Explanation — Your application program tried to write data to a disk location on the file server, but an application running on another workstation had the disk location physically locked.

Action — Try your operation later when the disk lock operation is not in use.

Network Error: IO error in directory area during *<operation>*. **File =** *<drive>:<filename>*. **Abort, Retry, Fail? or Abort, Retry?**

Source Shell

Explanation The file server detected an error reading or writing the directory entry for the file on the disk drive. This error indicates a hardware failure in the file server.

Action See "Hardware Errors" on page 435 in Appendix A, "Troubleshooting."

Network Error: IO error network disk during *<operation>*. **File =** *<drive>:<filename>*. **Abort, Retry, Fail? or Abort, Retry?**

Source Shell

Explanation The file server detected an error reading or writing the file indicated in the message on the specified disk drive. This error indicates a hardware failure in the file server.

Action See "Hardware Errors" on page 435 in Appendix A, "Troubleshooting."

Network Error: no read privilege during *<operation>*. **File =** *<drive>:<filename>*. **Abort, Retry, Fail? or Abort, Retry?**

Source Shell

Explanation The user has not been granted the Read right to the specified file or directory.

Action Have the network supervisor or Workgroup Manager assign the user the Read right to the specified file or directory.

Network Error: no write privilege or file read only during *<operation>*. **File =** *<drive>:<filename>*. **Abort, Retry, Fail? or Abort, Retry?**

Source Shell

Explanation Either you tried to write to a file that has been flagged Read-Only, or you did not have the Write right to that file.

Action Have the network supervisor flag the file as a Read/Write file or assign you the Write right to the file or directory.

Network Error: out of directory handles during *<operation>*. File = *<drive>*:*<filename>*. Abort, Retry, Fail? or Abort, Retry?

Source Shell

Explanation The workstation is trying to use more than 255 directory handles. Either the current workstation application or a TSR (terminate-and-stay-resident) program has a bug that requests too many directory handles.

Action Reboot the workstation. If the error reoccurs, contact the vendor of the application or the TSR.

Note: If the file server is running out of memory, the server cannot allocate all 255 directory handles for each attached workstation. The shell will then return this message when a request for a directory handle is made and the file server does not have enough memory to grant the request. In this case, however, a number of other system alerts will be generated as well. If you suspect low memory in the file server, use SYSCON to view the "File Server Error Log" and use MONITOR to view the memory statistics.

Network Error: out of disk space during *<operation>*. File = *<drive>*:*<filename>*. Abort, Retry, Fail? or Abort, Retry?

Source Shell

Explanation The disk drive has run out of available disk storage space.

Action See "Locked Device Errors" on page 440 in Appendix A, "Troubleshooting."

Network Error: out of dynamic work space during *<operation>*. File = *<drive>*:*<filename>*. Abort, Retry, Fail? or Abort, Retry?

Source Shell

Explanation The file server has run out of dynamic memory work space. NetWare v3.12 allocates 2 MB of memory for Alloc Short Term Memory, which should be more than enough. Either the operating system is corrupted, or a loadable module is requesting more Alloc Short Term Memory than it should.

Action Complete one or more of the following:

- If you suspect a corrupted operating system, copy SERVER.EXE from the *NetWare v3.12 Operating System_1* diskette to the file server boot directory, and reboot the file server.
- If you suspect a loadable module, load MONITOR and select "Resource Utilization." Check each resource tag for resources using "Alloc Short Term Memory." The number "In Use" should not be more than about 20,000 bytes. If a module is using more, unload that module and contact the vendor.
- If all loadable modules are using a reasonable number of bytes of allocated memory, you can increase the amount of Alloc Short Term memory with the "Maximum Alloc Short Term Memory" parameter in SET. See "SET" in *System Administration*.

Network Error: out of file handles during *<operation>*. File = *<drive>*:*<filename>*. Abort, Retry, Fail? or Abort, Retry?

Source Shell

Explanation The shell has run out of available file handles.

Action Increase the number of file handles in the workstation's NET.CFG using the "FILE HANDLES" option. Then reboot the workstation and load the shell again.

Network error on server *<name>*. Check network cabling or server status.

Source VLM.EXE

Explanation This is a critical communications error between the workstation and the file server. A communications error can be caused by a hardware or software failure.

Action See "Hardware Errors" on page 435 in Appendix A, "Troubleshooting." If the problem persists, contact your Novell Authorized Reseller.

Network Error on SERVER <*servername*>: Attempted access to illegal or down server. Abort, Retry?

Source Shell

Explanation Either the shell does not have a connection to the file server or you typed the name of the file server incorrectly. The error may also occur if an invalid server number was used or if the server has been flagged "not used" in the shell's server table.

Action Check the cable connection. Change the default drive to a network drive and try the command again. Type the file server's name correctly. If you are on a multiserver network, run WHOAMI to determine which servers the shell is attached to, or run SLIST to view a list of currently running file servers.

Network Error on SERVER <*servername*>: Connection no longer valid. Abort, Retry?

Source Shell

Explanation The file server received a packet and returned it to the shell, but the specified connection ID did not exist in the file server. If the shell remains unattached to the file server for longer than 15 minutes, the file server's watchdog timer will terminate the connection.

A router (file server or bridge) that has gone down or has an unconnected or bad cable can also break the connection.

Action Abort the connection; then log in again. The shell will build a new connection, if possible. If the problem persists, check the cables.

Network Error on SERVER <*servername*>: Error locating router. Abort, Retry?

Source Shell

Explanation When a network read or write error occurs and the retry option is selected, the shell will try to find an alternate route to the destination file server. This error indicates that the previously used route is now bad and no alternate route is available. This may also be caused by routers (file servers or bridges) that are corrupted.

Action Check the cables and make sure the connection is not lost. Run SLIST to see which servers are in the router servicing the workstation.

Network Error on SERVER <*servername*>: Error reading from network. Abort, Retry?

Source Shell

Explanation The shell encountered problems when it tried to receive and decode a NetWare packet. This error indicates a hardware problem with the connections, cables, terminators, or network boards.

Action See "Hardware Errors" on page 435 in Appendix A, "Troubleshooting."

Network Error on SERVER <*servername*>: Error receiving from network. Abort, Retry?

Source Shell

Explanation A reply packet was not received within a given timeout period. The server may have been brought down abnormally.

Action If the network is busy, retry the command. You can also increase the number of retries and timeout values in NET.CFG. Check the file server console to make sure the file server has not been brought down abnormally.

Network Error on SERVER <*servername*>: Error sending on network. Abort, Retry?

Source Shell

Explanation The shell was trying to send a packet to the file server, but IPX was unable to complete the request.

Action See "Hardware Errors" on page 435 in Appendix A, "Troubleshooting."

Network Error on SERVER <*servername*>: Error writing to network. Abort, Retry?

Source Shell

Explanation The shell encountered problems when it tried to format and send a NetWare packet. This error indicates a hardware problem with the connections, cables, terminators, or network boards.

Action See "Hardware Errors" on page 435 in Appendix A, "Troubleshooting."

Network Error on SERVER <*servername*>: Reply invalid header. Abort, Retry?

Source: Shell

Explanation: This error can be caused by any of the following:

- A bad checksum was found in the reply packet header.
- The reply was not a file server reply.
- The workstation's memory is corrupted.
- Interference occurred in the cables.

Action: Check the workstation's memory and the network's cabling.

Network Error on SERVER <*servername*>: Reply invalid sequence number. Abort, Retry?

Source: Shell

Explanation: The reply sequence number did not match the request sequence number. This error indicates that the workstation's memory is corrupted or that the shell received a bad IPX packet. Bad packets can be caused by faulty cables or cable interference.

Action: Check the workstation's memory and the network's cabling.

Network Error on SERVER <*servername*>: Reply invalid slot. Abort, Retry?

Source: Shell

Explanation: A routing error occurred that was caused by corrupted workstation memory, faulty cables, cable interference, or an invalid slot definition (either on the file server or on the workstation).

Action: Check the workstation's memory and the network's cabling.

Network Error on SERVER <*servername*>: Unknown communications error code. Abort, Retry?

Source: Shell

Explanation: An unknown error was found in the reply packet. The error did not match any known errors. Normally, this is caused by packet corruption through interference, bad cables, etc.

Action Infrequent errors may be caused by interference. If the interference is frequent or bothersome, check all cables, boards, etc.

Network printer number expected.

Source CAPTURE

Explanation The Printer flag (option) was used in the CAPTURE command, but the printer number was either missing or invalid. Valid printer numbers are 0 through 4.

Action Specify a valid number (0 through 4) after the Printer flag (option).

Network Spooler Error: (probably out of space on SYS: volume)

Source Shell

Explanation Although the shell knew about the job, the job was deleted while data was being spooled. The SYS: volume may be out of space, or something may have happened to the print job created by the spool function.

Action Run CHKVOL or VOLINFO to view available space on the SYS: volume. If the SYS: volume is running out of space, remove unused files on the volume or add another hard disk.

New password has been used previously.

Source ATTACH

Explanation You tried to change your password to a password you used previously on the file server.

The network supervisor can require periodic password changes for any or all accounts on the file server to protect the file server from access by unauthorized persons. The network supervisor can also restrict users from changing their passwords to passwords they have used previously.

Action The file server keeps track of the passwords that you have used previously. Therefore, you will need to use a password that you have not already used with your account.

New password is too short.

Source ATTACH, LOGIN, MAP

Explanation You tried to define a password that is shorter than the required minimum length for system passwords. The network supervisor can restrict individual passwords to a minimum length.

Action Use a longer password.

New password is too short. Please try again.

Source CAPTURE

Explanation You tried to define a password that is shorter than the required minimum length for system passwords. The network supervisor can restrict individual passwords to a minimum length.

Action Use a longer password.

New password not retyped correctly.

Source CAPTURE, LOGIN, MAP, SETPASS, VOLINFO

Explanation The new password was not retyped correctly. Your password was not changed.

Action Retype the new password correctly.

New password on server *<servername>* has been used previously, password not changed.

Source SETPASS

Explanation You tried to change your password to a password you used previously on the file server.

The network supervisor can require periodic password changes for any or all accounts on the file server to protect the file server from access by unauthorized persons. The network supervisor can also restrict users from changing their passwords to passwords they have used previously.

Action The file server keeps track of the passwords you have used previously. Therefore, you will need to use a password that you have not already used with your account.

New password was too short for server <*servername*>, password not changed.

Source SETPASS

Explanation You tried to define a password that is shorter than the required minimum length for system passwords. (The network supervisor can restrict individual passwords to a minimum length.)

Action Use a longer password.

No account balance for file server <*servername*>.

Source PSERVER

Explanation Accounting has been installed on the specified file server, and an error has occurred that has given the print server a zero balance. Accounting was probably installed with a version of SYSCON earlier than v3.0.

Action Copy a 3.0 or later version of SYSCON to the specified file server. Then either delete the print server and re-create it or remove accounting and then restore it.

- To delete the print server, run PCONSOLE, select "Print Server Information," and delete the print server from the list. Then re-create the print server.
- To delete accounting, run SYSCON and select "Accounting" and then "Accounting Servers." Delete all servers from the list. Press <Escape> and answer "Yes" to the prompt to remove accounting. Then reinstall accounting.

No connection to file server <*servername*>, or file server does not exist.

Source ALLOW

Explanation You are not logged in or attached to the specified file server.

Action Log in or attach to a valid server.

No connection to Server <*servername*>.

Source LISTDIR

Explanation You tried to use utilities on a file server you are neither logged in nor attached to.

Action Do one or both of the following:

- Use the WHOAMI utility to list the file servers you are logged in or attached to; then specify one of these file servers when you execute the utility.

- Use the ATTACH utility to attach to the file server you want to specify in the given utility. Then map a drive to the file server, and use the new drive mapping in your command.

No connection to specified file server.

Source FLAG, SMODE

Explanation You tried to execute a command on a file server other than your default file server, but you are not attached to that file server.

Action You do not need to *log in* to the other file server; you only need to *attach* to the file server. If you *log in* to another file server, the connection to your current default file server (and any connections you may have to other file servers) will be lost.

However, if you *attach* to an additional file server, you will retain all your current connections, and you will be able to execute a command successfully on that file server.

No credit left for file server *<servername>*.

Source PSERVER

Explanation Accounting was installed on the specified file server with a version of SYSCON earlier than v3.0.

Action Copy a 3.0 or later version of SYSCON to the specified file server. Then either delete the print server and re-create it, or remove accounting and then restore it.

- To delete the print server, run PCONSOLE, select "Print Server Information," and delete the print server from the list. Then re-create the print server.

- To delete accounting, run SYSCON and select "Accounting" and then "Accounting Servers." Delete all servers from the list. Press <Escape> and answer "Yes" to the prompt to remove accounting. Then reinstall accounting.

No default queue name can be found.

Source NPRINT

Explanation One of the following occurred:

- No print queue was specified in the command, and the file server does not have a default print queue mapped to printer 0.
- No print queues have been defined on the file server.

Action If no print queues have been defined on the file server, use PCONSOLE to define a print queue. If you are using NetWare v3.12, you must also use the SPOOL console command to set up a default queue for CAPTURE and NPRINT.

No default queue name can be found on server *<servername>*.

Source CAPTURE

Explanation One of the following occurred:

- No print queue was specified in the command, and the file server does not have a default print queue mapped to printer 0.
- No print queues have been defined on the file server.

Action If no print queues have been defined on the file server, use PCONSOLE to define a print queue. If you are using NetWare 3.12, you must also use the SPOOL console command to set up a default queue for CAPTURE and NPRINT.

No directories matching *<pattern>* found.

Source FLAGDIR

Explanation The pattern specified in the command does not match any existing directories.

Action Use LISTDIR to view the directory structure. Try again using a pattern that matches existing directories.

No disks can be found to upgrade. Ensure that the correct disk drivers have been loaded. The In-Place Upgrade process is now being aborted.

Source 2XUPGRADE

Explanation The upgrade process cannot find any disks that need upgrading. This situation occurs when disk drivers are not loaded, or when all of the disks have been upgraded to NetWare v3.1*x* already, or when the disks do not have any NetWare partitions.

Action Load the appropriate disk drivers and restart the upgrade process.

No Entries Found!

Source ALLOW

Explanation No directories or files were found in the specified path.

Action Use NDIR to view the files and directories in the path. Then try the command again using a valid file or directory name.

No EXECUTABLE files could be found with pattern "*<pattern>*"

Source SMODE

Explanation You either mistyped the filename or specified an executable file that does not exist. This error could also occur if you specified an invalid directory name or if you mistyped the directory name.

Action Do one or both of the following:

- Use the NDIR command to list the files. Then retype the filename using an executable filename listed in the directory.
- Type the directory path correctly.

No Expanded Memory Manager present. Cannot continue initialization.

Source Shell

Explanation The Expanded Memory Manager (EMM) driver must be loaded before the shell will load. This EMM driver has not been loaded.

Action Load the EMM driver according to the vendor's documentation and make sure the expanded memory is active. Then load the shell.

No extended information available for local drive.

Source FLAG

Explanation You tried to flag a file as either Transactional, Indexed, or both, but the file was on a local drive. You cannot use the FLAG utility to flag files on local drives.

Action None. This message is for information only.

No extended information available for local drive. Exiting to system.

Source SMODE

Explanation You tried to assign a search mode to a file, but the file was on a local drive. You cannot use the SMODE utility to flag files on local drives.

Action None. This message is for information only.

No Extended Memory Manager present. Cannot continue initialization.

Source Extended memory shell

Explanation The shell could not find an XMS driver.

Action Load the XMS driver before loading the extended memory shell.

No files found matching <*pattern*>.

Source NPRINT

Explanation You used an NPRINT command to print files that match the pattern, but NPRINT could not find any files that match the pattern.

Action Make sure you are in the correct directory; then use the NDIR utility to list the names of files in the directory from which you want to print files. Use a pattern that will satisfy the NPRINT command.

No match found for pattern <*pattern*>.

Source VERSION

Explanation You used a wildcard pattern with the VERSION command, but no files were found that match the pattern.

Action Try the VERSION command with a different pattern.

No matching data remain for the given scan parameters.

Source SMDR

Explanation This is not an error.

Action None. This message is for information only.

No more IPX sockets are available.

Source PSERVER (.EXE, .NLM, or .VAP)

Explanation All the sockets on the workstation are in use.

Action The default value for the "IPX SOCKETS" parameter is 20. Increase the current value by at least ten in the SHELL.CFG file and then reboot the print server.

No NetWare v2.1*x* or v2.2 volumes can be found on any of the disks. Check for disk drivers that are loaded without any disks attached. The In-Place Upgrade process is now being aborted.

Source 2XUPGRADE

Explanation Either no volumes were found, or the volumes found were already labeled as NetWare v3.1*x* volumes. This situation occurs when incorrect disk drivers are loaded, or when hard disks have been accidently disconnected from their drivers.

Action Make sure that the correct disk drivers are loaded and that the disks have not already been upgraded. Also check for loose cables to the hard disks.

No one logged into server *<servername>* **station** *<station number>*.

Source SEND

Explanation No one is logged in at the station number indicated.

Action Use the USERLIST command to find the correct station number.

No print servers are operating.

Source RPRINTER

Explanation No print servers are currently running.

Action Try again when a print server is running.

No response from file [or given] server.

Source ATTACH, LISTDIR, LOGIN, MAP, PSERVER (.EXE, .NLM, or .VAP)

Explanation You tried to attach to, log in to, or issue a command on a file server on the internetwork. The file server did not respond for one of the following reasons:

- The file server lost power or was shut off before the DOWN command was used.
- A broken or loose connection exists on the internetwork between your file server and the other file server.

When a file server is brought down with the DOWN command, the DOWN command sends a message to all other file servers on the internetwork, informing them that the file server is no longer active on the internetwork.

However, if a file server is shut off without the DOWN command being used, all other file servers on the internetwork assume that the file server is still on the internetwork, even though it is not.

In this situation, you will still see the file server name with the SLIST command, even though the file server is no longer active on the internetwork. The file server can be seen with SLIST up to 15 minutes after it has lost its power or abends. You will see this error message if you try to log in to or issue a command on the file server.

Action Try the command again when the file server has been brought back up.

No response from the print server.

Source PSC

Explanation The print server cannot respond at this time.

Action Check the print server monitor for a system message. If the print server continues to hang, reboot it.

No socket available for remote printers. Remote printers will not be initialized.

Source PSERVER.EXE

Explanation All the sockets on the workstation are in use.

Action The default value for the "IPX SOCKETS" parameter is 20. Increase the current value by at least 10 in the NET.CFG file, and then reboot the print server.

No such property exists.

Source TSA

Explanation An invalid property was specified.

Action Make sure the property you want is valid; then try again.

No such volume.

Source FLAGDIR

Explanation The volume in the path you typed does not exist.

Action Retype the command, specifying an existing volume.

No trustee for the specified directory.

Source REMOVE, REVOKE

Explanation The trustee has not been granted a trustee assignment to the specified directory. If the trustee has rights to the directory, those rights have been granted at a higher level.

Action None. This message is for information only.

No trustee for the specified file.

Source REMOVE, REVOKE

Explanation The trustee has not been granted a trustee assignment to the specified file. If the trustee has rights to the directory, those rights have been granted at a higher level.

Action None. This message is for information only.

No user name matches the pattern *<pattern>*.

Source USERLIST

Explanation No username matches the pattern given in the USERLIST command.

Action Use a different pattern.

No users named *<username>*.

Source — USERLIST

Explanation — The username specified in the USERLIST command is not logged in or is misspelled.

Action — Use the USERLIST command to list all logged-in users. If you want to see a list of users on a file server you are attached to, type USERLIST servername/.

Not attached to the specified server

Source — RIGHTS

Explanation — You tried to execute a command on a file server other than your default file server, but you are not attached to that file server.

Action — Use the ATTACH command to attach to the file server; then try the command again.

Not authorized to service queue *<servername> <queue>*. Queue will not be serviced by printer *<number> <printer name>*.

Source — PSERVER (.EXE, .NLM, or .VAP)

Explanation — The print server is not authorized to service the specified queue.

Action — Run PCONSOLE and select "Print Queue Information." Then select the specified queue from the "Print Queue" list. Select "Queue Servers" and then press <Insert> to add the print server to the list of authorized print servers.

Not Changed

Source — ALLOW

Explanation — The file or directory rights specified in the ALLOW command were not modified.

Action — You must have Access Control rights to give rights to other users.

Not enough memory for buffer for printer *<number>* *<printer name>*. Printer not initialized. Requested buffer size was *<size>* K.

Source PSERVER (.EXE, .NLM, or .VAP)

Explanation The file server or workstation that is running PSERVER does not have enough memory to do one of the following:

- Run the print server
- Service remote printers
- Add services
- Add the specified user to the notify list of the specified printer
- Add the specified printer

Action Add more memory to the file server or workstation, or free memory by doing one of the following:

- To free memory in the file server, see "Insufficient Server Memory Errors" on page 440 in Appendix A, "Troubleshooting."
- To free memory in the workstation, see "Insufficient Workstation Memory Errors" on page 442 in Appendix A, "Troubleshooting."

Not enough memory for communications with remote printers. Remote printers will not be initialized.

Source PSERVER (.EXE, .NLM, or .VAP)

Explanation The file server or workstation that is running PSERVER does not have enough memory to do one of the following:

- Run the print server
- Service remote printers
- Add services

- Add the specified user to the notify list of the specified printer
- Add the specified printer

Action — Add more memory to the file server or workstation, or free memory by doing one of the following:

- To free memory in the file server, see "Insufficient Server Memory Errors" on page 440 in Appendix A, "Troubleshooting."
- To free memory in the workstation, see "Insufficient Workstation Memory Errors" on page 442 in Appendix B, "Troubleshooting."

Not enough memory to add queue <*servername*> <*queue*> to printer <*number*> <*printer name*>. Queue will not be serviced by this printer.

Source — PSERVER (.EXE, .NLM, or .VAP)

Explanation — The file server or workstation that is running PSERVER does not have enough memory to do one of the following:

- Run the print server
- Service remote printers
- Add services
- Add the specified user to the notify list of the specified printer
- Add the specified printer

Action — Add more memory to the file server or workstation, or free memory by doing one of the following:

- To free memory in the file server, see "Insufficient Server Memory Errors" on page 440 in Appendix A, "Troubleshooting."
- To free memory in the workstation, see "Insufficient Workstation Memory Errors" on page 442 in Appendix A, "Troubleshooting."

Not enough memory to add *<user>* to notify list for printer *<number>* *<printer name>*.

Source PSERVER (.EXE, .NLM, or .VAP)

Explanation The file server or workstation that is running PSERVER does not have enough memory to do one of the following:

- Run the print server
- Service remote printers
- Add services
- Add the specified user to the notify list of the specified printer
- Add the specified printer

Action Add more memory to the file server or workstation, or free memory by doing one of the following:

- To free memory in the file server, see "Insufficient Server Memory Errors" on page 440 in Appendix A, "Troubleshooting."
- To free memory in the workstation, see "Insufficient Workstation Memory Errors" on page 442 in Appendix A, "Troubleshooting."

Not enough memory to initialize printer *<number>* *<printer name>*.

Source PSERVER (.EXE, .NLM, or .VAP)

Explanation The file server or workstation that is running PSERVER does not have enough memory to do one of the following:

- Run the print server
- Service remote printers
- Add services
- Add the specified user to the notify list of the specified printer
- Add the specified printer

Action Add more memory to the file server or workstation, or free memory by doing one of the following:

- To free memory in the file server, see "Insufficient Server Memory Errors" on page 440 in Appendix A, "Troubleshooting."
- To free memory in the workstation, see "Insufficient Workstation Memory Errors" on page 442 in Appendix A, "Troubleshooting."

Not enough memory to validate directory.

Source OS

Explanation The file server had enough memory to read the directory tables, but it did not have enough memory to validate the directories. Before you dismounted the volume, you received a warning that you were running out of memory and that you could not remount your volume because it had grown too much.

This error could occur at one of the following points in the volume mount:

- After comparing mirrored directory lengths
- During setup of extra directory structures
- During directory space restriction routines
- While adding directory trustees
- During maintenance routines

Action See "Insufficient Server Memory Errors" on page 440 in Appendix A, "Troubleshooting."

Not enough pages of expanded memory for installation

Source Shell

Explanation Too few expanded memory pages are available for the shell to load. Either there are not enough pages, or other programs are already using the pages.

Action	Check the Expanded Memory Manager to ensure that it is working properly. (See the vendor's documentation.) Programs using expanded memory may need to be unloaded.

Not enough room in DOS environment. Could not add "*<servername>*"

Source LOGIN, MAP

Explanation You are already attached to the maximum number of file servers. A workstation can be attached to no more than eight file servers at any one time.

Action If you need to log in to another file server, log out of a file server to which you are currently attached.

Not running on top of DOS version 2.*x*.

Source Shell

Explanation The shell version does not match the DOS version. You tried to load a shell that works with DOS version 2.*x*, but your workstation was booted with a version of DOS other than 2.*x*.

Action Upgrade your workstation to DOS version 3.*x* or later. Then upgrade your workstation shell with NETX, or install the VLMs that are shipped with NetWare v3.12.

Not running on top of DOS version 3.*x*

Source Shell

Explanation The shell version does not match the DOS version. You tried to load a shell that works with DOS version 3.*x*, but your workstation was booted with a version of DOS other than 3.*x*.

Action Upgrade your workstation shell with NETX, or install the VLMs that are shipped with NetWare v3.12.

Not running on top of DOS version 4.*x*.

Source Shell

Explanation The shell version does not match the DOS version. You tried to load a shell that works with DOS version 4.*x*, but your workstation was booted with a version of DOS other than 4.*x*.

Action Upgrade your workstation shell with NETX, or install the VLMs that are shipped with NetWare v3.12.

Number of buffers *<number1>*, Buffer size *<size>* bytes, Memory pool *<number2>* bytes

Source LSL

Explanation This information appears when the LSL has read configuration information from the NET.CFG file. (LSL does not display default values when it loads.)

- *<number1>* The number of communication buffers allocated by the LSL. Normally, the LSL does not need buffers; therefore, none should be allocated unless directed by a protocol's documentation. This number may be less than requested due to memory limits within the LSL.
- *<size>* The size of the LSL's communications buffers (106 bytes of this value are reserved for protocol and media headers). This value cannot be smaller than 618 bytes.
- *<number2>* The amount of memory allocated to the LSL's free memory pool. This free memory pool is used by protocols. This value may be smaller than requested due to memory limits within the LSL. The LSL first allocates the requested number of communications buffers and then allocates the free memory pool from the remaining memory. Normally, a free memory pool is not needed and should not be allocated.

Action None. This message is for information only.

Number of cache buffers is getting too low.

Source OS

Explanation The number of cache buffers has dropped below a preset value and the system is running out of memory. However, the requested cache buffer was allocated successfully.

Action See "Insufficient Server Memory Errors" on page 440 in Appendix A, "Troubleshooting."

Number of copies (1-999) expected.

Source CAPTURE

Explanation You used a Copies flag (option) in a CAPTURE command, but either you did not specify the number of copies to be made or you specified an illegal number of copies.

Action Retype the command, and specify the number of copies with the Copies flag (Copies=*number*). The *number* must be between 1 and 999.

Number of copies expected with the COPIES Flag.

Source NPRINT

Explanation You used a Copies flag (option) in an NPRINT command, but you did not specify the number of copies to be made.

Action Retype the command, and specify the number of copies with the Copies flag (Copies=*number*).

Number of segments in the volume does not match

Source OS

Explanation Two segments of the volume claim different numbers of segments. This error could occur for one of the following reasons:

- Two volumes on the file server have identical names and a segment from each volume is causing the error.
- The volume is corrupted.

Action If you have two volumes with the same name, unload the disk driver for the volume that you do not want to rename. Rename the other volume (the volume that is on the hard disk that still has its disk driver loaded). Then load the disk driver that you just unloaded. Mount both volumes.

If the volume is corrupted, run VREPAIR. If the volume cannot be fixed, load INSTALL, delete the volume, and re-create it.

Note: If you delete the volume, all data will be destroyed. You will have to restore the data from a backup.

Number of supported frame types too big.

Source OS

Explanation The driver passed in a number of supported media types to the operating system that exceeded the system's internal buffer limit of 32. You may be using an outdated driver.

Action Make sure your driver is certified for NetWare v3.12 and is functioning properly. If you have a current and functional driver, contact your Novell Authorized Reseller.

NWGetEffectiveDirectoryRights returned an error.

Source NCOPY

Explanation A network error prevented NCOPY from obtaining information about your effective rights.

Action Try again. If the problem persists, contact your Novell Authorized Reseller.

One or more of the parameters is null or invalid.

Source TSA

Explanation You specified invalid parameters.

Action Check the parameters and replace any null or invalid ones.

Open Volume Auditing Failed.

Source OS

Explanation The operating system failed when it attempted to open volume auditing. (No other information is available.)

Action Restart the server, or enter your password and continue with auditing disabled. If the problem persists, contact your Novell Authorized Reseller.

Operation aborted because BTRIEVE could not be accessed.

Source INSTALL

Explanation Although Btrieve is loaded, it could not be accessed. The installation process has terminated prematurely, and INSTALL will be unloaded.

Action Make sure that you have a version of Btrieve that is compatible with the v3.12 version of INSTALL. Unload and reload Btrieve to see if the problem persists. If the problem does continue, contact your Novell Authorized Reseller.

Operation aborted because BTRIEVE could not be loaded.

Source INSTALL

Explanation Btrieve could not be loaded. This could be caused by insufficient memory or by conflicts with exported functions.

Action The system console screen should indicate why Btrieve could not be loaded. Examine this screen to determine the necessary steps for resolving the conflict.

If the problem is due to insufficient memory, see "Insufficient Server Memory Errors" on page 440 in Appendix A, "Troubleshooting." If this is not the problem, contact your Novell Authorized Reseller.

Operation aborted because CLIB could not be loaded.

Source INSTALL

Explanation CLIB could not be loaded. This could be caused by insufficient memory or by conflicts with exported functions.

Action The system console screen should indicate why CLIB could not be loaded. Examine this screen to determine the necessary steps for resolving the conflict.

If the problem is due to insufficient memory, see "Insufficient Server Memory Errors" on page 440 in Appendix A, "Troubleshooting." If this is not the problem, contact your Novell Authorized Reseller.

Operation aborted because SYS:SYSTEM\\PRODUCTS.DAT could not be accessed.

Source INSTALL

Explanation In order to install products, the above file must be accessible.

Action Make certain volume SYS: is mounted. (Switch to the console screen and type "VOLUMES".) If it is mounted, restore the PRODUCTS.DAT file from backup or from some other source; then retry the action. If all these remedies fail, contact your Novell Authorized Reseller.

Out of memory for request structure in HotfixBlockingIO

Source OS

Explanation The system attempted to build a data structure to use in a Hot Fix operation. The system abended due to lack of memory resources.

Action Some NLMs or internal processes may have used up needed memory resources. Rebooting the file server should fix the problem. If the problem persists, add more memory to the file server and then reboot.

Out of server connections. User connect request failed.

Source: OS

Explanation: The server is operating at its maximum connection capacity. No additional connections are allowed until current connections are terminated.

Action: Try again later when other users have logged out of the system. A list of attached and logged in users is available from the "Connection Information" window for this server. Idle users can be cleared from the system with MONITOR.

Overlapping disk segments detected while adding free segments.

Source: INSTALL

Explanation: An internal system error has occurred.

Action: Try again. If the problem persists, contact your Novell Authorized Reseller.

Overlapping segment entry found starting at offset *<number>* on *<server>* for volume *<name>* segment *<number>*.

Source: OS

Explanation: When the operating system tried to mount the volume, it found an overlapping disk area. The operating system will discard the volume.

Action: None. This message is for information only.

Parameter Error: Too few parameters

Source MENU

Explanation The MENU command was not followed by the filename of a menu.

Action Include the name of the menu in the MENU command.

Password for user <*name*> on server <*servername*> has expired.

Source ATTACH, MAP

Explanation Your account is locked because your password has expired.

The network supervisor can require periodic password changes for any or all accounts on the file server to protect the file server from access by unauthorized persons. The network supervisor can also assign a grace period during which users can still use their old, expired passwords before having to choose new passwords.

Action If you use your current password during your grace period, change it before your grace period ends; otherwise, your network supervisor will have to change it for you.

Password has expired.

Source LOGIN, VOLINFO

Explanation Your account is locked because your password has expired.

The network supervisor can require periodic password changes for any or all accounts on the file server to protect the file server from access by unauthorized persons. The network supervisor can also assign a grace period during which users can still use their old, expired passwords before having to choose new passwords.

Action If you use your current password during your grace period, change it before your grace period ends; otherwise, your network supervisor will have to change it for you.

Password has expired.

Source CAPTURE, NPRINT

Explanation Your password has expired, but your supervisor has allowed you a specific number of grace logins with your old password.

Action Use the SETPASS command to change your password. If you use your current password during your grace period, change it before your grace period ends; otherwise, your network supervisor will have to change it for you.

Password has expired and all grace logins have been used.

Source ATTACH, LOGIN, MAP, VOLINFO

Explanation Your user account is locked because you did not change your expired password. The network supervisor can limit the number of times you can log in with an expired password.

Action The network supervisor, your Workgroup Manager, or your User Account Manager will need to unlock your account before you can log in.

Password has expired and grace period has also expired.

Source CAPTURE, NPRINT

Explanation Your user account is locked because you did not change your expired password. The network supervisor can limit the number of times you can log in with an expired password.

Action The network supervisor, your Workgroup Manager, or your User Account Manager will need to unlock your account before you can log in.

Password not unique.

Source LOGIN

Explanation You tried to change your password to a password you used previously on the file server. The network supervisor can restrict users from changing their passwords to passwords they have used previously. The file server keeps track of the passwords you have used previously.

Action Use a password that you have not already used with your account.

Password on server <*servername*> not changed.

Source CAPTURE, NPRINT

Explanation The file server returned a condition that the utility has not accounted for. Your password could not be changed.

Action Make sure the file server is still running, then try again.

Password too short.

Source LOGIN, MAKEUSER

Explanation You tried to define a password that is shorter than the required minimum length for system passwords. The network supervisor can restrict all system passwords to a minimum length.

Action Use a longer password.

Path does not exist.

Source TLIST

Explanation The path you specified was mistyped or does not exist.

Action Retype the path, starting with the volume name.

PIPE not found in resident portion of COMMAND.COM.

Source Shell

Explanation This is a warning. The piping feature provided by DOS could not be found in COMMAND.COM and thus will not be supported on the file server. The copy of COMMAND.COM that the shell is using is probably corrupted. If you try to use the PIPE feature, you will get the DOS error "Intermediate file error during pipe."

This warning may appear if the shell has been previously unloaded from memory. If this is the case, ignore the warning.

Action Copy an uncorrupted version of COMMAND.COM to the workstation's boot directory and reboot the workstation. Make sure that the COMMAND.COM version corresponds to the version of the NET*x*.COM file.

Please specify your action for the print server.

Source PSC

Explanation You used PSC without an option.

Action Specify an option when you use the PSC command.

Previous volume segment could not be found.

Source INSTALL

Explanation INSTALL could not read from the disk. The proper disk driver may not be loaded, the cabling may not be correct, or the drive parameters may be set incorrectly.

Action See "Volume I/O Errors" on page 441 in Appendix A, "Troubleshooting."

Previously loaded module was used re-entrantly

Source OS

Explanation The module you are trying to load has already been loaded. The system initialized another instance of the module.

Action None. This message is for information only.

Print queue *<servername>* *<queue>* cannot be serviced by printer *<number>* *<printer name>*.

Source PSERVER (.EXE, .NLM, or .VAP)

Explanation The file server returned a condition that prevented the specified queue from being serviced by the specified printer.

Action Contact your Novell Authorized Reseller.

Print queue *<servername>* *<queue>* cannot be serviced by printer *<number>* *<printer name>*, because a queue operator has disabled print servers from attaching to the queue.

Source PSERVER (.EXE, .NLM, or .VAP)

Explanation A print server operator has set the "Servers can service entries in queue" option in PCONSOLE to "No." This prevents print servers from attaching and servicing the specified queue.

Action Run PCONSOLE and set the "Servers can service entries in queue" option to "Yes." This allows print servers to attach and service the queue.

Print queue *<servername> <queue>* **cannot be serviced by printer** *<number> <printer name>*, **because the maximum number of print servers are already attached to the queue.**

Source PSERVER (.EXE, .NLM, or .VAP)

Explanation A print server queue can be serviced by up to 25 print servers. The maximum number of servers are already attached and servicing this queue.

Action If the print server needs to service this queue, have one of the other print servers detach from the queue.

Print queue *<servername> <queue>* **cannot be serviced by printer** *<number> <printer name>*, **because the print server is not attached to that file server.**

Source PSERVER (.EXE, .NLM, or .VAP)

Explanation The print server was attached to the file server when the specified printer was authorized to service the specified queue. However, the print server is not currently attached to the queue's file server.

Action Run PCONSOLE and attach the print server to the file server.

Print queue *<servername> <queue>* **is unknown. Queue will not be serviced by printer** *<number> <printer name>*.

Source PSERVER (.EXE, .NLM, or .VAP)

Explanation The specified queue was deleted and the specified printer's configuration file was not modified.

Action Run PCONSOLE. Either re-create the queue or delete the queue from the printer's configuration file.

Print queue *<servername> <queue>* **was not added to the list of queues to be serviced by printer** *<number> <printer name>*, **because it was already in the list.**

Source PSERVER (.EXE, .NLM, or .VAP)

Explanation Two queues in the list of queues to be serviced have the same name.

Action Run PCONSOLE, select "Print Server Information," and then select the print server. Select "Print Server Configuration" and then "Queues Service by Printer." Select the printer specified in the message. Delete the duplicate queue name in the list.

Print server *<print server>* **does not exist.**

Source CAPTURE

Explanation You specified both a print server and a queue in your CAPTURE command. The queue you specified is assigned to the print server, but the print server is no longer authorized to service the queue.

Action Use the PCONSOLE utility to attach the queue to the print server. Select "Print Queue Information." Then select the queue from the "Print Queue" list. Select "Queue Servers" and then press <Insert> to add the print server to the list of authorized print servers.

Print Server *<print server>* **has no available remote printer slots.**

Source RPRINTER

Explanation All defined remote printers are currently being used by other remote printers.

Action Run PCONSOLE and verify that the correct number of remote printers has been defined for the specified print server; then try again.

Print server is not authorized to login to file server *<servername>* **at this time.**

Source PSERVER (.EXE, .NLM, or .VAP)

Explanation The login property that allows logins only at specified times has been set. NetWare does not have a program that sets this property for print servers. Either your bindery is corrupted or you have used a third-party utility to set this property.

Action Complete one of the following.

- ◆ If you haven't used a third-party utility to set this property, run BINDFIX.
- ◆ If you have a third-party program that sets this property, use it to remove the station restriction.

Print server is not authorized to login to file server *<servername>* from this station.

Source PSERVER (.EXE, .NLM, or .VAP)

Explanation The login property that allows logins only from a specified station has been set. NetWare does not have a program that sets this property for print servers. Either your bindery is corrupted or you have used a third-party program to set this property.

Action Complete one of the following.

- ◆ If you haven't used a third-party utility to set this property, run BINDFIX.
- ◆ If you have a third-party program that sets this property, use it to remove the station restriction.

Print server *<print server>* is not up and running.

Source PSC

Explanation The print server specified in your command is not currently running.

Action Check the spelling of the print server in your command. Try the command again when the print server is running.

Print server's account on server *<servername>* has been disabled by intruder detection lock.

Source PSERVER (.EXE, .NLM, or .VAP)

Explanation The login property for intruder detection has been set. NetWare does not have a program that sets this property for print servers. Either your bindery is corrupted or you have used a third-party program to set this property.

Action Complete one of the following.

- ◆ If you haven't used a third-party utility to set this property, run BINDFIX.
- ◆ If you have a third-party program that sets this property, use it to remove the station restriction.

Print server's password on file server *<servername>* has expired. No more grace logins.

Source PSERVER (.EXE, .NLM, or .VAP)

Explanation The login properties that force expiration of passwords and limit grace logins have been set. NetWare does not have a program that sets these properties for print servers. Either your bindery is corrupted or you have used a third-party program to set this property.

Action Complete one of the following.

- ◆ If you haven't used a third-party utility to set this property, run BINDFIX.
- ◆ If you have a third-party program that sets this property, use it to remove the station restriction.
- ◆ Use PCONSOLE to change the print server's password.

Print server's password on file server *<servername>* has expired. Please change it.

Source PSERVER (.EXE, .NLM, or .VAP)

Explanation The login property that forces periodic changes in a password has been set. NetWare does not have a program that sets this property for print servers. Either your bindery is corrupted or you have used a third-party program to set this property.

Action — Complete one of the following.

- If you haven't used a third-party utility to set this property, run BINDFIX.
- If you have a third-party program that sets this property, use it to remove the station restriction.
- Use PCONSOLE to change the print server's password.

Printer <*printer*> has not been installed.

Source — PSC

Explanation — You specified a printer in your command that has not been defined with PCONSOLE.

Action — Check the printer number in your command. If the printer exists, use PCONSOLE to configure the print server to include this printer.

Printer <*printer number*> is busy.

Source — PSC

Explanation — The action you specified cannot be completed at the moment.

Action — Wait and try again. If the action must be completed now, use the "Pause" or "Stop" option before specifying the action.

Printer <*printer*> is not a remote printer.

Source — PSC

Explanation — Either "Private" or "Shared" was issued with PSC, but the printer specified is not a remote printer.

Action — Use the "Private" or "Shared" command with remote printers only. Check the printer number in the command.

Printer <*printer*> is not connected.

Source — PSC

Explanation — The printer has been defined with PCONSOLE, but it has not been connected.

Action The workstation must run RPRINTER to connect the remote printer to the print server.

Printer *<number>*, *<printer name>*, is of unknown type. Not installed.

Source PSERVER (.EXE, .NLM, or .VAP)

Explanation Either the configuration file for the specified printer is corrupted, or the primary configuration file for the specified printer is not on the file server running the print server.

Action Do one of the following:

- If you suspect a corrupted configuration file, run PCONSOLE, delete the printer, and create a new configuration for the printer.
- If the print server is not running on its default file server, either bring down the print server and reboot it using its default file server, or run PCONSOLE on the print server's current file server and define the specified printer on that file server.

Printer number expected.

Source PSC

Explanation You did not specify a printer number with PSC.

Action Specify the printer number with PSC, or set a default printer number with the SET PSC command.

Printer number expected with the PRINTER select flag.

Source NPRINT

Explanation You specified a Printer flag (option) as part of an NPRINT or CAPTURE command, but you omitted a printer number.

Action Include a printer number with the Printer flag (option).

Printer port requested by printer *<number> <printer name>*, is already in use. Printer not initialized.

Source PSERVER (.EXE, .NLM, or .VAP)

Explanation Two printers are configured to to use the same port address. The printer generating this message will not be initialized.

Action Use PCONSOLE to change the configuration of this printer so that it uses a unique port address.

Private is valid on NetWare 2.15 and above, except NetWare 386.

Source FLAGDIR

Explanation The Private flag is supported in NetWare 286 v2.15 and later, but not in NetWare v3.*x*.

Action Use the Private flag on file servers running the appropriate version of the software.

Problem with file *<filename>*. (TTS file...was not changed) length kept=0, had allocated=4096.

Source OS

Explanation The file server was brought down abnormally, probably due to a power failure. TTS prevented the specified file from becoming corrupted.

Action None. If the files are queue files (which begin with a Q_ and have an .SVR extension), a file must be added to the queue before the queue management file can be updated to the proper length.

Program Aborted.

Source NPRINT

Explanation A disk I/O error occurred that aborted the NPRINT job.

Action Load MONITOR and check the status of the hard disks.

Protocol ID could NOT be registered (error <*number*>).

Source OS

Explanation The PROTOCOLS REGISTER command was used to register a new protocol ID number, but the number could not be registered because of an error.

Action Another message should be displayed before this message to indicate why the command failed. Correct the problem accordingly.

PServer: No connections are available on the file server.

Source PSERVER.NLM

Explanation The print server needs one connection slot to run. All 250 connection slots are in use.

Action Wait until a user or other object has logged out. Load MONITOR and select "Connection Information" to view users who are attached but not logged in. Notify one of those users; then delete the connection.

PServer: Unable to get memory for print server stack.

Source PSERVER.NLM

Explanation The file server does not have enough memory to run the print server.

Action See "Insufficient Server Memory Errors" on page 440 in Appendix A, "Troubleshooting."

PServer: Unable to get resource tag for print server.

Source PSERVER.NLM

Explanation The file server does not have enough memory to run the print server.

Action See "Insufficient Server Memory Errors" on page 440 in Appendix A, "Troubleshooting."

PServer: Unable to open print server screen

Source PSERVER.NLM

Explanation The file server does not have enough memory to run the print server.

Action See "Insufficient Server Memory Errors" on page 440 in Appendix A, "Troubleshooting."

Q

Queue *<queuename>* does not exist on server *<servername>*.

Source CAPTURE

Explanation You either specified a queue that is not defined on the file server or mistyped the name of the queue.

Action Use the PCONSOLE utility to view the names of queues on the file server.

Queue *<name>* not found. It will be removed from the queue service list.

Source PCONSOLE

Explanation The queue no longer exists in the bindery, and is being removed from the Queue Service List. Normal operation should continue.

Action No action is necessary. This message is for information only.

Queue *<name>* not found. Normal operation should continue.

Source PCONSOLE

Explanation The queue no longer exists in the bindery, but still appears in the printer's Queue Service List. It can only be removed from the list by the network supervisor or equivalent.

Action No action is necessary. This message is for information only.

R

Read past end of read buffer.

Source OS

Explanation While an NLM was being loaded, a read error occurred because the system did not recognize the end-of-file marker.

Action Try to reload the original NLM. If the original NLM file is bad, contact the vendor of the NLM.

Redirected block *<old block>* to *<new block>* on partition *<number>*.

Source OS Media Manager

Explanation An I/O error occurred on one of the disks allocated to the designated partition. Hot Fix redirected the data to another physical disk block. There is full data integrity for the file being written. (See "Device numbering" in *Concepts* for an explanation of the partition number.)

Action No action is necessary unless this message appears every few minutes. If this is the case, load MONITOR and check the disk's Hot Fix statistics.

Disks that are rapidly using up their Hot Fix redirection blocks usually need to be repaired or replaced. See "General Disk I/O Errors" on page 438 in Appendix A, "Troubleshooting."

Redirection block table mismatch detected on *<partition number>*

Source OS

Explanation The operating system keeps two copies of the Hot Fix tables. When the operating system ran a consistency check on these tables, it determined that the tables do not match.

Action Complete one of the following:

If the hard disk is mirrored, complete the following steps.

1. Unmirror the disks with INSTALL and bring up the out-of-sync disk as a volume.

2. Delete the NetWare v3.12 partition on the hard disk that has inconsistent Hot Fix tables.

3. Re-create the NetWare v3.12 partition and remirror the disk to the volume created in Step 1.

If the hard disk is not mirrored, the operating system will self-correct the discrepancy by selecting the most accurate table. Some data corruption may occur. If necessary, restore the data from a backup.

Redirection error table mismatch detected on *<partition number>*

Source OS

Explanation The operating system keeps two copies of the Hot Fix tables. When the operating system ran a consistency check on these tables, it determined that the tables do not match.

Action Complete one of the following:

If the hard disk is mirrored, complete the following steps.

1. Unmirror the disks with INSTALL and bring up the out-of-sync disk as a volume.

2. Delete the NetWare v3.12 partition on the hard disk that has inconsistent Hot Fix tables.

3. Re-create the NetWare v3.12 partition and remirror the disk to the volume created in Step 1.

If the hard disk is not mirrored, the operating system will self-correct the discrepancy by selecting the most accurate table. Some data corruption may occur. If necessary, restore the data from a backup.

Redirection table inconsistencies on partition *<number>* can not be corrected.

Source OS Media Manager

Explanation The Hot Fix tables contain inconsistencies. All data on the partition has been lost.

Action Reset the Hot Fix tables for the partition.

Redirection table inconsistencies on partition *<number>* were corrected.

Source OS Media Manager

Explanation Hot Fix detected inconsistencies between redirection tables on mirrored drives. The tables on one disk were updated with the latest information on the other.

Action None. This message is for information only.

REMOVE does not work with local drives.

Source REMOVE

Explanation Floppy disk drives and hard disk drives on workstations do not have trustees or rights.

Action Use REMOVE only on network drives.

Rename Inhibit is valid only on NetWare 386.

Source FLAGDIR

Explanation The Rename Inhibit attribute is supported in NetWare v3.12.

Action Use the Rename Inhibit attribute on file servers running NetWare v3.12.

Reserved area is not zero filled.

Source OS, INSTALL

Explanation While mounting a volume, the operating system found that the reserved area of a segment definition was not zero-filled as it should be. Therefore, the segment was not included in the volume definition table.

Action Run VREPAIR. If the problem persists, make sure you have a backup of the volume. Delete the volume, re-create it using INSTALL, and restore the data from the backup.

RIP Socket was open when router was trying to open the RIP socket.

Source OS

Explanation Before the loader was ready to load, another NLM had already opened the RIP socket used by IPX. The offending NLM may be an unlicensed version.

Action Normally, no action is necessary; the loader will automatically override the offending NLM. However, if the problem persists, bring down the server and bring it back up without the offending NLM.

Router configuration error detected
Another router is claiming the same internet address

Source OS

Explanation Another router claims to have the same network and node address as one of the boards in this router. This is a configuration error and may cause network errors.

Action Find out which board has the incorrect network and node addresses; then change the configuration.

Router configuration error detected
<servername> **is claiming my same internet address**

Source OS

Explanation Another server on the network is claiming to be at the same address as this server because two file servers have been given the same IPX internal network number.

Action Assign each file server a unique network address.

Router configuration error detected
Router at node *<number1>* **claims network** *<number2>* **should be** *<number3>*

Source OS

Explanation This error occurs when two active servers use the same internetwork address. Users may not be able to locate servers on the network because of failed or improper routing of packets.

Action Bring down one of the servers and reconfigure it with a unique network address. If routing problems persist, issue RESET ROUTER commands to all routers.

Router configuration error detected. Another router is claiming the same internet address.

Source OS

Explanation Packet routing cannot be completed. This error occurs when an incorrect network number is issued by the BIND command to an IPX LAN driver. Another router claims to have the same network and node address as one of the network boards in this router.

This is a configuration error and may cause network errors. Users may not be able to locate servers because of failed or improper routing of packets.

Action Find out which board has the incorrect network and node addresses; then change the configuration. Reissue the BIND command at the system console using the network number shown in the message.

Router configuration error detected. Node *<address>* (*<name>*) claims network *<number1>* should be *<number2>*.

Source OS

Explanation Packet routing cannot be completed. The BIND command issued to bind IPX to a LAN driver specified an incorrect network number. Other bridges or servers on the network think that the cabling system has a different network number. You may not be able to locate servers because of failed or improper routing of packets.

Action Unbind the LAN driver; then bind the LAN driver with the correct number displayed in the message. Reissue the BIND command at the system console using the network number shown in the alert message. Two or more servers will detect this condition. Set the network address correctly, or the condition will reoccur.

RPRINT$$.EXE not found.

Source RPRINTER

Explanation RPRINTER was not installed properly. Both files (RPRINTER.EXE and RPRINT$$.EXE) should be installed in the same directory.

Action Copy RPRINTER.EXE and RPRINT$$.EXE to the same directory. Otherwise, you must set SMODE on RPRINTER.EXE so that the search path will be used to find RPRINT$$.EXE. RPRINT$$.EXE must be in the search path.

S

SAP Socket was open when router was trying to open the SAP socket.

Source OS

Explanation Before the loader was ready to load, another NLM had already opened the SAP socket used by IPX. The offending NLM may be an unlicensed version.

Action Normally, no action is necessary; the loader will automatically override the offending NLM. However, if the problem persists, bring down the server and bring it back up without the offending NLM.

SBACKUP: Unable to allocate the *<resource name>* resource tag.

Source SBACKUP

Explanation SBACKUP cannot allocate a required server resource. You may not have enough server memory. You should have a minimum of 8 MB of RAM on the server.

Action See "Insufficient Server Memory Errors" on page 440 in Appendix A, "Troubleshooting."

SBACKUP: Unable to open SBACKUP screen.

Source SBACKUP

Explanation SBACKUP cannot create a user screen. You may not have enough server memory. You should have a minimum of 8 MB of RAM on the server.

Action See "Insufficient Server Memory Errors" on page 440 in Appendix A, "Troubleshooting."

Script Error: Could not interpret line. *<line>*

Source LOGIN

Explanation The syntax of the line in the login script is incorrect. You may have forgotten quotation marks, used improper capitalization, or split a long command (longer than one line) with a hard return. Long commands should be allowed to wrap.

Action Consult "Appendix A" in *Installation and Upgrade* for the correct syntax for the line.

Searchable subdirectory too deep in tree.

Source PURGE

Explanation During a recursive purge (PURGE /ALL) on a NetWare v3.12 server, the directory tree cannot be over 28 levels deep. This messages indicates that PURGE found a subdirectory 29 levels deep.

Action To purge directories that are deeper than 29 levels, go to the directory that is 28 levels deep and execute PURGE from that directory.

Selected server <*name*> not allowed, server <*name*> only.

Source SBACKUP

Explanation You specified a path for log files that is not on the current server. Log files may not be redirected to another server.

Action Select a directory for the log files on the current server.

Semi-permanent memory allocator is out of memory.

Source OS

Explanation A request for semipermanent memory failed because the file server is out of memory.

Action See "Insufficient Server Memory Errors" on page 440 in Appendix A, "Troubleshooting."

Server <*servername*> battery is low. Repair or replace battery.

Source UPS

Explanation The UPS module detected a low battery condition.

Action Make sure the battery is connected properly. Test the battery condition with a battery tester. If the battery is bad, replace it.

Server *<servername>* is unknown at this time.

Source CAPTURE, REMOVE

Explanation You mistyped the name of the file server, specified a file server that is not on the network, or specified a file server that has been brought down for system maintenance.

This message could also indicate problems with network boards, active or passive hubs, or cabling.

Action Use the SLIST command or the SYSCON utility to list all the file servers that your station recognizes. Type the name of the file server correctly.

If the file server has been brought down for maintenance, try the command later when the file server has been brought back up. If you still have problems, ask your network supervisor for help.

Server *<servername>* not found.

Source SEND, SLIST

Explanation You tried to attach to the file server, but it did not respond for one of the following reasons:

- The file server is not cabled to the internetwork.
- The file server has been brought down by the network supervisor for system maintenance.
- You mistyped the name of the file server.

Action Use the SLIST command or the SYSCON utility to list all the file servers on the internetwork. Type the name of the file server correctly.

If the file server has been brought down for maintenance, try the command later when the file server has been brought back up. If you still have problems, ask your network supervisor for help.

Server <*servername*> on battery power. <*number*> min. remaining.

Source UPS

Explanation Commercial power has failed, and the server is running off the battery.

Action Save any open files and log out from the server within the specified number of minutes, or you will be logged out automatically.

Server error in retrieving queue ID.

Source CAPTURE

Explanation The file server returned a condition that CAPTURE has not accounted for. This condition prevented CAPTURE from getting information about the queue.

Action Make sure the file server is still running, and try again. If the problem persists, contact your Novell Authorized Reseller.

Server is out of memory.

Source SBACKUP

Explanation SBACKUP cannot access enough memory to allocate memory from the dynamic memory pool in the server. The backup process cannot continue.

Action See "Insufficient Server Memory Errors" on page 440 in Appendix A, "Troubleshooting."

Short term memory allocator is out of memory. <*Number*> attempts to get more memory failed.

Source OS

Explanation The request for short-term memory failed because the file server is out of memory.

Action See "Insufficient Server Memory Errors" on page 440 in Appendix A, "Troubleshooting."

Specified path <*path*> not found.

Source FLAG, GRANT, REMOVE, REVOKE, TLIST

Explanation Your command contained an undefined drive letter.

Action Retype your command, including a defined drive letter. Use the MAP command to view a list of defined drives.

Specified path <*path*> not locatable.

Source CHKVOL, LISTDIR, RIGHTS, SMODE

Explanation Your command contained an undefined drive letter.

Action Retype your command, including a defined drive letter. Use the MAP command to view a list of defined drives.

Station <*connection number*> attempted to use an unencrypted password call.

Source OS

Explanation The indicated station could not log in. An application or utility attempted to log in, verify a password, or change a password without first encrypting the password. The server is configured to accept only encrypted passwords.

Action Try one or more of the following:

- Replace the application or utility with one that encrypts passwords when making calls to log in, verify, or change passwords. If the utility is a NetWare v2.*x* utility, replace it with a NetWare v3.*x* utility.

- Use the SET server utility's "Allow Unencrypted Passwords" parameter to configure the server to accept unencrypted passwords.

Station <*number*> file lock threshold exceeded. Total violations <*number*>.

Source OS

Explanation The number of open files and file locks on the server for the specified station exceeded the limit specified. The total violations number indicates the total number of requests to lock a record that failed.

Action Use the SET console command to increase the number of file locks per connection:

```
SET MAXIMUM FILE LOCKS PER CONNECTION=<number>
   Minimum = 10
   Maximum = 1000
   Default = 250
```

Increasing the number of file locks will increase the amount of memory used by the server. You may need to add memory or free up existing memory. See "Insufficient Server Memory Errors" on page 440 in Appendix A, "Troubleshooting."

Station <*number*> record lock threshold exceeded. Total violations <*number*>.

Source OS

Explanation The number of record locks on the server for the specified station exceeded the limit specified. Applications that request record locks do not function properly until record locks are released by other applications.

The total violations number indicates the number of requests that failed to lock a record because the record lock threshold limit was exceeded.

Action Use the SET console command to increase the number of record locks:

```
SET MAXIMUM RECORD LOCKS PER CONNECTION=<number>
   Minimum = 100
   Maximum = 200,000
   Default = 20,000
```

Increasing the number of record locks will increase the amount of memory required by the server. You may need to add memory or free up existing memory. See "Insufficient Server Memory Errors" on page 440 in Appendix A, "Troubleshooting."

Subdirectory entry and first directory block do not match.

Source OS

Explanation While verifying subdirectory entries, the system scanned the subdirectory number vector table of the current volume. The value of the current element in the table does not have a value of -1 (which indicates a subdirectory); therefore, the attempt to mount the volume has been aborted.

Action Run VREPAIR. If the problem persists, make sure you have a backup of the volume. Delete the volume, re-create it using INSTALL, and restore the data from the backup.

Subdirectory entry refers to invalid directory block.

Source OS

Explanation The operating system encountered a problem while mounting a volume. A test of the subdirectory first block entry did not return with the correct value. The entry contained a value not equal to zero, indicating the wrong directory block or corruption.

Action Run VREPAIR. If the problem persists, make sure you have a backup of the volume. Delete the volume, re-create it using INSTALL, and restore the data from the backup.

Supervisor has disabled the login function for this server.

Source MAP

Explanation Your user account on the file server is locked.

The network supervisor can disable the login function temporarily to prevent users from logging in or attaching to the file server during system maintenance. Most likely, the network supervisor of the file server is doing maintenance work on the file server.

Action This condition is usually only temporary. Try to log in to the file server after the login function has been enabled.

Supervisor has disabled the login function on file server <*servername*>. Access denied.

Source VOLINFO

Explanation Your user account on the file server is locked.

The network supervisor can disable the login function temporarily to prevent users from logging in or attaching to the file server during system maintenance. Most likely, the network supervisor of the file server is doing maintenance work on the file server.

Action This condition is usually only temporary. Try to log in to the file server after the login function has been enabled.

Supervisor has the system bindery locked.

Source ATTACH, CHKVOL, FLAG, RENDIR, REMOVE, REVOKE, SEND, SETPASS

Explanation The system bindery on the file server is inaccessible. The network supervisor may be doing maintenance work on the system. The system bindery contains the names of users, their rights, file servers to which they are attached, etc.

Action The system bindery is usually locked only momentarily. Wait a few minutes and try the command again.

Syntax error in configuration information, closing ']' was not found

Source OS

Explanation The beginning square bracket ([ ) was found in the hardware configuration for the BIND command, but the closing square bracket ( ]) was missing.

Action Include the closing square bracket in the hardware configuration.

Syntax error, unexpected input <*string*>.

Source OS

Explanation Some settable parameters require a time value setting, ranging from fractions of a second to seven days. This error indicates an improperly typed time value spelling, such as "1 hour #$." The pound and dollar signs will cause this message to be displayed. If the pound and dollar sign were deleted, the parameter would be set for one hour with no errors displayed.

Action — Enter the correct time value for the settable parameter at the command line, or modify the AUTOEXEC.NCF file.

Syntax error, unexpected input (<*name*>) Time parameter NOT changed

Source — OS

Explanation — A SET command was issued with a parameter that requires a time value, but the value was entered in an unrecognizable format.

Action — Type SET without a parameter to view the acceptable values for the parameter. Retype the parameter with a valid time value. (Each unit of time must be followed by its name: days, hour, minutes, seconds. Abbreviations cannot be used.)

System file lock threshold exceeded. <*number*> file open or lock requests failed.

Source — OS

Explanation — The number indicates the requests that failed to open or lock a file because the limit was exceeded. The number of open files and file locks on the server exceeded the maximum specified by the SET utility's "Maximum File Locks" parameter. (The default is 10,000.) The file open or lock requests are not being serviced.

Action — Increase the number of file locks using the SET MAXIMUM FILE LOCKS command. For more information, see "SET" in *Utilities Reference*.

System record lock threshold exceeded. <*number*> record lock requests failed.

Source — OS

Explanation — The number of record locks on the server exceeded the maximum specified. Applications that lock records will not function properly. The number in the message indicates the total number of record lock requests for the station that failed because the limit was exceeded.

Action Use the SET console command to increase the number of system record locks:

```
SET MAXIMUM RECORD LOCKS=<number>
  Minimum = 10
  Maximum = 10,000
  Default = 500
```

Increasing the number of record locks will increase the amount of memory required by the server. You may need to add memory or free up existing memory. See "Insufficient Server Memory Errors" on page 440 in Appendix A, "Troubleshooting."

T

Tab expansion size expected with the TAB flag.

Source NPRINT

Explanation You used a Tab flag (option) in your command, but you did not specify a number.

Action Include a valid number (0 through 18) with the Tab flag (option) in the command.

Tab size expected.

Source CAPTURE

Explanation You used the Tab flag (option) in your command, but you did not specify a valid number (1 through 18).

Action Specify a valid tab size (1 through 18) with the Tab flag (option) in the command.

Tab size must be 1–18.

Source CAPTURE

Explanation You used the Tab flag (option) in your command, but you did not specify a valid number (1 through 18).

Action Specify a valid tab size (1 through 18) with the Tab flag (option) in the command.

The bindery cannot be closed.

Source TSA

Explanation For some reason, the bindery cannot be closed.

Action Make sure that you have Supervisory rights to the server. Also make sure the bindery is not being used.

The bindery file on the server <*servername*> is locked.

Source NPRINT

Explanation The system bindery of the file server is inaccessible. The network supervisor of that file server may be doing maintenance work on the system. The system bindery contains the names of users, their rights, file servers to which they are attached, etc.

Action The system bindery is usually locked only momentarily. Wait a few minutes and try the command again.

The bindery of server "<*servername*>" is locked.

Source CAPTURE

Explanation The system bindery of the file server is inaccessible. The network supervisor of that file server may be doing maintenance work on the system. The system bindery contains the names of users, their rights, file servers to which they are attached, etc.

Action The system bindery is usually locked only momentarily. Wait a few minutes and try the command again.

The bindery property at offset <*offset number*> cannot be read.

Source 2XUPGRADE

Explanation A bindery property could not be read from the file NET$BIND.SYS. The NetWare v2.1*x* bindery may have been corrupted, or the NET$BIND.SYS file may have failed to open.

Action At this point, the file system has been upgraded to NetWare v3.1*x*, but it has no bindery. Restore your server to NetWare v2.1*x*, and replace your two bindery files (NET$BIND.SYS and NET$BVAL.SYS) with an uncorrupted version of the bindery from your backups before restarting the upgrade.

The block allocation size does not match.

Source INSTALL

Explanation INSTALL found two volume segments with the same name, but the block sizes of the two do not match. Two volumes on the same server cannot have the same name.

Action — Bring the disks that contain these volumes online one at a time, rather than at the same time. If one of the volumes is old and no longer needed, delete it to avoid the problem in the future.

The command line contained illegal characters.

Source — CAPTURE

Explanation — You may have typed a character while you were pressing the Control key. This will produce a "control character." Control characters such as ^C and ^E are special characters used for formatting text in word processing programs, controlling printers, transmitting data, etc. These characters should not be included in commands.

Action — Retype your command.

The connection information on the destination server could not be obtained.

Source — NPRINT

Explanation — The file server returned a condition that prevented NPRINT from getting your username.

Action — Make sure the file server is still running, and try again. If the problem persists, contact your Novell Authorized Reseller.

The connection is invalid or does not exist.

Source — TSA

Explanation — No connection has been established, or the old connection is invalid.

Action — Reestablish the connection and proceed.

The connection with the print server has been lost.

Source — RPRINTER

Explanation — RPRINTER could not get information on the status of the connection.

Action — Make sure the print server is still running, and run RPRINTER again.

The console has been secured, path specifiers are no longer allowed

Source OS

Explanation After the console has been secured, no paths can be specified when loading files. Only the currently known search paths will be used.

Action Copy the loadable module into a currently defined search path, such as SYS:SYSTEM. Then load the module.

The conventional memory block for the EMS stack cannot be resized. The VLM.EXE file cannot be loaded. DOS memory is probably corrupt. Reboot your computer and then try to load the VLM.EXE again.

Source VLM.EXE

Explanation This error indicates that the DOS memory chain has been corrupted.

Action Because the DOS memory chain has been corrupted, it is unsafe to continue operating the computer. The best solution is to reboot the computer; then try to load VLM.EXE.

The data set handle is invalid.

Source TSA

Explanation The data set may not exist.

Action Verify that the data set exists.

The data set name is invalid.

Source TSA

Explanation An invalid file or directory name was specified.

Action Specify a valid data set name for the specified name space.

The data set was excluded by the selection list.

Source TSA

Explanation The specified file or directory was excluded by the selection criteria.

Action Change the selection criteria in SBACKUP.

The destination server is busy.

Source NPRINT

Explanation The file server to which you sent your print job is too busy to process your print job at this time.

Action An "Abort or Retry" message should also appear. Type "A" to abort the print job or "R" to retry the print job.

The destination server <*servername*> is unknown at this time.

Source NPRINT

Explanation You mistyped the name of the file server, specified a file server that is not on the network, or specified a file server that has been brought down for system maintenance.

Action Use the SLIST command or the SYSCON utility to list the file servers on the network. Type the name of the file server correctly.

If the file server has been brought down for maintenance, try the command later when the file server has been brought back up. If you still have problems, ask your network supervisor for help.

The Directory Entry Table cannot be read as needed to update new object ID's. Trustee rights and file owner information will be lost.

Source 2XUPGRADE

Explanation The directory cannot be read into memory. Information such as file ownership and trustee rights are lost.

Action Reassign file ownership and trustee rights by using the FILER and GRANT commands, or by using SYSCON.

The Directory Entry Table cannot be read due to a bad disk block. The In-Place Upgrade process is now being aborted.

Source 2XUPGRADE

Explanation The NetWare v2.1*x* Directory Entry Table (DET) could not be read from the disk. The disk has a bad block. Without the DET, files and directories will be lost or corrupted.

Action Reboot the server and run the NetWare v2.1*x* VREPAIR utility. (You may need to run VREPAIR several times until the problem is fixed.)

The Directory Entry Table cannot be written to as needed to update new object ID's. Trustee rights and file owner information will be lost.

Source 2XUPGRADE

Explanation The directory cannot be written to. Information such as file ownership and trustee rights are lost.

Action Reassign file ownership and trustee rights by using the FILER and GRANT commands, or by using SYSCON.

The disk device lock has been revoked by the operating system. This hard disk may have just failed.

Source 2XUPGRADE

Explanation The disk device information was temporarily lost by the operating system. This may have been caused by a hard disk failure.

Action Make sure that your hard disk is still working.

The disk which contains the SYS: volume cannot be written to. The In-Place Upgrade process is now being aborted.

Source 2XUPGRADE

Explanation The first disk, which contains the SYS: volume, cannot be written to. The upgrade is aborted.

Action Refer to another message that should appear with this one.

The disk's Partition Table cannot be written to (status = *<status number>***). The Disk Modification Phase cannot be completed without first modifying the Partition Table to recognize NetWare v3.1*x* partitions. The In-Place Upgrade process is now being aborted.**

Source 2XUPGRADE

Explanation This error occurs after the disk is first written to at the start of Phase 3. The status indicates the cause of the failure. If the status is equal to 2 or 3, then no data has been lost. Otherwise, all data on this disk may be lost.

Action If you have lost your volumes, restore the disk from your backups, then upgrade using another upgrade method.

The DOS partition will be placed on the same EXTERNAL hard disk as the SYS: volume. Many computers cannot boot from a DOS partition on an external hard disk.

Source — 2XUPGRADE

Explanation — The SYS: volume is on an external hard disk such as a Disk Coprocessor Board (DCB) or an IDE disk. The DOS partition is placed on the same external hard disk as the SYS: volume.

The requested DOS partition will still be created; however, DOS currently does not support external hard disks. A DOS partition makes booting a NetWare v3.1*x* server considerably faster; however, it is not necessary for NetWare v3.1*x*

Action — Do one of the following:

- If you have a Novell 386 AE server with a DCB controller, do nothing. It is one of the few computers that can boot from a DOS partition on an external DCB disk.
- Complete the upgrade; then add a new internal hard disk for the SYS: volume and the DOS partition. Ignore error message 141. It will be issued at the start of Phase 4 since the bindery is stored on the SYS: volume.
- Reconfigure the server before performing the upgrade, placing the SYS: volume on an internal hard disk, especially if you plan to upgrade later to NetWare v4.0.

The extended attributes cannot be read.

Source — TSA

Explanation — For some reason, the extended attributes for a file cannot be read.

Action — Make sure that you have specified a valid file and that you have appropriate user access rights.

The FAT chain used to define the FAT has an invalid forward reference.

Source — OS

Explanation — A File Allocation Table (FAT) chain is a list of directory block locations. This error probably indicates file system corruption.

Action — Run VREPAIR. If the problem persists, make sure you have a backup of the volume. Delete the volume, re-create it using INSTALL, and restore the data from the backup.

The FAT chain used to define the FAT is invalid.

Source — OS

Explanation — A File Allocation Table (FAT) chain is a list of directory block locations. This error probably indicates file system corruption.

Action — Run VREPAIR. If the problem persists, make sure you have a backup of the volume. Delete the volume, re-create it using INSTALL, and restore the data from the backup.

The FAT chain used to define the FAT overlaps on itself.

Source — OS

Explanation — A File Allocation Table (FAT) chain is a list of directory block locations. This error probably indicates file system corruption.

Action — Run VREPAIR. If the problem persists, make sure you have a backup of the volume. Delete the volume, re-create it using INSTALL, and restore the data from the backup.

The file *<filename>* not found.

Source — NPRINT

Explanation — Either you do not have a search drive mapped to the directory where the file resides, or the file does not exist on the file server volume.

Action — Use the MAP command or the SESSION utility to map a search drive to the directory in which the file resides. You can use the SYSCON utility to permanently enter this mapping in your login script.

The file "DIRSTAMP.SYS" cannot be found. The Directory Entry Table is either corrupt or it is from a version of NetWare not supported by this upgrade program. The In-Place Upgrade process is now being aborted.

Source 2XUPGRADE

Explanation The file DIRSTAMP.SYS is used to store information about Macintosh files. This file could not be found when a portion of the NetWare v2.1*x* Directory Entry Table (DET) was accessed. Without this file, the directories cannot be read.

Action If the DET is corrupted, reboot the server and run the NetWare v2.1*x* VREPAIR utility to repair it. Make sure that you are upgrading from NetWare v2.1*x* or v2.2 only. (You may need to run VREPAIR several times until the problem is fixed.)

The file "DIRSTAMP.SYS" cannot be read. Volume *<volume name>***:'s FAT Table is corrupt. The In-Place Upgrade process is now being aborted.**

Source 2XUPGRADE

Explanation DIRSTAMP.SYS is the first file on every v2.*x* volume. If the File Allocation Table (FAT) is corrupted, then this file will not be read properly. This error message aborts the upgrade, preventing the paddle wheel from spinning endlessly while in the Disk Analysis phase.

If the FAT is corrupted, then a symptom may be that only the first 4 KB of each file can be read, causing utilities to "hang" abnormally after being loaded.

Action Your server may have some serious hardware problems. Bring up your v2.*x* server and get it into a working state before retrying the In-Place Upgrade.

The File Server bindery object has been renamed from "*<old server name>***" to "***<new server name>***" to correspond with the server's new name.**

Source 2XUPGRADE

Explanation The name of the server is stored inside the bindery. When the v3.*x* server operating system was loaded, the server was given a different name than that of the v2.*x* server. The file server bindery object was renamed to reflect the newly given name.

This prevents the SLIST utility from erroneously seeing the old server name, which is no longer available.

Action — If you do not like the server's new name, then simply bring down the server and bring it back up again, giving it the desired name. You may need to change a line inside the AUTOEXEC.NCF file in the SYS:SYSTEM directory.

The file server has reached its maximum number of connections.

Source — ATTACH, LOGIN

Explanation — Each file server has a limited number of connection slots. A NetWare v3.*x* file server can have up to 250 users connected.

Action — Try again after a user has logged out of the file server.

The file server's bindery is locked. Unable to attach to file server *<servername>*.

Source — PSERVER (.EXE, .NLM, or .VAP)

Explanation — The system bindery must be opened to allow new users or objects to log in or attach to the file server. The network supervisor probably has the bindery locked while doing maintenance work. The system bindery contains the names of users, their rights, file servers to which they are attached, etc.

Action — The system bindery is usually locked only momentarily. Wait a few minutes and try the command again.

The first entry of a file's FAT chain is invalid.

Source — OS

Explanation — A File Allocation Table (FAT) chain is a list of directory block locations. This error probably indicates file system corruption.

Action — Run VREPAIR. If the problem persists, make sure you have a backup of the volume. Delete the volume, re-create it using INSTALL, and restore the data from the backup.

The given base drive is not defined.

Source — NPRINT

Explanation — The drive you specified in your command is not a defined network drive.

Action: Use the MAP command or the SESSION utility to establish a new network drive mapping; then specify the newly-mapped drive in your command.

The handle tag is invalid or the pointer is null.

Source: TSA

Explanation: This handle is not valid.

Action: None. This message is for information only.

The Hot Fix Redirection Area in the NetWare v3.1*x* disk partition cannot be created. The In-Place Upgrade process is now being aborted.

Source: 2XUPGRADE

Explanation: A call to the operating system that creates the Hot Fix redirection area has failed. Your hard disk may be faulty.

Action: Make sure that your hard disk is still working.

The ID number of the specified queue could not be obtained.

Source: NPRINT

Explanation: The system bindery was locked when NPRINT tried to send a print job to the printer. The system bindery contains the names of users, their rights, file servers to which they are attached, etc.

Action: The system bindery is usually locked only momentarily. Wait a few minutes and try the command again.

The In-Place Upgrade process has been aborted by the user. The In-Place Upgrade process is now being aborted.

Source: 2XUPGRADE

Explanation: During the upgrade process, the user is given the option to abort the upgrade. This option is given only in Phases #1 and #2. The In-Place Upgrade NLM is unloaded, and the user is returned to the console prompt (:).

Action: None. This message is for information only.

The IPX interface does not support checksums. The IPXNCP.VLM file will load successfully without using checksums. Make sure the installed IPXODI.COM is version 2.01 or later and that it is not bound to a board configured to use the ETHERNET_802.3 frame format.

Source IPXNCP.VLM

Explanation IPXNCP.VLM will load without supporting checksums. For checksum to be supported, the loaded IPXODI.COM file must support checksums. Either the loaded version of IPXODI.COM does not have checksum support, or the protocol bound to IPX does not support checksums.

Action Because IPXNCP.VLM will load without support for checksums, no action is required at this point. However, to avoid receiving this message the next time the IPXNCP.VLM file is loaded, either load IPXODI.COM with checksum support enabled, or add "CHECKSUM=OFF" to the NET.CFG file.

See "Configuring Your DOS Workstation" in *Workstation for DOS and Windows* for more information about the NET.CFG file.

The IPX interface is not loaded. The IPXNCP.VLM file cannot be loaded. Load the IPXODI.COM file first and then try loading the IPXNCP.VLM file.

Source IPXNCP.VLM

Explanation An attempt was made to load the IPXNCP.VLM file without having previously loaded the IPX interface.

Action Load IPXODI.COM before attempting to load IPXNCP.VLM.

The IPX socket for large internet packets could not be opened. The IPXNCP.VLM file will load successfully without using large internet packets. Configure the IPXODI.COM file for enough sockets in the NET.CFG file or add LARGE INTERNET PACKETS=OFF to the NET.CFG file; then load the IPXNCP.VLM file.

Source IPXNCP.VLM

Explanation This message is only a warning. The DOS Requester will function properly without the use of large internet packets.

The large internet packet protocol, which is a part of the IPXNCP.VLM module, requires an IPX socket in order to function properly. The request to open a socket failed indicating that not enough IPX sockets are available.

Action If large internet packets are desired, make sure that the IPX interface is configured for enough sockets in the NET.CFG file before loading the DOS Requester. If large internet packets are not desired, add "LARGE INTERNET PACKETS=OFF" to the "NETWARE DOS REQUESTER" section of the NET.CFG file.

See "Configuring Your DOS Workstation" in *Workstation for DOS and Windows* for more information about the NET.CFG file.

The IPX sockets could not be opened. The IPXNCP.VLM file cannot be loaded. Configure the IPXODI.COM file for enough sockets in the NET.CFG file and then try to load the IPXNCP.VLM file.

Source IPXNCP.VLM

Explanation The IPXNCP.VLM file failed to open the IPX sockets needed in order to run. The IPXNCP.VLM module requires four or more IPX sockets be available.

Action Increase the number of IPX sockets available by using the "IPX SOCKETS=" parameter in the NET.CFG file; then reload IPXODI.COM and then IPXNCP.VLM.

The loaded VLM.EXE file has a different version. VLM.EXE cannot be unloaded. Make sure the VLM.EXE file you are using has the same version number and then try to unload VLM.EXE.

Source VLM.EXE

Explanation An attempt was made to unload the VLM.EXE file using the /U parameter. This message indicates that the version of the VLM.EXE file that is currently loaded in memory is not the same version as the one being used to attempt the unload function. This is unsafe and is therefore not allowed by the VLM.EXE file.

Action Use the same version of the VLM.EXE file to attempt the unload as was previously loaded in memory; otherwise, the VLM.EXE file that is loaded in memory can be removed only by rebooting the computer.

The loaded VLM.EXE file indicates it is unsafe to execute an unload for VLM number *<number>*. VLM.EXE will not be unloaded. Unload all memory resident programs (TSRs) that were loaded after the VLM.EXE file and then try to unload VLM.EXE.

Source VLM.EXE

Explanation An attempt was made to unload the VLM.EXE file using the /U parameter. This message indicates that the loaded VLM.EXE file has refused to unload. This usually is caused by interrupts being used after the VLM.EXE file was loaded. Another possible cause is that a VLM is in an unsafe state to unload.

Action Unload all the TSR (terminate-and-stay-resident) programs that were loaded after the VLM.EXE file; then try to unload VLM.EXE. Make sure all loaded VLMs are in a safe state for unloading.

The Logical Partition on disk #*<disk number>* cannot be opened. Trustee rights and file owner information on this disk will be lost.

Source 2XUPGRADE

Explanation The disk's logical partition, which stores the system tables and volume segments, cannot be opened. The bindery has been upgraded successfully at this point; however, the trustees and the file ownership information cannot be recorded.

Action Reassign file ownership and trustee rights by using the FILER and GRANT commands, or by using SYSCON.

The Logical Partition on this disk cannot be opened (status = *<status number>*). The In-Place Upgrade process is now being aborted.

Source 2XUPGRADE

Explanation The disk's logical partition, which stores the system tables and volume segments, cannot be opened. The status number in the message indicates the underlying cause of the error.

Action Make sure that your hard disk is still working.

The maximum levels of directories has been reached.

Source LISTDIR

Explanation The LISTDIR program encountered subdirectories beyond 50 levels deep. The maximum level of subdirectories that LISTDIR will process is 50.

Action None. This message is for information only.

The maximum number of connections allowed through the SMDR (64) has been exceeded.

Source SMDR

Explanation The SMDR allows a maximum of 64 simultaneous connections.

Action Eliminate unneeded connections; then try the operation again.

The maximum number of upgradable disks (32) has been exceeded. This disk (disk #<*disk number*>) will not be upgraded.

Source 2XUPGRADE

Explanation The In-Place Upgrade utility will upgrade a maximum of 32 disks. NetWare v2.1*x* and v2.2 supported only 32 disks per server, while NetWare v3.*x* supports up to 2,048.

Action After completing the In-Place Upgrade for the first 32 disks, unload the disk drivers for the disks that have been upgraded; then run the upgrade again.

The message file <*name*> is invalid. The program cannot be loaded.

Source VLM.EXE and VLMs (AUTO, BIND, CONN, FIO, GENERAL, IPXNCP, NDS, NETX, NMR, NWP, PRINT, REDIR, RSA, SECURITY, TRAN)

Explanation The .MSG file is invalid. This problem could be the result of a corrupted file, a bad translation, or an outdated file version.

Action Either update the .MSG file with a valid copy or delete the file. The DOS Requester will use the default messages that are bound to the binary files.

The mirror copies of the FAT don't match.

Source OS

Explanation A File Allocation Table (FAT) is an index to one or more disk allocation blocks in which a file is located. This error probably indicates file system corruption.

Action Run VREPAIR. If the problem persists, make sure you have a backup of the volume. Delete the volume, re-create it using INSTALL, and restore the data from the backup.

The Mirror Information Table in the NetWare v3.*x* disk partition cannot be created. The In-Place Upgrade process is now being aborted.

Source 2XUPGRADE

Explanation Your hard disk is probably going bad. The table containing disk mirroring information, located inside the Hot Fix redirection area, cannot be created. Version 1.00 of the In-Place Upgrade NLM did not create the Mirror Information Table. The v3.1*x* INSTALL NLM automatically creates this table if it does not already exist.

Action Make a backup of your hard disk's data; then try to salvage your hard disk. If you cannot salvage the disk, replace it and restore the data from your backup. See "Hardware Errors" on page 435 in Appendix A, "Troubleshooting."

The mirrored partitions on this system are not all synchronized.

Source OS Media Manager

Explanation During remirroring, one device was found to be out of sync. Until all of the mirrors are synchronized, single device or network board failure can cause file service disruption.

Action None. This message is for information only.

The name space path has not been updated.

Source TSA

Explanation A valid path was not found in the path list for the selected name space.

Action Make sure that a valid DOS path exists; then try again.

The name space type does not exist or is invalid.

Source TSA

Explanation An invalid name space type was specified.

Action Specify a valid name space type, and make sure support for the specified name space type is loaded on the specified volume.

The named module is already registered to SMDR.

Source SMDR

Explanation SMS resources (TSAs, for example) can only be loaded once per server. Subsequent attempts to load multiple copies will result in this error message.

Action None. This message is for information only.

The named TSA is not loaded on the SMDR. Load the TSA; then try again.

Source SMDR

Explanation The TSA you want to connect to is not loaded on the target machine. The name of the SMDR is the same as the name of the server it is running on. Either you specified the wrong SMDR name, or the TSA is not loaded.

Action Make sure you are using the correct SMDR name; then load the TSA and try the operation again.

The named SMDR is unknown, does not exist, or is not loaded.

Source SMDR

Explanation You may have typed an invalid SMDR name, or one that is outside your SAP advertising scope and is therefore "invisible."

Action Make sure that the SMDR is loaded and that you specified the name correctly.

The NetWare DOS Named Pipes Extender is currently loaded. The NetWare Requester for DOS cannot be loaded. Unload the NetWare DOS Named Pipes Extender; then load the NetWare Requester for DOS files.

Source CONN.VLM

Explanation The DOS Requester cannot be loaded after the NetWare DOS Named Pipes Extender. The NetWare DOS Pipes Extender has been loaded in this machine. To use both the DOS Requester and NetWare DOS Named Pipes Extender, load the DOS Requester before the DOS Named Pipes Extender.

Action Type "DOSNP /U" to unload the DOS Named Pipes Extender; then load the DOS Requester before reloading the DOS Named Pipes Extender.

The NetWare operating system produced an internal error while attempting to release the disk device.

Source 2XUPGRADE

Explanation The upgrade process is unable to give the hard disk resource back to the operating system.

Action This may be a symptom of an operating system failure. Reboot the system and restart the upgrade process.

The NetWare partition could not be located, the selected action cannot be completed.

Source INSTALL

Explanation The installation program cannot find a NetWare disk partition.

Action If no disk partitions have been created, create one. See "General Disk I/O Errors" on page 438 in Appendix A, "Troubleshooting."

The NetWare v2.1*x* or v2.2 bindery files cannot be opened. User accounts, including passwords, will not be upgraded. The In-Place Upgrade process is now being aborted.

Source 2XUPGRADE

Explanation At this point, the file system has been upgraded to NetWare v3.1*x*, but it has no bindery. The NetWare v2.1*x* bindery consists of two files located in the SYS:SYSTEM directory: NET$BIND.SYS (for objects and properties), and NET$BVAL.SYS (for property data sets).

These bindery files contain the names of users, their rights, their passwords, etc. One or both of these files could not be found or opened.

This error can be produeced when the server has enough memory to upgrade the file system, but not enough memory to mount the SYS: volume afterwards. This happens when the Permanent Memory Pool and the Alloc Memory Pool take memory but do not release it back to the cache buffers.

Simply rebooting the server to free these memory pools may solve the problem.

Action — Reboot the server; then restart the upgrade process with the new /BINDERY option. The /BINDERY option skips directly to the Bindery phase of the In-Place Upgrade.

The Network is inactive or you are not connected properly.

Source — Shell

Explanation — The workstation attached to a file server successfully when the shell was loaded and being initialized, but the initialization was not completed.

Action — Make sure the shell program is valid. Check the cable connections.

The new NetWare v3.1*x* partition number cannot be found after writing it to the disk's Partition Table. This disk cannot be upgraded. The disk has been restored to its original state BEFORE the upgrade so no data has been lost. This error may have been produced by faulty hardware.

Source — 2XUPGRADE

Explanation — This error occurs after the disk is first written to at the start of Phase 3. It has been known to occur on certain faulty PS/2 Model 80 system boards that handle 32-bit addressing incorrectly (ECA 048).

The following PS/2 Model 8580 system boards may produce this message:

Serial No. 111, Range: 600 - 6101499
Serial No. 121, Range: 45000 - 49999
Serial No. 121, Range: 9000 - 9014999
Serial No. 311, Range: 65000 - 6553499
Serial No. 321, Range: 92000 - 9215499

Action Check the serial number of your PS/2 Model 80 system board. Replace your system board if it has one of the above serial numbers. After your hardware is working correctly, retry the upgrade.

The new password has been used previously.

Source MAP, NPRINT

Explanation You tried to change your password to a password you used previously on the file server.

The network supervisor can require periodic password changes for any or all accounts on the file server to protect the file server from access by unauthorized persons. The network supervisor can also restrict users from changing their passwords to passwords they have used previously.

Action The file server keeps track of the passwords you have used previously. Therefore, you will need to use a password that you have not already used with your account.

The new password has been used previously. Please try again.

Source CAPTURE

Explanation You tried to change your password to a password you used previously on the file server.

The network supervisor can require periodic password changes for any or all accounts on the file server to protect the file server from access by unauthorized persons. The network supervisor can also restrict users from changing their passwords to passwords they have used previously.

Action The file server keeps track of the passwords you have used previously. Therefore, you will need to use a password that you have not already used with your account.

The new password is too short.

Source NPRINT

Explanation You tried to define a password that is shorter than the required minimum length for passwords. The network supervisor can restrict all passwords to a minimum length.

Action Use a longer password.

The new screen for the In-Place Upgrade cannot be opened.

Source 2XUPGRADE

Explanation The resources needed to open a new screen for the upgrade process are not available.

Action Unload all unnecessary NLMs from memory so the required resources can be freed up.

The number of megabytes specified on the command line for a DOS partition is too large. 32 megabytes are being reserved for a DOS partition.

Source 2XUPGRADE

Explanation You used the /P parameter on the command line with an invalid number for the size of the DOS partition. Valid numbers include 0 through 32 only, with no fractions. Because the number entered was greater than the maximum of 32 MB, the maximum was assigned instead.

Action If you do not want a 32MB DOS partition, unload the upgrade process and start over. Do this by pressing the <Alt><Esc> keys to return to the console prompt; then type "UNLOAD 2XUPGRDE."

The number of segments in the volume does not match.

Source INSTALL

Explanation INSTALL found two volumes with the same name, but the two volumes don't have a matching number of volume segments (which means they are different volumes). Two volumes on the same server cannot have the same name.

Action Bring the disks that contain these volumes online one at a time, rather than at the same time. If one of the volumes is old and no longer needed, delete it to avoid the problem in the future.

The object ID or name that was backed up does not match the current object ID or name.

Source TSA

Explanation The object ID or name for the restore does not match the object ID or name for the backup. Restore is probably being performed on a different server than the server that was used for the backup. This results in an object on both servers with a different ID.

Action None. This message is for information only.

The Open option is not used.

Source TSA

Explanation The Open option mode type string is not being used.

Action None. This message is for information only. However, you may add the mode type string if you wish (for example, NO_DATA_STREAMS_STR).

The Open mode option is out of range (<*number*> i.e. <0 or >23).

Source TSA

Explanation An invalid Open mode option was specified.

Action Specify a range within allowable parameters.

The operating system is unable to get the required resource and/or process tags to begin the upgrade.

Source 2XUPGRADE

Explanation The upgrade process was unable to get the necessary resources to run the upgrade. These resources, such as memory pools, are managed by the NetWare operating system.

Action Unload all unnecessary NLMs from memory so that the required resources can be freed up.

The parameter specified for the following option was out of range and has been adjusted.

Source
: VLM.EXE and VLMs (AUTO, BIND, CONN, FIO, GENERAL, IPXNCP, NDS, NETX, NMR, NWP, PRINT, REDIR, RSA, SECURITY, TRAN)

Explanation
: A configurable parameter has been configured too high or too low to be valid. The parameter is specified on the line following the message.

Action
: Check and correct the parameter specified in the NET.CFG file. For more information about the NET.CFG file, see "Configuring Your DOS Workstation" in *Workstation for DOS and Windows*.

The preferred connection could not be established. Check the PREFERRED SERVER and PREFERRED TREE statement specified in the NET.CFG file. Also check the server's status before continuing.

Source
: VLM.EXE

Explanation
: An attempt was made to connect to a specific server. This attempt failed. Either the server is not running at this time or, in the preferred server case, it may be unknown by the initial server's bindery.

Action
: Make sure the spelling of the preferred server is correct. Check the server status to see that it is up and running. Finally, check to see if any restrictions have been made at the server to isolate the server from your network.

The print queue <*queuename*> can not be found.

Source
: NPRINT

Explanation
: You either specified a queue that is not defined on your file server or mistyped the name of the queue.

Action
: Use the PCONSOLE utility to see which queues are defined on your file server. Type the queue name correctly in your command.

The print queue is full. Try again.

Source: NPRINT

Explanation: The print queue is full. The queue can handle 100 print jobs at a time.

Action: Try again later or specify another queue.

The print queue is halted. Try again.

Source: NPRINT

Explanation: The queue operator has flagged the queue so that no new print jobs can be added to the queue.

Action: Try again when the flag has been removed.

The print server's account on file server <*servername*> has been disabled.

Source: PSERVER (.EXE, .NLM, or .VAP)

Explanation: The login property that disables an account has been set. NetWare does not have a program that sets this property for print servers. Either your bindery is corrupted, or you have used a third-party program to set this property.

Action: Complete one of the following:

- If you don't have a third-party program that sets this property, run BINDFIX.
- If you have a third-party program that sets the disable property, use it to reenable the account.

The printer number specified must be in the range 0–15.

Source: RPRINTER

Explanation: You entered an invalid printer number. The printer number must be between 0 and 15.

Action: Verify the printer number with PCONSOLE before trying to enter the command again from the command line.

The PRINT.VLM file has not been loaded. The NETX.VLM file will load successfully without print services. To enable printing services, load the PRINT.VLM file before loading the NETX.VLM file.

Source NETX.VLM

Explanation This message is only a warning. For full NetWare shell compatibility, the PRINT.VLM file must be loaded. Otherwise, problems will arise when using pre-v4.0 NetWare print utilities.

Action For full print functionality, load PRINT.VLM before loading NETX.VLM.

The program cannot scan file entry information.

Source TSA

Explanation The file scan failed.

Action Specify a valid file name for the requested name space. Also make sure that you have appropriate user access rights.

The program cannot scan for trustees.

Source TSA

Explanation The TSA could not scan for a trustee list.

Action Make sure that you have appropriate user access rights and that your entry index is valid; then try again.

The program cannot set file information.

Source TSA

Explanation The TSA cannot set file information.

Action Make sure that you have appropriate user access rights. Also make sure the information to be set is valid.

The program cannot write extended attribute (<*value*>).

Source TSA

Explanation The TSA could not write the extended attribute(s).

Action Make sure the extended attributes and the file or directory are valid. Also make sure that you have appropriate user access rights.

The program was processing a record or subrecord and did not find the Trailer field.

Source TSA

Explanation Your data has been corrupted; the trailer field of a record is missing.

Action Clean your tape heads and check your hardware; then try again. If the problem persists, contact your Novell Authorized Reseller.

The program's attempt to scan failed, probably because an invalid path was specified.

Source TSA

Explanation An invalid path was specified.

Action Specify a valid path for the requested name space. Also make sure that you have appropriate user access rights.

The random passwords file named "NEW.PWD" cannot be created. No passwords will be assigned to the users.

Source 2XUPGRADE

Explanation User passwords cannot be transferred from NetWare v2.1*x*'s bindery to NetWare v3.1*x*'s bindery. New user passwords were generated, but could not be saved into a file named NEW.PWD in SYS:SYSTEM. Users are given no passwords because passwords cannot be recorded.

Action Manually assign users new passwords after the upgrade is completed, using the SYSCON utility from a workstation.

The read/write request exceeds 128Kb.

Source TSA

Explanation An intermodule communication request exceeds the 128KB limit.

Action Restructure the read/write request into pieces of 128 KB or smaller.

The requested function is not supported by this TSA.

Source TSA

Explanation The requested function is not supported on the selected TSA.

Action Request a valid function, or select another TSA that supports the requested function.

The scan type is out of range (<*number*> i.e. <0 or >31).

Source TSA

Explanation An invalid scan type was specified.

Action Correct the scan type and try again.

The SECURITY.VLM file has not been loaded. The NWP.VLM file will load successfully without NCP signature support. Load the SECURITY.VLM file before loading the NWP.VLM file or add SIGNATURE LEVEL=0 to the NET.CFG file; then load NWP.VLM.

Source NWP.VLM

Explanation This message is only a warning. The DOS Requester will function properly without NCP authentication. For NCP authentication to operate properly, the SECURITY.VLM module must be loaded before NWP.VLM. Either the NWP.VLM is being loaded before SECURITY.VLM, or SECURITY.VLM did not load successfully.

Action If NCP authentication is desired, make sure that the SECURITY.VLM is configured to load before NWP.VLM and that it loads successfully before attempting to load NWP.VLM. If NCP authentication is not desired, add "SIGNATURE LEVEL=0" to the "NETWARE DOS REQUESTER" section of the NET.CFG file.

The SECURITY.VLM file must be loaded before any other NetWare Protocol Module. The SECURITY.VLM file will not be loaded. Load the SECURITY.VLM file before loading any NetWare Protocol Modules.

Source SECURITY.VLM

Explanation This message is only a warning. The DOS Requester will function properly without the use of NCP authentication. The SECURITY.VLM file must be loaded before any NetWare Protocol Modules (such as BIND.VLM or NDS.VLM) to function properly.

Action If authentication is desired, load the SECURITY.VLM after TRAN.VLM and before any NetWare Protocol Module (such as BIND.VLM or NDS.VLM); then set the "SIGNATURE LEVEL=" parameter in the NET.CFG file. If NCP authentication is not desired, set "SIGNATURE LEVEL=0" in the NET.CFG file.

See "Configuring Your DOS Workstation" in *Workstation for DOS and Windows* for more information about the NET.CFG file.

The selected disk cannot be formatted at this time. There is not enough memory available.

Source INSTALL

Explanation This message is self-explanatory.

Action See "Insufficient Server Memory Errors" on page 440 in Appendix A, "Troubleshooting."

The selected disk cannot be tested at this time. There is not enough memory available to begin another test.

Source INSTALL

Explanation Either a previous test is being conducted on the disk, or you do not have sufficient memory.

Action See "Insufficient Server Memory Errors" on page 440 in Appendix A, "Troubleshooting." Otherwise, wait until a previous test is completed.

The selected print server could not be found.

Source RPRINTER

Explanation The print server specified in the command is not currently running.

Action Use PCONSOLE to verify the correct spelling of the print server's name.

The selected print server does not respond.

Source RPRINTER

Explanation The print server probably went down during the initialization process.

Action Try again when the print server is running.

The selected remote printer has an unknown printer type.

Source RPRINTER

Explanation The RPRINTER and PSERVER programs come from different releases of the print server.

Action Check the version of RPRINTER and PSERVER with VERSION. Reinstall the programs so that they are both the same version.

The selected remote printer is already in use.

Source RPRINTER

Explanation You selected the printer from the command line, but that printer is already being used by another workstation.

Action Use the RPRINTER menu to select a printer. (At the command line, type "RPRINTER" without any parameters.) Or select a different printer number.

The selected volume cannot be located.

Source INSTALL

Explanation An internal system error has occurred.

Action Try again. If the problem persists, contact your Novell Authorized Reseller.

The selection type is out of range (<*number*> i.e. <0 or >31).

Source TSA

Explanation An invalid selection type was specified.

Action Correct the selection type, and try again.

The sequence number is invalid.

Source TSA

Explanation An invalid sequence number was specified.

Action Correct the sequence number, and try again.

The server in the filespec does not match the specified server flag <*flag*>.

Source CAPTURE

Explanation You used a Create flag (option) in your CAPTURE command, but you specified a drive mapped to a file server other than your default file server. You can create a file with the CAPTURE command only on your default file server.

Action If you use a drive in your file specification, make sure that the drive is mapped to a directory on your default file server.

The server is unable to allocate sufficient memory.

Source SMDR

Explanation You do not have enough server memory.

Action See "Insufficient Server Memory Errors" on page 440 in Appendix A, "Troubleshooting."

The session file <*name*> is corrupt.

Source SBACKUP

Explanation The backup session's log file does not have valid header information. This file can no longer be used.

Action Complete the restore session without a session log file.

The SMDR received an encrypted password it could not decode.

Source SMDR

Explanation When SMS resource users (such as SBACKUP) attempt to connect to remote SMS resources (TSAs, for example), the password is encrypted and packed into an SMSP datagram.

If the data is corrupted before it is sent, during transmission, or after it is received, the decryption routine will not recognize the data, and the connect attempt will fail.

Action Try to reconnect. If the problem persists, contact your Novell Authorized Reseller.

The SMDR was unable to encrypt the password.

Source SMDR

Explanation When SMS resource users (such as SBACKUP) attempt to connect to remote SMS resources (TSAs, for example), the password is encrypted and packed into an SMSP datagram.

If the data is corrupted before it is sent, during transmission, or after it is received, the decryption routine will not recognize the data, and the connect attempt will fail.

Action Try to reconnect. If the problem persists, contact your Novell Authorized Reseller.

The source drive is not defined.

Source MAP

Explanation You tried to map a drive to a second drive, but the second drive is not defined as a network drive.

Action Do one or both of the following:

- Use the MAP utility to define the second drive as a network drive; then retry the command.
- Map the second drive to a drive that is already defined as a network drive. For example, if V is a defined drive, use the following map command:

```
MAP V:=H:
```

If this error occurs during login, the MAP command in question is located in your login script. Use the SYSCON utility to access your login script, and map the second drive to a network directory.

The specified action is not supported.

Source PSC

Explanation The option specified in the command is not supported by PSC.

Action Try again. Type the options correctly.

The specified form name could not be found.

Source NPRINT

Explanation You either specified a form name that is not defined on your file server or mistyped the name of the form.

Action Use the PCONSOLE utility to see which forms are currently defined on your file server. Type the name of the form correctly.

The specified print definition could not be found.

Source NPRINT

Explanation You either specified a printer definition that is not defined with your user account or mistyped the name of the printer job.

Action Use the PRINTCON utility to see which jobs are currently defined with your user account. Type the name of the print job correctly.

The specified queues not matched.

Source NPRINT

Explanation You specified a queue and a printer in your command that are not assigned to each other. When a queue is defined and configured on the file server, it is assigned to a printer. Any output sent to a particular queue will be printed on the printer to which the queue is assigned.

Action Specify the printer or the queue, but *not* both. If you specify a queue, the output will be sent to the printer to which the queue is assigned. If you specify a printer, the output will be placed in the default queue assigned to the printer.

The specified server cannot be found.

Source CHKVOL

Explanation You mistyped the name of the file server, specified a file server that is not on the network, or specified a file server that has been brought down for system maintenance.

Action Use the SLIST command to list all the file servers that your station recognizes. Type the name of the file server correctly. If the file server has been brought down for maintenance, try the command when the file server has been brought back up. If you still have problems, ask your network supervisor for help.

The specified user account on server *<servername>* has expired or has been disabled by the Supervisor.

Source CAPTURE, NPRINT

Explanation This message could occur for one of the following reasons:

- Your account has expired. The network supervisor can limit your account to a specific period, after which the account will expire and will no longer be accessible.
- Your account has been disabled. The network supervisor can disable your account for any reason.
- You did not type your password correctly. The network supervisor can limit the number of failed attempts to log in to your account.

  In other words, if the maximum number of failed login attempts for your account is three and you type your password incorrectly during four consecutive login attempts, the operating system will consider you an intruder and will disable your account.

Action The network supervisor will need to enable your account before you can access the account again.

The specified user's account balance on server *<servername>* has dropped below the minimum.

Source CAPTURE, NPRINT

Explanation Your account balance on the file server has expired. You cannot log in to this account until your account balance has been brought up to date.

Action Ask the network supervisor to reconcile your user account.

The specified volume not found.

Source CHKVOL

Explanation You either specified a volume that does not exist on the file server or mistyped the volume name. A volume name, such as SYS:, must be followed by a colon.

Action: Use the VOLINFO utility or the CHKVOL * command to see which volumes are defined. When you specify a volume name in a command, always type a colon (:) after the volume name.

The supervisor has disabled logins on file server *<servername>*.

Source: PSERVER (.EXE, .NLM, or .VAP)

Explanation: The print server cannot log in to the file server because logins have been disabled on the specified file server.

Action: Try again when logins have been reenabled.

The supervisor has disabled the login function for this server.

Source: ATTACH, LOGIN, MAP

Explanation: Your user account on the file server is locked.

The network supervisor can disable the login function temporarily to prevent users from logging in or attaching to the file server during system maintenance. Most likely, the network supervisor of the file server is doing maintenance work on the file server.

Action: This condition is usually only temporary. Try to log in to the file server after the login function has been enabled. If you are using CAPTURE or NPRINT, attach to another file server and use its printer.

The Supervisor has disabled the login function on server *<servername>*.

Source: CAPTURE, NPRINT

Explanation: Your user account on the file server is locked.

The network supervisor can disable the login function temporarily to prevent users from logging in or attaching to the file server during system maintenance. Most likely, the network supervisor of the file server is doing maintenance work on the file server.

Action: This condition is usually only temporary. Try to log in to the file server after the login function has been enabled. If you are using CAPTURE or NPRINT, attach to another file server and use its printer.

The Supervisor has the system bindery locked.

Source CHKVOL, LISTDIR, LOGIN, MAP

Explanation The system bindery on the file server is inaccessible. The network supervisor may be doing maintenance work on the system. The system bindery contains the names of users, their rights, file servers to which they are attached, etc.

Action The system bindery is usually locked only momentarily. Wait a few minutes and try the command again.

The SYS: volume cannot be found. Without this volume, NetWare v3.1*x* will not operate.

Source 2XUPGRADE

Explanation The SYS: volume was not present on any of the disks. Both NetWare v2.1*x* and v3.*x* require a volume named SYS: in which to store system files. The upgrade process is not automatically aborted because some users may want to upgrade disks that were not connected to the server after the initial upgrade.

Action After pressing any key to continue, type "Y" to continue with the upgrade without the SYS: volume, or type "N" to exit the upgrade.

The target server requires NetWare 2.10 or later in order to work.

Source CAPTURE

Explanation You are using the latest version of a command line utility, but you tried to use this utility on a file server that is not using the latest version of the operating system.

Action You can use this utility only on file servers that are using NetWare v2.1 or later.

The target service agent and the data requestor versions are incompatible.

Source SBACKUP

Explanation SBACKUP cannot attach to the requested TSA because incompatible module versions are being used.

Action See *Server Backup* for more information.

The total volume size does not match.

Source INSTALL

Explanation INSTALL found two volume segments with the same name, but the sizes of the two volumes do not match. Two volumes on the same server cannot have the same name.

Action Bring the disks that contain these volumes online one at a time, rather than at the same time. If one of the volumes is old and no longer needed, delete it to avoid the problem in the future.

The transport mechanism has failed.

Source TSA

Explanation The intermodule communication layer has failed.

Action Check the LAN communication between machines, and reestablish the connection.

The UPS battery for server *<servername>* is recharging. The status is no longer low.

Source UPS

Explanation After the network supervisor troubleshoots a low battery, the battery recharges.

Action None. This message is for information only.

The UPS battery recharge for server *<servername>* is complete.

Source UPS

Explanation After a battery recharge is complete, the file server console displays this message.

Action None. This message is for information only.

The VLM.EXE file *<version>* is currently loaded.

Source VLM.EXE

Explanation This message is displayed during the VLM.EXE file diagnostics display. (The diagnostics display is accessed by running VLM.EXE with the /D parameter.) This message indicates that the VLM.EXE file of the given version is currently loaded into memory.

Action None. This message is for information only.

The VLM.EXE file cannot use conventional memory. VLM.EXE will use an alternate memory scheme.

Source VLM.EXE

Explanation An attempt was made to load the VLM.EXE file in conventional memory using the /MC parameter. This message indicates that insufficient conventional memory is available to load the VLMs.

The VLM.EXE file will attempt to use an alternate type of memory—either expanded memory (EMS) or extended memory (XMS)—before failing to load.

Action Because the VLM.EXE file will attempt to use an alternate memory type, no action is required at this point.

However, to avoid this message the next time the VLM.EXE file is loaded, either make sure there is sufficient conventional memory to support the VLMs desired, or do not specify the /MC parameter when loading VLM.EXE.

The VLM.EXE file cannot use extended memory (XMS). VLM.EXE will use an alternate memory scheme.

Source VLM.EXE

Explanation An attempt was made to load the VLM.EXE file in extended memory (XMS) using the /MX parameter. This message indicates that either no XMS 2.0 extended memory manager is present, or insufficient extended memory is available to load the VLMs.

The VLM.EXE file will attempt to use an alternate type of memory—either expanded memory (EMS) or conventional memory—before failing to load.

Action Because the VLM.EXE file will attempt to use an alternate memory type, no action is required at this point.

However, to avoid this message the next time the VLM.EXE file is loaded, either make sure an extended memory manager is loaded with sufficient memory to support the VLMs desired, or do not specify the /MX parameter when loading VLM.EXE.

The VLM.EXE file is already loaded. VLM.EXE cannot be reloaded. If you want to load VLM.EXE with a different configuration, unload VLM.EXE first with the /U parameter and then try loading the VLM.EXE file.

Source VLM.EXE

Explanation The VLM.EXE file has already been loaded into memory. There cannot be two copies of the VLM.EXE file loaded in memory at the same time.

Action If the VLM.EXE file is being reloaded in an attempt to reconfigure the VLMs already loaded, you must first unload VLM.EXE using the /U parameter; then reload VLM.EXE.

The VLM.EXE file is not currently loaded.

Source VLM.EXE

Explanation This message is displayed during the VLM.EXE file diagnostics display. (The diagnostics display is accessed by running VLM.EXE with the /D parameter.) This message indicates that the VLM.EXE file is not currently loaded into memory.

Action None. This message is for information only.

The VLM.EXE file is not loaded. VLM.EXE cannot be unloaded.

Source VLM.EXE

Explanation An attempt was made to unload the VLM.EXE file using the /U parameter. This message indicates that the VLM.EXE file is not currently loaded in memory.

Action The action that caused this message to occur is invalid, so no further action is required.

The VLM.EXE file is testing the VLMs.

Source VLM.EXE

Explanation This message is used to show the progress the VLM.EXE file is making in configuring the VLMs to be loaded. Because this process can take a few seconds, the progress is displayed using a period (.) to indicate each VLM being tested.

Action None. This message is for information only.

The VLM.EXE file is using conventional memory.

Source	VLM.EXE
Explanation	This message indicates that the VLM.EXE file will be loading the VLMs into conventional memory.
Action	None. This message is for information only.

The VLM.EXE file is using expanded memory (EMS).

Source	VLM.EXE
Explanation	This message indicates that the VLM.EXE file will be loading the VLMs into expanded memory (EMS).
Action	None. This message is for information only.

The VLM.EXE file is using extended memory (XMS).

Source	VLM.EXE
Explanation	This message indicates that the VLM.EXE file will be loading the VLMs into extended memory (XMS).
Action	None. This message is for information only.

The volume cannot be locked at this time. Another process is using it—perhaps a surface test is being done. The selected action cannot be completed.

Source	INSTALL
Explanation	This message is self-explanatory.
Action	See "Locked Device Errors" on page 440 in Appendix A, "Troubleshooting."

The volume flags do not match.

Source	INSTALL
Explanation	INSTALL found two volume segments with the same name, but the volume flags of the two do not match. Two volumes on the same server cannot have the same name.
Action	Bring the disks that contain these volumes online one at a time, rather than at the same time. If one of the volumes is old and no longer needed, delete it to avoid the problem in the future.

The Volume Definition Table on <*disk label*> has invalid entries.

Source INSTALL

Explanation The data on the disk is corrupted or unreadable.

Action A confirmation question will follow this message. Choosing to fix the volume definition table will destroy the invalid entries. If you think that valid data exists on the volumes in question, do not fix the table. See "General Disk I/O Errors" on page 438 in Appendix A, "Troubleshooting."

There are no accessible drives with NetWare partitions.

Source INSTALL

Explanation The installation program cannot find a NetWare disk partition.

Action If no disk partitions have been created, make one. See "General Disk I/O Errors" on page 438 in Appendix A, "Troubleshooting."

There are no available NetWare partitions compatible with the selected drive.

Source INSTALL

Explanation No disk partitions were found of suitable size to be mirrored with the selected disk partition (drive).

Action Mirroring requires at least two disks that contain disk partitions of approximately the same size. You may need to install an additional disk in order to mirror. If this is not the problem, you may have a disk problem. See "General Disk I/O Errors" on page 438 in Appendix A, "Troubleshooting."

There are no free areas available for a volume.

Source INSTALL

Explanation Either there are no free areas on the disk, or the free areas are too small to be of any benefit.

Action Get another disk, or delete one of the existing volumes.

There are no more response buffers available.

Source — PSERVER (.EXE or .VAP)

Explanation — The print server has run out of memory for handling communication packets.

Action — Bring down the print server and reboot it. If the problem persists, contact your Novell Authorized Reseller.

There are not enough SPX connections to run the print server.

Source — PSERVER.EXE

Explanation — The workstation does not have enough SPX connections to run PSERVER.

Action — Add the following line to the NET.CFG file in the workstation's boot directory:

```
SPX CONNECTIONS = 50
```

Reboot the workstation and then run PSERVER.

There is a missing or invalid value for '<*parameter*>' on line <*number*> of the configuration file. This entry will be ignored. Correct the line specified in the configuration file before continuing.

Source — VLM.EXE and VLMs (AUTO, BIND, CONN, FIO, GENERAL, IPXNCP, NDS, NETX, NMR, NWP, PRINT, REDIR, RSA, SECURITY, TRAN)

Explanation — The configuration file NET.CFG contains a configuration keyword that has an invalid parameter or that does not specify a parameter. This invalid line will be ignored by the configuration process.

Action — Because this line will be ignored, no action is required at this point. However, to avoid this message the next time the VLM.EXE file is loaded, delete or correct the line specified by the error message.

There is a missing or invalid ON/OFF value for '*<parameter>*' on line *<number>* of the configuration file. This entry will be ignored. Correct the line specified in the configuration file before continuing.

Source: VLM.EXE and VLMs (AUTO, BIND, CONN, FIO, GENERAL, IPXNCP, NDS, NETX, NMR, NWP, PRINT, REDIR, RSA, SECURITY, TRAN)

Explanation: The configuration file NET.CFG contains a configuration keyword that is defined to use either an "ON" or "OFF" parameter, but a different parameter or no parameter has been specified. This invalid line will be ignored by the configuration process.

Action: Because this line will be ignored, no action is required at this point. However, to avoid this message the next time the VLM.EXE file is loaded, delete or correct the line specified by the message.

There is already a print server named *<print server>* running.

Source: PSERVER (.EXE, .NLM, or .VAP)

Explanation: All print servers on your network must have unique names.

Action: Run PCONSOLE and rename the duplicate print server.

There is an unrecognized entry '*<entry>*' on line *<number>* of the configuration file. This entry will be ignored. Correct the line specified in the configuration file before continuing.

Source: VLM.EXE

Explanation: The configuration file NET.CFG contains a configuration keyword under a header where it does not belong. This invalid line will be ignored by the configuration process.

Action: Because this line will be ignored, no action is required at this point. However, to avoid this message the next time the VLM.EXE file is loaded, delete or correct the line specified by the message.

There is insufficient memory to load the VLMs. The VLM.EXE file cannot be loaded. Reconfigure the VLMs to be loaded in the NET.CFG file and then try to load the VLM.EXE file.

Source: VLM.EXE

Explanation: The VLM.EXE file can use expanded memory (EMS), extended memory (XMS), or conventional memory. This message indicates that there is not enough of any one of these to support the VLMs to be loaded.

Action: Check the amount of memory available (ncluding expanded memory and extended memory). Some memory managers provide dynamic memory pools by converting extended memory to expanded memory or vice versa. Other memory managers require you to configure the amount and type of memory desired.

In either case, make sure there is enough memory of one type to support the VLMs to be loaded or reduce the number of VLMs to be loaded. You can do this by using the "VLM=" statement in the NET.CFG file or by renaming the VLMs that are not desired.

There is no accounting balance for the specified user account on server *<servername>*.

Source: CAPTURE, NPRINT

Explanation: You tried to access a file server on which you have no account balance.

Action: Ask the network supervisor to establish an account balance for you on that server.

There is no default file server. You must specify a file server name.

Source: PSERVER (.EXE or .VAP)

Explanation: You are attached, but not logged in, to a file server.

Action: Specify the file server and print server name in the PSERVER command.

There is no free space on this drive for a NetWare partition.

Source INSTALL

Explanation Either there are no free areas on the disk, or the free areas are too small to be of any benefit.

Action Get another disk, or delete one of the existing partitions.

There was not enough memory to hold the PrintDef escape sequences.

Source CAPTURE

Explanation Your workstation does not have enough memory to hold the escape sequences contained in the PRINTDEF definition.

Action Try another PRINTDEF definition that uses fewer escape sequences. See "Insufficient Workstation Memory Errors" on page 442 in Appendix A, "Troubleshooting."

This data set name is already in use.

Source TSA

Explanation The TSA cannot overwrite the existing data set because the data set is being used.

Action Change the SBACKUP selection to "Overwrite parent/child," or change the destination path.

This hard disk contains more than 8 volumes. NetWare v3.1*x* allows a maximum of only 8 volumes per hard disk. The In-Place Upgrade process is now being aborted.

Source 2XUPGRADE

Explanation NetWare v2.1*x* allows for a maximum of 16 volumes per hard disk, while NetWare v3.1*x* is limited to a maximum of 8 volumes per hard disk.

Action Use an upgrade method other than this In-Place Upgrade process.

This login attempt has been denied.

Source TSA

Explanation For some reason, the login attempt failed.

Action Make sure that you have specified a valid username and password for the selected server; then try again.

This logout attempt cannot be completed.

Explanation For some reason, the logout attempt failed.

Action Make sure that you have no work in progress; then try again.

This machine does not have an 80386 microprocessor. NetWare v3.12 CANNOT BE RUN ON THIS MACHINE!!!

Source OS

Explanation You are trying to run the NetWare v3.12 operating system on a non-386 or -486 computer.

Action Use a 386 or 486 computer.

This module is already loaded and cannot be loaded more than once.

Source OS

Explanation The module specified in the LOAD command has already been loaded, and can be loaded only once.

Some types of modules can be loaded only once, other modules can be loaded more than once (multiple copies can exist in memory), and other modules can be loaded reentrantly (only one copy exists in memory, but it can be used in multiple instances).

For example, one LAN driver can handle multiple network boards of the same type.

Action None. Thie message is for information only.

This NetWare server has insufficient free hard disk space to complete the upgrade. The In-Place Upgrade process is now being aborted.

Source 2XUPGRADE

Explanation Your server does not have enough free hard disk space to run the upgrade. You will need about 10% more disk space per volume to accommodate the NetWare v3.1*x* file system than was required for NetWare v2.1*x*. The SYS: volume may need more than 10% free disk space to accommodate the optional DOS partition.

NetWare v3.1*x* directories use up to four times more disk space than NetWare v2.1*x* directories.

Action Remove nonsystem files until approximately 10% of each volume on the disk is free, or specify a smaller DOS partition size during the upgrade.

This NetWare server has insufficient memory to complete the upgrade. The In-Place Upgrade process is now being aborted.

Source 2XUPGRADE

Explanation Your server does not have enough free memory to run the upgrade. Servers using large hard disks or having many directories may need additional memory when upgrading.

The upgrade process uses approximately 8 KB of memory for each directory, 3 KB for every 19 directory entries (files, directories, trustee entries), and 2 KB for each megabyte on your hard disk. A server may require more memory to do the In-Place Upgrade than is needed to operate the server on a day-to-day basis.

Action See "Insufficient Server Memory Errors" on page 440 in Appendix A, "Troubleshooting."

This NetWare server may have insufficient memory to complete the upgrade process. Either temporarily add more memory and restart the upgrade process, or continue with the upgrade. If you continue, the upgrade process will perform a more complete memory requirements check as it builds the new file system in memory. Your server has sufficient memory if you make it to the PHASE #3: DISK MODIFICATION screen.

Source 2XUPGRADE

Explanation An equation has been implemented in the System Analysis phase to quickly estimate the memory requirements of an In-Place Upgrade before entering the Disk Analysis phase. This equation may estimate that your server needs slightly more memory than it actually needs.

The Disk Analysis phase performs a more accurate calculation of needed memory, but can take up to two hours per hard disk to compute.

Action If the difference between how much memory your server actually has is close to the memory needed estimate, you may want to continue the upgrade to see if the Disk Analysis phase completes without aborting due to lack of memory. Otherwise, temporarily install more memory in your server and restart the upgrade.

This program cannot allocate a directory handle.

Source TSA

Explanation For some reason, the TSA could not allocate a directory handle.

Action Make sure that you have specified a valid directory path for the desired name space. Also make sure that you have appropriate user access rights.

This program cannot create a directory entry.

Source TSA

Explanation For some reason, the TSA could not create the specified directory entry.

Action Make sure that you have specified a valid directory path for the name space, and that you have appropriate user access rights.

This program cannot create a file.

Source TSA

Explanation For some reason, the TSA could not create the specified file.

Action Make sure that you have specified a valid directory path for the name space, and that you have appropriate user access rights.

This program cannot delete a data set.

Source TSA

Explanation For some reason, the specified data set could not be deleted.

Action Make sure that you have specified a valid data set name and that you have appropriate user access rights. Also make sure the file is not already in use.

This program cannot get the data stream name.

Source TSA

Explanation For some reason, the TSA could not read the requested data stream name.

Action Make sure that you have specified a valid data set name for the name space. Also make sure that the name space is supported on the volume and that you have appropriate user access rights.

This program cannot get the directory object name.

Source TSA

Explanation For some reason, the specified object was not found in the bindery.

Action Make sure that you have specified a valid bindery object, and that you have appropriate user access rights.

This program cannot get the entry index.

Source TSA

Explanation For some reason, the TSA could not get an entry index for the requested file or directory.

Action Make sure that you have specified a valid data set name for the name space. Also make sure that the name space is supported on the volume and that you have appropriate user access rights.

This program cannot get the name space entry name.

Source TSA

Explanation For some reason, the TSA could not read the name space entry name for the requested file or directory.

Action Make sure that you have specified a valid data set name for the name space. Also make sure that the name space is supported on the volume and that you have appropriate user access rights.

This program cannot get the name space size information.

Source TSA

Explanation For some reason, the TSA could not read the name space information size.

Action Make sure that you have specified a valid data set name for the name space. Also make sure that the name space is supported on the volume and that you have appropriate user access rights.

This program cannot get the NetWare server information.

Source TSA

Explanation For some reason, the TSA failed to read the file server information.

Action Make sure the server version matches the TSA version you are using.

This program cannot get the volume-supported name space information.

Source TSA

Explanation For some reason, the TSA could not read the list of supported name spaces for the requested volume.

Action Make sure that you have specified a valid volume name. Also make sure that the volume is mounted and that you have appropriate user access rights.

This program functions only under SFT NetWare version 2.1 or greater

Source SECURITY

Explanation You are using the latest version of a command line utility, but you are trying to use the command on a file server that is not using the latest version of NetWare.

Action Use NetWare v2.1*x* command line utilities only on file servers that are running the NetWare v2.1*x* operating system.

This program has encountered a buffer underflow and cannot get the entire field.

Source TSA

Explanation The TSA received an end-of-data error before the correct number of bytes were read. The data may be corrupted.

Action Check the data to ensure it is correct. Repeat the session if necessary.

This scan type is not used.

Source TSA

Explanation An invalid or unused scan type was specified.

Action Try again, using a valid scan type.

This selection type is not used.

Source TSA

Explanation An invalid or unused selection type was specified.

Action Try again, using a valid selection type.

This utility works on NetWare 386 servers only.

Source ALLOW

Explanation The NetWare v3.*x* operating system is the only operating system that supports ALLOW. The NetWare 286 operating system does not use inherited rights.

Action Use ALLOW only with NetWare v3.*x*.

This version of the loader doesn't support this NLM compression format (version <*version*>).

Source OS

Explanation The operating system tried to load an NLM that is in an unsupported compression format.

Action Make sure that any compressed NLMs you want to load are in compression format v1.10.

Timeout value (0-1000) expected.

Source CAPTURE

Explanation You did not specify a value for the Timeout flag.

Action Specify a Timeout value.

TLI Transport Timeout Failure.

Source SBACKUP

Explanation A failure occurred in transport layer interface (TLI) communication (timeout). SBACKUP could not communicate with a remote Storage Management Services (SMS) module (for example, TSA311 or TSA312).

Action Make sure that communication exists between the server on which SBACKUP is loaded and the server on which the other SMS modules are loaded. Also make sure that transport layer NLMs are loaded and functional on both servers.

TLIST does not work with local drives.

Source TLIST

Explanation TLIST does not work with local drives, because local drives do not have trustees.

Action Check your drive letter. Try the command again using a network drive.

Too many parameters on command line.

Source RIGHTS

Explanation Your command contained too many parameters. You cannot specify the same parameter more than once in the command.

Action Include each parameter only once in the command.

Too many stations are already attached to server *<servername>* using the specified user account. The Supervisor has limited the number of active concurrent connections.

Source CAPTURE, NPRINT

Explanation The network supervisor has limited the number of workstations that can be logged in with this username.

Action Try again when someone else using this username has logged out.

Too much cache is configured. The FIO.VLM file will reduce the cache blocks by *<number>* blocks and load successfully. Check the CACHE BUFFERS and BUFFER SIZE parameters in the NET.CFG file; then load the FIO.VLM file.

Source VLM.EXE, FIO.VLM

Explanation The amount of cache available in DOS is limited by conventional memory. The parameters determining the amount of memory to be used are CACHE BUFFERS and BUFFER SIZE. These two buffers cannot be configured to use more than 64 KB of memory. One of these parameters must be reduced.

Action Reduce the "CACHE BUFFERS" or "BUFFER SIZE" parameter in the NET.CFG file. See "Configuring Your DOS Workstation" in *Workstation for DOS and Windows* for more information about the NET.CFG file.

Total volume size does not match

Source OS

Explanation Two segments of the volume claim different numbers of segments. This error can occur for one of the following reasons:

- Two volumes on the file server have identical names and a segment from each volume is causing the error.
- The volume is corrupted.

Action If you have two volumes with the same name, unload the disk driver for the volume that you do not want to rename. Rename the other volume (the volume that is on the hard disk that still has its disk driver loaded). Then load the disk driver that you just unloaded. Mount both volumes.

If the volume is corrupted, run VREPAIR. If the volume cannot be fixed, load INSTALL, delete the volume, and re-create it.

Note: If you delete the volume, all data will be destroyed. You will have to restore the data from a backup.

Transaction Tracking System NOT Available.

Source SETTTS

Explanation TTS is not installed on the file server.

Action Use SETTTS only on file servers that have TTS installed. In NetWare v2.*x*, TTS is optional. In NetWare v3.12, TTS is installed automatically.

Transaction Tracking System not installed on server "*<servername>*".

Source SETTTS

Explanation TTS is not installed on the specified file server.

Action Use SETTTS only on file servers that have TTS installed. In NetWare v2.*x*, TTS is optional. In NetWare v3.12, TTS is installed automatically.

TTS cannot allocate sufficient memory

Source OS

Explanation Your server may not have enough memory.

Action See "Insufficient Server Memory Errors" on page 440 in Appendix A, "Troubleshooting."

TTS cannot allocate memory to do the transaction backouts.

Source OS

Explanation Your server may not have enough memory.

Action See "Insufficient Server Memory Errors" on page 440 in Appendix A, "Troubleshooting."

TTS disabled because of directory error on TTS backout file.

Source OS

Explanation There is not enough memory space available on the volume for the directory.

Action Increase the percentage of volume space that can be used by the directory.

TTS disabled because of error allocating more disk space for the backout file.

Source OS

Explanation The backout volume is full.

Action Try adding another drive to the backout volume, deleting or compressing existing files on the backout volume, or moving files from the backout volume to another volume. (Increasing disk space on volumes other than the backout volume will not help.)

TTS disabled because of error growing TTS memory tables.

Source OS

Explanation Your server may not have enough memory.

Action See "Insufficient Server Memory Errors" on page 440 in Appendix A, "Troubleshooting."

TTS disabled because of error reading backout file.

Source OS

Explanation The Transaction Tracking System (TTS) could not read the backout file. TTS was disabled because it could not reliably back out any transactions. TTS protection is gone, but completed transactions are intact.

Action No action is necessary. You may continue without TTS protection.

TTS disabled because of error reading backout file during record generation.

Source OS

Explanation The Transaction Tracking System (TTS) may have disabled itself because it failed to generate records to be written to a file. This failure occurred when TTS could not read the backout file for some reason. The problem could be a hardware failure, a power failure, or a corrupted file.

Action See"Hardware Errors" on page 435 and "Power Supply Errors" on page 437 in Appendix A, "Troubleshooting." If you suspect file corruption, delete the file and restore from a backup.

TTS disabled because of error writing to file during backout.

Source OS

Explanation The Transaction Tracking System (TTS) had a problem writing to the actual database for which it was backing out transactions, so it disabled itself to prevent further problems. The database is probably corrupted.

Action Try to determine whether the database application can read the database. Some database programs have recovery utilities that can detect and repair corruption.

TTS disabled because of error writing volume definition information.

Source OS

Explanation This error indicates possible hardware failure.

Action See "Hardware Errors" on page 435 in Appendix A, "Troubleshooting."

TTS disabled because of too many defined volumes.

Source OS

Explanation The Transaction Tracking System (TTS) can track transactions on only a certain number of volumes. This number has been exceeded.

Action Combine volumes so that the number is within the limit set by TTS.

TTS disabled by operator.

Source OS

Explanation Someone issued the DISABLE TTS command from the file server console.

Action No action is necessary. This message is generated to the screen, and to the TTS$LOG.ERR file, for a chronological record of when TTS was disabled, and to indicate that it was disabled by the operator rather than by TTS itself (as is the case when the TTS runs out of disk space).

TTS exceeded the limit of number of active transactions *<number>* transactions delayed

Source OS

Explanation Because the limit of active transactions was exceeded, the Transaction Tracking System (TTS) must delay additional requests to complete transactions until the number of active transactions comes within the limit.

Action No action is required. If the limit of active transactions is adjustable, you may be able to increase it if it hasn't already been set to the maximum. See "SETTTS" in *Utilities Reference* for more information.

TTS has been shut down.

Source OS

Explanation This alert is for information purposes only.

Action No action is necessary unless you want to initialize TTS. See "SETTTS" in *Utilities Reference* for more information.

TTS not initialized.

Source OS

Explanation This alert is for information purposes only.

Action No action is necessary unless you want to initialize TTS. See "SETTTS" in *Utilities Reference* for more information.

TTS ran out of memory expanding transaction node tables *<number>* memory allocation requests failed

Source OS

Explanation The system has run out of memory for more transactions.

Action See "Insufficient Server Memory Errors" on page 440 in Appendix A, "Troubleshooting."

Two subdirectories reference the same first directory block.

Source OS

Explanation The operating system encountered a problem while mounting a volume because two subdirectories reference the same directory block.

Action Run VREPAIR. If the problem persists, make sure you have a backup of the volume. Delete the volume, re-create it using INSTALL, and restore the data from the backup.

Two volume segments with the same sync value have mismatched data. *<description>*.

Source INSTALL

Explanation INSTALL found multiple instances of the same volume. This probably occurred because two physical disks each contain a volume with the same name.

Action Since a given server may have only one volume with the same name, you must take one of the physical disks offline. You may delete one of the volumes and then bring the disks online simultaneously.

U

Unable to add a field to a form.

Source INSTALL

Explanation INSTALL was unable to complete an operation to build a screen presentation. This could be caused by insufficient memory.

Action See "Insufficient Server Memory Errors" on page 440 in Appendix A, "Troubleshooting."

Unable to add an option to a menu.

Source INSTALL

Explanation INSTALL was unable to build a menu on the screen. This could be caused by insufficient memory.

Action See "Insufficient Server Memory Errors" on page 440 in Appendix A, "Troubleshooting."

Unable to allocate *<number>* byte buffer.

Source VERSION

Explanation Your workstation does not have enough memory to run the utility or command.

Action See "Insufficient Workstation Memory Errors" on page 442 in Appendix A, "Troubleshooting."

Unable to allocate *<number>* bytes of memory.

Source ATTACH, CASTOFF, CASTON, LOGIN, LOGOUT, MAP, PURGE, SETPASS, USERLIST, WHOAMI

Explanation Your workstation does not have enough memory to run the utility or command.

Action See "Insufficient Workstation Memory Errors" on page 442 in Appendix A, "Troubleshooting."

Unable to allocate a process resource tag in CCreateProcess.

Source OS

Explanation The operating system was unable to create a process resource tag because it is out of memory.

Action See "Insufficient Server Memory Errors" on page 440 in Appendix A, "Troubleshooting."

Unable to allocate a semaphore resource tag in CAllocateSemaphore.

Source OS

Explanation The operating system was unable to create the semaphore resource tag because it is out of memory.

Action See "Insufficient Server Memory Errors" on page 440 in Appendix A, "Troubleshooting."

Unable to allocate a timer resource tag in InitializeTimer.

Source OS

Explanation The operating system was unable to create a timer resource tag because it is out of memory.

Action See "Insufficient Server Memory Errors" on page 440 in Appendix A, "Troubleshooting."

Unable to allocate an alloc resource tag in InitializeMemory.

Source OS

Explanation The operating system was unable to create an alloc resource tag because it is out of memory.

Action See "Insufficient Server Memory Errors" on page 440 in Appendix A, "Troubleshooting."

Unable to allocate memory.

Source INSTALL

Explanation The server is out of memory.

Action See "Insufficient Server Memory Errors" on page 440 in Appendix A, "Troubleshooting."

Unable to allocate memory for buffer; the volume definitions were NOT updated on the disk.

Source INSTALL

Explanation The server is out of memory.

Action See "Insufficient Server Memory Errors" on page 440 in Appendix A, "Troubleshooting."

Unable to allocate memory for data trees.

Source OS

Explanation The operating system was unable to allocate memory for data trees because it is out of memory.

Action See "Insufficient Server Memory Errors" on page 440 in Appendix A, "Troubleshooting."

Unable to allocate memory for NLM unpacking.

Source OS

Explanation The operating system was unable to allocate memory for unpacking the NLM because it is out of memory.

Action See "Insufficient Server Memory Errors" on page 440 in Appendix A, "Troubleshooting."

Unable to allocate memory to mount volume <*name*>.

Source OS

Explanation The operating system was unable to mount the volume because it is out of memory.

Action See "Insufficient Server Memory Errors" on page 440 in Appendix A, "Troubleshooting."

Unable to append <*name*> to the current list.

Source SBACKUP

Explanation You may not have enough server memory. You should have a minimum of 8 MB of RAM on the server.

Action See "Insufficient Server Memory Errors" on page 440 in Appendix A, "Troubleshooting."

Unable to append a boolean field.

Source SBACKUP

Explanation SBACKUP cannot add a Boolean field item to the current form (data entry screen). You may not have enough server memory." You should have a minimum of 8 MB of RAM on the server.

Action See "Insufficient Server Memory Errors" on page 440 in Appendix A, "Troubleshooting.

Unable to append a hot spot field.

Source SBACKUP

Explanation SBACKUP cannot add the Hot Spot field item to the form (data entry screen). You may not have enough server memory. You should have a minimum of 8 MB of RAM on the server.

Action See "Insufficient Server Memory Errors" on page 440 in Appendix A, "Troubleshooting."

Unable to append a prompt field.

Source SBACKUP

Explanation SBACKUP cannot add the Prompt field to the form (data entry screen). You may not have enough server memory. You should have a minimum of 8 MB of RAM on the server.

Action See "Insufficient Server Memory Errors" on page 440 in Appendix A, "Troubleshooting."

Unable to append a string field.

Source SBACKUP

Explanation SBACKUP cannot add a string to the current screen. You may not have enough server memory. You should have a minimum of 8 MB of RAM on the server.

Action See "Insufficient Server Memory Errors" on page 440 in Appendix A, "Troubleshooting."

Unable to append date field.

Source SBACKUP

Explanation An SBACKUP screen interface processing error occurred during the program's attempt to add a date field to the screen. You may not have enough server memory. You should have a minimum of 8 MB of RAM on the server.

Action See "Insufficient Server Memory Errors" on page 440 in Appendix A, "Troubleshooting."

Unable to append time field.

Source SBACKUP

Explanation An SBACKUP screen interface processing error occurred while adding a time field to the screen. You may not have enough server memory. You should have a minimum of 8 MB of RAM on the server.

Action See "Insufficient Server Memory Errors" on page 440 in Appendix A, "Troubleshooting."

Unable to append to a menu.

Source SBACKUP

Explanation SBACKUP cannot add another item to the menu. You may not have enough server memory." You should have a minimum of 8 MB of RAM on the server.

Action See "Insufficient Server Memory Errors" on page 440 in Appendix A, "Troubleshooting.

Unable to append to the form.

Source SBACKUP

Explanation An SBACKUP screen interface error occurred during the program's attempt to process the current screen form. You may not have enough server memory. You should have a minimum of 8 MB of RAM on the server.

Action See "Insufficient Server Memory Errors" on page 440 in Appendix A, "Troubleshooting."

Unable to attach to file server *<servername>*.

Source PSERVER (.EXE, .NLM, or .VAP)

Explanation A network error prevented the print server from attaching to the specified file server.

Action Try again. If the problem persists, contact your Novell Authorized Reseller.

Unable to attach to print server *<print server>*. Error *<number>*.

Source RPRINTER

Explanation A network error (indicated by the specified number) prevented RPRINTER from attaching to the specified print server.

Action Try again. Check the configurations in the NET.CFG file. The following parameters should have been configured for at least the values indicated:

```
IPX SOCKETS = 20
SPX CONNECTIONS = 50
```

These values may need to be increased by 10, depending upon what other applications are loaded in the workstation.

After setting the parameters in the NET.CFG file, reboot the workstation.

Unable to attach to server *<servername>*.

Source CAPTURE

Explanation You mistyped the name of the file server, specified a file server not cabled to your network, or specified a file server that has been brought down for system maintenance.

Action Use the SLIST command or the SYSCON utility to see which file servers are on your network. Type the file server name correctly.

Unable to build selection list, error *<code>*.

Source SBACKUP

Explanation SBACKUP cannot build a data set (probably a file or directory) selection list. You may not have enough server memory.

Action See "Insufficient Server Memory Errors" on page 440 in Appendix A, "Troubleshooting."

Unable to change attributes.

Source FLAGDIR

Explanation A network error prevented FLAGDIR from changing the attributes.

Action Make sure the file server is still running, and try again. If the problem persists, contact your Novell Authorized Reseller.

Unable to close data set: *<message>*.

Source SBACKUP

Explanation SBACKUP cannot close the data set (probably a file or directory) just processed.

Action Check your user access rights and the file attributes for the data set.

Unable to complete initialization process.

Source RPRINTER

Explanation This is a status message and is the second message in a pair.

Action Refer to the message that preceded this status message for a solution to the problem.

Unable to connect to the selected print server at this time

Source RPRINTER

Explanation A network error prevented the remote printer from connecting to the print server.

Action Try again. Make sure the print server you are trying to attach to is still running. If the specified print server is running and the problem persists, contact your Novell Authorized Reseller.

Unable to create capture file in specified directory.

Source — CAPTURE

Explanation — You used CAPTURE with the Create option and specified a directory in which you do not have the Create right.

Action — Use the RIGHTS command to view your effective rights in the directory. Specify a directory in which you have the Create right.

Unable to create directory <*name*>.

Source — INSTALL

Explanation — The specified directory could not be created.

Action — See "File I/O Errors" on page 441 in Appendix A, "Troubleshooting."

Unable to create display portal. Probable cause, not enough memory.

Source — PSERVER

Explanation — The file server does not have enough memory to run PSERVER.

Action — Add more memory to the file server, or unload loadable modules that are not being used.

Unable To Create File.

Source — INSTALL

Explanation — An error probably occurred while allocating memory, or an error occurred while accessing the disk.

Action — See "Insufficient Server Memory Errors" on page 440 and "General Disk I/O Errors" on page 438 in Appendix A, "Troubleshooting."

Unable to create file <*name*> on server.

Source — INSTALL

Explanation — One of the following problems may exist: (1) the disk is full, (2) the disk is write-protected, or (3) the path specification is invalid.

Action — Insert a disk with more free space on it. If the disk is write-protected, remove the write protection; or you may specify a different path.

Unable to create file <*name*>. One of the following problems may exist: (1) the disk is full, (2) the disk is write-protected, or (3) the path specification is invalid.

Source INSTALL

Explanation Refer to the message for possible explanations.

Action Insert a disk with more free space on it. If the disk is write-protected, remove the write protection; or you may specify a different path.

Unable to create VOL$LOG.ERR on <*volume name*>

Source OS

Explanation The system cannot log the error messages it produces. The VOL$LOG.ERR file (the volume's error file) could not be created because the volume is out of room, or because a disk error occurred. Historical error information for this volume will not be recorded at the server.

Action See "Locked Device Errors" on page 440 in Appendix A, "Troubleshooting."

Unable To Create volume <*name*>.

Source INSTALL

Explanation An error probably occurred while allocating memory, or an error occurred while accessing the disk.

Action See "Insufficient Server Memory Errors" on page 440 and "General Disk I/O Errors" on page 438 in Appendix A, "Troubleshooting."

Unable to delete the file after printing.

Source NPRINT

Explanation You used the Delete flag with the NPRINT command; however, the file server could not delete the specified file for one of the following reasons:

- The file was locked by another user or application.
- The file was deleted by another user or application after it was printed.

- You do not have the Delete right to the file.
- The file is flagged Delete Inhibit.

Action: If the file was not successfully deleted with the NPRINT command, use the DOS DEL command or the DOS ERASE command to delete the file.

Unable to detach from file server. (<*value*>)

Source: ATTACH

Explanation: An error occurred when you tried to detach from the file server. The <*value*> is the error number that can be used to trace the error.

Action: Try again or reboot the workstation. If the problem persists, record the error value and contact your Novell Authorized Reseller.

Unable to find a free block to redirect the FAT block.

Source: INSTALL

Explanation: The volume may be full, or the drive parameters may not be set up correctly. This message could also indicate a bug in the program.

Action: If possible, try specifying a larger volume size. Also check your drive parameters. If the problem persists, contact your Novell Authorized Reseller.

Unable to find a free block during Directory block allocation.

Source: INSTALL

Explanation: The volume may be full, or the drive parameters may not be set up correctly. This message could also indicate a bug in the program.

Action: If possible, try specifying a larger volume size. Also check your drive parameters. If the problem persists, contact your Novell Authorized Reseller.

Unable to find a free block during FAT block allocation.

Source: INSTALL

Explanation: An internal system error has occurred.

Action: Try again. If the problem persists, contact your Novell Authorized Reseller.

Unable to find a free block to redirect the Directory block.

Source INSTALL

Explanation The volume may be full, or the drive parameters may not be set up correctly. This message could also indicate a bug in the program.

Action If possible, try specifying a larger volume size. Also check your drive parameters. If the problem persists, contact your Novell Authorized Reseller.

Unable to find an unmapped drive.

Source CHKVOL

Explanation You tried to map a drive, but all 26 available drive designations have been used.

Action Use the DEL or REM options of the MAP command to remove unnecessary drive mappings.

Unable to find file *<filename>*.

Source VERSION

Explanation You used a filename with the VERSION command, but that filename was not found in the current directory or in any of your search paths.

Action Check the spelling of the filename. If correct, change to the directory that contains the file and try again.

Unable to find load file *<name>*

Source OS

Explanation The specified load file could not be found. Perhaps the file is not in the specified directory or search path. Files with filename extensions .NLM, .NAM, .LAN, and .DSK will be checked if no extension was specified. If an extension was specified, only files with that extension will be checked.

Action Make sure the file exists in the directory. Check the spelling and extension of the file.

Unable to find the end of the file.

Source NCOPY

Explanation The source file was not copied because it is corrupted.

Action Check the source file.

Unable to get a buffer for data transfer.

Source SBACKUP

Explanation SBACKUP cannot access enough dynamic memory from the server to complete data transfer; SBACKUP will terminate.

Action See "Insufficient Server Memory Errors" on page 440 in Appendix A, "Troubleshooting."

Unable to get connection list. (<*value*>)

Source ATTACH, CASTOFF, CASTON, LOGOUT, WHOAMI

Explanation The ATTACH utility was unable to get the connection list. The <*value*> is the error number that can be used to trace the error.

Action Try again. If this doesn't work, reboot the workstation and try again. If the problem persists, record the error value and contact your Novell Authorized Reseller.

Unable to get connection status. (<*value*>)

Source LOGOUT, PURGE, WHOAMI

Explanation The PURGE utility was unable to get the connection status from the file server. The <*value*> is the error number that can be used to trace the error.

Action Try again. If this doesn't work, reboot the workstation and try again. If the problem persists, record the error value and contact your Novell Authorized Reseller.

Unable to get default server

Source SYSTIME

Explanation You tried to execute a command on a file server, but you are not logged in or attached to that file server.

Action Log in or attach to a file server.

Unable to get header and/or offset, error *<code>*.

Source SBACKUP

Explanation SBACKUP expected to read a record header from the media, and failed. The media may be damaged, or the device may be malfunctioning.

Action Check the media for damage; then restart the session. Also make sure that the device is operating correctly.

Unable to get object ID of print server *<print server>*.

Source PSERVER (.EXE, .NLM, or .VAP)

Explanation The bindery, which must be opened to get object IDs, is locked or corrupted. The bindery is usually locked only momentarily.

Action Try again in a few minutes. Run BINDFIX if the problem persists.

Unable to get one name, error *<code>*.

Source SBACKUP

Explanation SBACKUP expected to read a data set name from the media and failed. The media may be damaged, or the device may be malfunctioning.

Action Check the media for damage; then restart the session and make sure that the device is operating correctly.

Unable to get the data set name, error *<code>*.

Source SBACKUP

Explanation An internal error has occurred. The DOS name space name for the data set could not be read.

Action None. This message is for information only.

Unable to get the internetwork address for the indicated print server at this time.

Source RPRINTER

Explanation The bindery is locked, and RPRINTER is unable to access necessary bindery information. Usually, the bindery is locked only momentarily.

Action — Try again. If the problem persists, run BINDFIX. If running BINDFIX does not solve the problem, contact your Novell Authorized Reseller.

Unable to initialize IPX.

Source — PSERVER.EXE

Explanation — The IPXODI.COM file, which contains both IPX and SPX, has not been loaded.

Action — Load IPXODI.

Unable to initialize SPX.

Source — PSERVER.EXE

Explanation — The IPXODI.COM file, which contains both IPX and SPX, has not been loaded.

Action — Load IPXODI.

Unable to initialize system auditing on volume *<name>*. Volume mount aborted.

Source — OS

Explanation — The operating system cannot initialize system auditing on the named volume, because it cannot open the audit file or the audit file is already at its maximum size.

Action — Check the size of the audit file before continuing.

Unable to list target service agents: *<TSA message>*.

Source — SBACKUP

Explanation — No TSAs have been loaded on the selected target server.

Action — Make sure that TSAs are loaded on the selected server or workstation. You might also need to unload the Storage Management Data Requester (SMDR) and any other files you are prompted to unload; then reload the TSA.

Unable to locate segment link.

Source INSTALL

Explanation An internal system error has occurred.

Action Try again. If the problem persists, contact your Novell Authorized Reseller.

Unable to login to file server <*servername*>.

Source PSERVER (.EXE, .NLM, or .VAP)

Explanation The specified file server returned a condition that prevented the print server from logging in to the file server.

Action Try again. If the problem persists, contact your Novell Authorized Reseller.

Unable to map: <*string*> Limit of 16 search drives exceeded.

Source LOGIN

Explanation You either exceeded the maximum number of allowable search drives with a MAP command (a maximum of 16 search drives can be defined at any one time) or used improper syntax in your MAP command format.

Action Type MAP at the command line to see how many search drives are currently defined. If you already have 16 search drives defined, you will have to remove a search drive mapping before you can define another one.

If you have less than 16 search drive mappings defined, you probably have a syntax error in your MAP command.

If this error occurs when you log in, use the SYSCON utility to access your login script; then correct the problem.

Unable to open AUDIT configuration file error. Press enter to continue.

Source OS

Explanation The operating system failed when attempting to open the audit configuration file.

Action Restart the server. If the problem persists, contact your Novell Authorized Reseller.

Unable to open data set for backup. *<message>*.

Source SBACKUP

Explanation SBACKUP cannot open the requested data set (probably a file or directory) for backup (read mode). The data set may be locked by another application, or may be flagged Execute Only; or, you may not have user access rights.

Action Check the data set's flags and your user access rights. If these are not the problem, wait a moment until the data set is no longer in use or locked by another application; then try the command again.

Unable to open data set for restore: *<message>*.

Source SBACKUP

Explanation This error could have a variety of causes.

Action Make sure that the desired "Overwrite" option is selected and the data set is not in use. Also check your user access rights and the attributes for the data set.

Unable to open file *<name>*.

Source INSTALL

Explanation This error could result from inadequate disk space on a NetWare volume or from a corrupted floppy disk.

Action See "File I/O Errors" on page 441 in Appendix A, "Troubleshooting." If the error occurred while accessing a floppy diskette, make sure all files can be read from a workstation. If not, contact your Novell Authorized Reseller.

Unable to open file NET$ACCT.DAT to add audit record

Source OS

Explanation A disk I/O has failed.

Action See "General Disk I/O Errors" on page 438 in Appendix A, "Troubleshooting."

Unable to parse path *<path>*.

Source SBACKUP

Explanation You specified a directory path for the log file that either was typed incorrectly or does not exist.

Action Check the log file path for spelling errors, and make sure that the specified volumes and directories exist.

Unable to pop the current list. An attempt to restore an internal list failed. Usually, the SBACKUP will abort.

Source SBACKUP

Explanation An internal error occurred in SBACKUP.

Action Exit SBACKUP and try the operation again. If the problem persists, contact your Novell Authorized Reseller.

Unable to purge files. (*<value>*)

Source PURGE

Explanation An error occurred when PURGE tried to purge a file. The *<value>* is the error number that can be used to trace the error.

Action Try again. If this doesn't work, reboot the workstation and try again. If the problem persists, record the error value and contact your Novell Authorized Reseller.

Unable to push the current list. The list stack is full. SBACKUP can't perform the function you requested.

Source SBACKUP

Explanation SBACKUP cannot add another list. You may not have enough server memory.

Action Unload any unneeded NLMs and try again. If the problem persists, try adding more memory to the server. You should have a minimum of 8 MB of RAM on the server.

Unable to put first name in data set name, *<message>*.

Source SBACKUP

Explanation SBACKUP cannot begin a data set (probably a file or directory) name list with the requested name. You should have a minimum of 8 MB of RAM on the server.

Action Make sure that the data set name exists and is valid for the specified name space. If you suspect a memory problem, see "Insufficient Server Memory Errors" on page 440 in Appendix A, "Troubleshooting."

Unable to put name in the data set name: *<name>*.

Source SBACKUP

Explanation No name could be assigned to the data set name in the list.

Action Make sure that you are using a valid data set name. Also check the number of open files and the available memory on your server. See "Data Set" in *Concepts* for more information.

Unable to read configuration file for printer *<number>*. Printer not initialized.

Source PSERVER (.EXE, .NLM, or .VAP)

Explanation The configuration file for the specified printer is corrupted.

Action Run PCONSOLE, delete the printer from the print server, and then re-create the printer.

Unable to read data set. *<data set name>*.

Source SBACKUP

Explanation SBACKUP encountered a problem reading the data set (probably a file or directory) from the disk. The data set on the backup media may not be correct.

Action Make sure that the data set is not corrupted; then try the backup again.

Unable To Read Drive Information.

Source INSTALL

Explanation An error occurred when the program attempted to access information on a disk drive.

Action See "General Disk I/O Errors" on page 438 in Appendix A, "Troubleshooting."

Unable to read file *<name>*.

Source INSTALL

Explanation INSTALL could not read from a DOS or NetWare disk. If it is a floppy disk, it may be bad, may not be inserted correctly, or may not contain the desired file. If it is a hard disk, the proper disk driver may not be loaded, the cabling may not be correct, or the drive parameters may be set incorrectly.

Action Make sure that you have a readable disk. Then check for the possible explanations listed above. See "General Disk I/O Errors" on page 438 in Appendix A, "Troubleshooting." If the problem persists, contact your Novell Authorized Reseller.

Unable to read volume definition table from NetWare partition on *<drive name>*

Source OS

Explanation The volume definition table on the specified drive could not be read because of a disk error. Consequently, the volume could not be mounted.

Action Check the disk drive and the cable. See "Hardware Errors" on page 435 in Appendix A, "Troubleshooting." If these suggestions do not solve the problem, see "General Disk I/O Errors" on page 438 in Appendix C.

Unable to register router tracking screen pause routine.

Source OS

Explanation This message refers to the key input pause routine activated by using the TRACK ON command. For some reason, the routine cannot be executed.

Action No action is necessary. The operating system will continue operating normally.

Unable to register the SBACKUP resources, error *<code>*

Source SBACKUP

Explanation SBACKUP cannot register the required resources from the NetWare operating system. You may not have enough server memory." You should have a minimum of 8 MB of RAM on the server.

Action See "Insufficient Server Memory Errors" on page 440 in Appendix A, "Troubleshooting.

Unable to scan next data set: *<message>*.

Source SBACKUP

Explanation SBACKUP cannot read the scan information for the requested data set (probably a file or directory).

Action Check your user access rights and the file attributes for the data set. Also make sure that the file is not in use.

Unable to select printer *<number>* on print server *<print server>*. Error *<number>*

Source RPRINTER

Explanation An error prevented RPRINTER from selecting the specified printer configuration on the specified print server.

If you are loading RPRINTER from a batch file that executes every time you boot your workstation, this message will return with an error code of 776. RPRINTER is trying to reconnect before SPX has timed out and removed your printer from the print server's table.

Action Complete one of the following:

- If you are loading from a batch file, add the following line to the file just above the line that loads RPRINTER:

  ```
  RPRINTER print_server_name printer_number -r
  ```

  Replace *print_server_name* with the name of your print server. Replace *printer_number* with the number of your printer. The -r option unloads your remote printer from the print server's table.

- ◆ If you are not loading from a batch file, run PCONSOLE to verify that the printer number specified in your command is a valid, configured printer on the print server you specified. If the printer number is valid, record the error number and contact your Novell Authorized Reseller.

Unable to set the archive status. *<message>*.

Source SBACKUP

Explanation SBACKUP cannot set (or reset) the Archive status flag on the data set just processed.

Action None. The Archive status will be left as is; the status was probably set to indicate that the file has been modified.

Unable to set up drive for mirroring.

Source INSTALL

Explanation An error occurred when the program attempted to write mirroring information to a disk drive.

Action Verify that the drive can be accessed, and that a NetWare disk partition exists on it. See "General Disk I/O Errors" on page 438 in Appendix A, "Troubleshooting."

Unable to start a data set scan. *<message>*.

Source SBACKUP

Explanation SBACKUP cannot find any data sets that match those specified.

Action Check your "scan begin" criteria for valid syntax and format.

Unable to unregister router tracking screen pause routine.

Source OS

Explanation This message refers to the key input pause routine deactivated by using the TRACK OFF command. For some reason, the routine cannot be deactivated.

Action No action is necessary. The operating system will continue operating normally.

Unable to write data set: *<message>*.

Source SBACKUP

Explanation SBACKUP cannot write the requested data set.

Action Make sure that you have user access rights and that the data set is not already in use.

Unable to write out partition information—ccode = *<number>*.

Source INSTALL

Explanation While writing the partition information to the disk drive, the operating system reported an error to INSTALL.

Action See "General Disk I/O Errors" on page 438 in Appendix A, "Troubleshooting."

Unable to write out partition table information. The returned error was *<number>*.

Source INSTALL

Explanation While writing the partition information to the disk drive, the operating system reported an error from INSTALL.

Action See "General Disk I/O Errors" on page 438 in Appendix A, "Troubleshooting."

Unable to write out the file.

Source INSTALL

Explanation INSTALL could not write to a DOS or NetWare disk. If it is a floppy disk, it may be bad, write protected, or not inserted correctly. If it is a hard disk, the proper disk driver may not be loaded, the cabling may not be correct, or the drive parameters may be set incorrectly.

Action Make sure that you have a writable disk. Then check for the possible explanations listed above. See "Volume I/O Errors" on page 441 in Appendix A, "Troubleshooting." If the problem persists, contact your Novell Authorized Reseller.

Unable to write to file <*name*>. One of the following problems may exist: (1) the target disk is full, or (2) the disk is write-protected.

Source INSTALL

Explanation Refer to the message for possible explanations.

Action Insert a disk with more free space on it. If the disk is write-protected, remove the write protection; or you may specify a different path.

Unable to write to file <*name*>.

Source INSTALL

Explanation The target disk may be full, or the disk may be write-protected.

Action Insert a disk with more free space on it. If the disk is write-protected, remove the write protection; or you may specify a different path.

Unable to write to VOL$LOG.ERR on <*volume name*>

Source OS

Explanation The system was unable to write to the volume's error file because of a disk failure.

Action Another message should appear that indicates what went wrong. Correct the problem according to the information in the message. See "Hardware Errors" on page 435 in Appendix A, "Troubleshooting."

UnCloneMirrorGroup was called

Source OS

Explanation A clone is a data structure created to track I/Os of a device that has been removed or is nonfunctional. This usually relates to mirrored disk devices. The abend occurred because of a lack of memory resources for the data structures.

Action Other processes in the server have used up all the available resources. Rebooting the server should clear up the problem. If this or other messages with similar memory-caused abends appear frequently, add more memory to the server. See "Insufficient Server Memory Errors" on page 440 in Appendix A, "Troubleshooting."

Unexpected end of directory file FAT chain at sequence *<number>*.

Source INSTALL

Explanation An internal system error has occurred.

Action Try again. If the problem persists, contact your Novell Authorized Reseller.

Unexpected end of FAT file FAT chain at sequence *<number>*.

Source INSTALL

Explanation An internal system error has occurred.

Action Try again. If the problem persists, contact your Novell Authorized Reseller.

Unexpected path error *<number>*.

Source ALLOW

Explanation A network error prevented ALLOW from obtaining information about the path.

Action Try again. If the problem persists, contact your Novell Authorized Reseller.

UNIX Hard Link flags don't match between the name spaces.

Source OS

Explanation The name spaces cannot be linked because their flags do not match.

Action Make sure that the UNIX hard link flags match before attempting to link the name spaces.

UNIX Hard Link flags set with no UNIX name space.

Source OS

Explanation You attempted to create a hard link before loading the UNIX name space.

Action Load the UNIX name space before creating a hard link.

Unknown attribute: *<attribute>*.

Source FLAGDIR

Explanation You used an invalid flag (option) in your command.

Action Use a valid flag (option) in your command.

Unknown attribute encountered in command line.

Source FLAG, SMODE

Explanation You used an invalid flag (option) in your command.

Action Use a valid flag (option) in your command.

Unknown communications error code

Source Shell

Explanation An error was found in the reply packet that did not match any known errors. Normally, this is caused by packet corruption through interference, bad cables, etc.

Action Infrequent errors may be caused by interference; if errors are frequent or bothersome, check all cables, boards, etc.

Unknown error (<*value*>) doing attach.

Source ATTACH

Explanation An error has occurred that the operating system cannot identify. The <*value*> is the error number that can be used to trace the error.

Action Record the error value and contact your Novell Authorized Reseller.

Unknown error returned. (<*value*>)

Source ATTACH

Explanation An error has occurred that the operating system cannot identify. The <*value*> is the error number that can be used to trace the error.

Action Record the error value and contact your Novell Authorized Reseller.

Unknown error returned by ATTACH

Source ATTACH, MAP

Explanation You upgraded a NetWare 286 v2.1*x* file server to NetWare v3.12, but you failed to change the users' passwords.

Action Log in as SUPERVISOR and run SYSCON. Change your users' passwords.

Unknown file server.

Source ATTACH, CHKVOL, LOGIN, MAP, RENDIR

Explanation You mistyped the name of the file server, specified a file server that is not on the network, or specified a file server that has been brought down for system maintenance.

Action Use the SLIST command or the SYSCON utility to list the file servers that your station recognizes. Type the name of the file server correctly.

If the file server has been brought down for maintenance, try the command when the file server has been brought back up. If you still have problems, ask your network supervisor for help.

Unknown flag in the flag list.

Source NPRINT

Explanation You specified a flag (option) that the operating system cannot recognize in a command.

Action Use a valid flag (option) in your command.

Unknown Packet Type!

Source OS

Explanation The router received an unknown packet. This message appears on the console screen when the TRACK ON console command has been issued.

Action None. This message is for information only.

Unknown set parameter name *<name>*

Source OS

Explanation A SET command was issued, but the specified parameter name was unknown.

Action Check the spelling of the parameter name. Type "SET" without a parameter to view the acceptable values for the parameter.

Unknown set parameter name *<string>* (type SET for a list of valid parameter names)

Source OS

Explanation A SET command was entered, but the system could not find the command in its table of keywords.

Action Type "SET" for a valid list of parameter keywords.

Unknown volume.

Source RENDIR

Explanation You either specified a volume that does not exist on the file server, or mistyped the volume name. A volume name, such as SYS:, must be followed by a colon.

Action If you are not sure which volumes are defined on your file server, use the VOLINFO utility or the CHKVOL * command to see which volumes are defined. When you specify a volume name in a command, always type a colon (:) after the volume name.

Unsupported frame type setting ignored

Source OS

Explanation The LOAD command was used to load a LAN driver. The "FRAME=" option was specified in the command, but the LAN driver supports only one frame type. This option is not supported in the command.

Action Do not specify the "FRAME=" option for this LAN driver.

Unsynchronized partition *<logical partition number>*.

Source OS

Explanation The hard disks in the specified logical partition are no longer synchronized. Synchronization has probably failed because of Hot Fix failure (all the redirection blocks on one of the disks are full), hardware failure, or device deactivation. (See "Device numbering" in *Concepts* for an explanation of the number.)

Action Load MONITOR. Check each disk for Hot Fix and hardware failure.

UPS cannot open the IPX socket. Load IPX before loading UPS.

Source UPS

Explanation UPS was unable to open an IPX socket.

Action Load IPX before loading UPS.

UPS is shutting down server *<servername>*. Commercial power has failed and the battery is too low.

Source UPS

Explanation The UPS module automatically brought down file server *<servername>* because the commercial power has failed and the battery is too low or discharge time has expired.

Action Turn off the power switches on the file server and its monitor, disks, and any other electronic equipment you may have on the affected electrical circuits. This will prevent the electronic components from being damaged by voltage transients when the line power comes back on.

Open files that were not saved properly may be lost or damaged.

User *<servername>/<username>* does not exist.

Source SEND

Explanation You either specified a user who does not exist on the file server, or mistyped the user's name.

Action Use the SYSCON utility to view the list of network users.

User *<servername>/<username>* has not logged in.

Source SEND

Explanation You specified a valid user who is not currently logged in to the file server.

Action If you are not certain which users are logged in to the file server, use the SESSION utility or the USERLIST command to view the list of current network users. If the user you were trying to send a message to is not listed, wait until the user is listed, and try again.

User "*<username>*" not found.

Source GRANT, MAKEUSER, REMOVE, REVOKE

Explanation You either specified a user that does not exist on *<servername>*, or mistyped the user's name.

Action Use the SYSCON utility to view the list of network users.

User or group "*<name>*" not found.

Source GRANT, REMOVE, REVOKE

Explanation You either specified a username or a group name that is not defined on the network, or mistyped the name of the user or the group.

Action Use the SYSCON or SESSION utility or the USERLIST command to see which users are defined on the network. Use the SYSCON or SESSION utility to see which groups (or trustees) are defined on the network.

User *<name>* on station *<number>* cleared by connection watchdog. Connection cleared due to communication or station failure.

Source OS

Explanation The user at the workstation is no longer attached to the server. The server has purged the connection and all associated system resources are freed.

If the SET server utility's "Display Watchdog Logouts" parameter has been set to ON, this message will appear when a station is turned off or rebooted before the user has logged out.

Action During a normal workstation power down or reboot, no action is required. If the station is failing to receive or send watchdog packets, check the cabling and cable termination points. On slow networks (wide area networks or networks with T-links or modem connections), workstations may have their connections cleared if the interval between watchdog packets is too small.

If the loss of contact is unexpected, potential problems can be isolated from the network map. Look for routers that are offline or inoperative.

For information on the watchdog feature, see "SET" in *Utilities Reference*.

V

Volume *<server>*/*<volume>* **almost out of disk space**

Source OS

Explanation The volume is about to run out of disk space. Users should save files currently in use to another volume or to another server to prevent data loss.

Action See "Locked Device Errors" on page 440 in Appendix A, "Troubleshooting."

Volume *<name>* **already has the maximum number of segments (***<number>***).**

Source INSTALL

Explanation You may create a new volume using this segment, but you may not add it to any existing volume.

Action Proceed as appropriate for your situation.

Volume *<name>* **could not be mounted. Some or all volume segments can not be located.**

Source OS

Explanation The volume specified in the MOUNT command could not be mounted. The volume has segments on more than one hard disk, and at least one of the hard disks is not responding.

Action Make sure all disk drivers have been loaded. See "Hardware Errors" on page 435 in Appendix A, "Troubleshooting."

Volume *<name>* **could not be mounted. There are already** *<number>* **volumes mounted. No more volumes can be mounted.**

Source OS

Explanation Mounting another volume would exceed the allowed limit for volumes concurrently mounted.

Action Dismount one or more volumes and try the MOUNT server utility again.

Volume *<name>* dismounted due to drive deactivation

Source OS

Explanation The specified volume was dismounted for one of the following reasons:

- A disk driver was unloaded.
- A disk failure occurred.
- The operating system initiated the driver unload.
- The volume is offline and unavailable to users.

Action Make sure the disk driver is loaded. See "Hardware Errors" on page 435 in Appendix A, "Troubleshooting."

Volume "*<volume>*" does not exist.

Source MAP, NCOPY

Explanation You asked for information about a volume that does not appear in the network's list of mounted volumes.

Action Use the VOLINFO or FILER utility or the CHKVOL * command to list the volumes mounted on the network; then try the command again.

Volume *<name>* DOS Type (*<number>*) does not match the file server DOS Type (*<number>*).

Source OS

Explanation Different language types can be specified for your file system by the LCONFIG.SYS file. The default is English.

After upgrading your system, you attempted to remount a volume that had a previously specified language type different from the language type your server is now using. If you do not change the language for your volume, this error occurs.

Action If you are using a language type other than English, make sure that the LCONFIG.SYS and SERVER.MSG files are both in your server's boot directory.

If you are trying to change from one of the other languages to English, you may get errors that need to be fixed by running VREPAIR.

Volume <*name*> first segment (<*number*>) does not start at block 0.

Source: OS, INSTALL

Explanation: The first segment of a volume must start with block 0. While mounting the specified volume, which is distributed over multiple physical disks, the operating system could not find the first segment. The segment that it found is not the first segment in the volume because it does not begin with block 0.

One reason why the operating system may not be able to find the segment is that the disk was corrupted. Another reason is that the operating system may not be able to access the disk at all because of a hardware problem on the network.

Action: Back up all data on the affected disk before troubleshooting the problem. See "General Disk I/O Errors" on page 438 and "Hardware Errors" on page 435 in Appendix A, "Troubleshooting."

Volume <*name*> has invalid segment <*number*>.

Source: INSTALL

Explanation: An invalid volume has been found. This volume has become corrupted in some way.

Action: Delete the volume, and restore the data from backups. If this fails, contact your Novell Authorized Reseller.

Volume <*name*> has multiple definitions for segment <*number*>.

Source: OS, INSTALL

Explanation: While mounting a volume, the operating system found multiple definitions for the specified segment, indicating that the current synchronization value is invalid. The operating system will discard the invalid synchronization value.

Action: None. This message is for information only.

Volume *<name>* has multiple sync definitions. All definitions except *<number>* discarded.

Source OS

Explanation While checking a volume definition during mounting of the volume, the operating system discarded all unneeded synchronization values.

Action None. This message is for information only.

Volume *<name>* is missing segment *<number>*.

Source OS

Explanation While checking a volume definition during mounting of the volume, the operating system found that a segment was missing. Segments are consecutively numbered.

Action None. This message is for information only. If the problem persists, contact your Novell Authorized Reseller.

Volume *<name>* last segment (*<number>*) ends at block *<number>* instead of *<number>*

Source OS, INSTALL

Explanation The segment ends at a block that is incorrect, based on the operating system's calculation of where the segment begins and how large it is.

Action None. This message is for information only.

Volume *<name>* not found in existing volumes list.

Source OS, INSTALL

Explanation The operating system cannot find a volume that it attempted to discard.

Action None. This message is for information only.

Volume *<server>/<volume>* out of disk space *<number>*k of disk space is in use by deleted files No deleted files have been deleted long enough to purge yet

Source OS

Explanation When the volume is out of disk space, this message will be broadcast to all users on the system. All attempts to write to files will fail because of insufficient disk space.

The second line of the message indicates that deleted files have not yet been purged. The third line indicates that all the deleted files cannot be purged yet because the preset purge time has not elapsed.

Users may not be able to save files they are using, and may lose data.

Action See "Locked Device Errors" on page 440 in Appendix A, "Troubleshooting."

Volume *<server>/<volume>* out of disk space There are no deleted files using disk space

Source OS

Explanation When the volume is out of disk space, this message will be broadcast to all users on the system. All attempts to write to files will fail because of insufficient disk space.

Action See "Locked Device Errors" on page 440 in Appendix A, "Troubleshooting."

Volume *<name>* segment *<number>* ends at block *<number>* and segment *<number>* starts at block *<number>*.

Source OS

Explanation The volume segments are not contiguous.

Action Back up all data before troubleshooting the problem. Make sure that the operating system can see all disks over which the volume is distributed, and that none have been corrupted. Run VREPAIR. Delete the volume, re-create it using INSTALL, and restore the data from the backup.

Volume *<name>* **last segment** *<number>* **ends at block** *<number>* **instead of** *<number>*.

Source INSTALL

Explanation The volume segments are not contiguous.

Action Back up all data before troubleshooting the problem. Make sure that the operating system can see all disks over which the volume is distributed, and that none have been corrupted. Run VREPAIR. Delete the volume, re-create it using INSTALL, and restore the data from the backup.

Volume *<name>* **still operational despite drive deactivation.**

Source OS

Explanation One of the disk drives in the volume has gone down. However, the volume's integrity has not been compromised sufficiently to bring the entire volume down.

Action See "Hardware Errors" on page 435 in Appendix A, "Troubleshooting."

Volume *<name>* **sync** *<number>* **not found in volume's sync list.**

Source OS, INSTALL

Explanation While attempting to discard an unneeded or invalid synchronization value, the operating system found that the value was not in the volume's synchronization list.

Action None. This message is for information only.

Volume Definition Table Mirror Mismatch

Source OS

Explanation Four copies of the Volume Segment Definition table are kept on each NetWare partition. This error indicates that these copies do not match.

Action Run the INSTALL program and select "Volume Options."

Volume Definition Tables on <server> are out of sync.

Source INSTALL

Explanation Four copies of the Volume Segment Definition table are kept on each NetWare partition. This error indicates that these copies do not match.

Action Run the INSTALL program and select "Volume Options."

Volume directory is too large (over 2 million files).

Source OS

Explanation While allocating directory tables during a volume mount, the system found the number of directory entries for the volume exceeded 2,000,000 entries. This error probably indicates corruption.

Action Run VREPAIR. If the problem persists, make sure you have a backup of the volume. Delete the volume, re-create it using INSTALL, and restore the data from the backup.

Volume flags do not match

Source OS

Explanation Two segments of the volume claim that the volume has different flags. This error could occur for one of the following reasons:

- Two volumes on the file server have identical names and a segment from each volume is causing the error.
- The volume is corrupted.

Action If you have two volumes with the same name, unload the disk driver for the volume that you do not want to rename. Rename the other volume (the volume that is on the hard disk that still has its disk driver loaded). Then load the disk driver that you just unloaded. Mount both volumes.

If the volume is corrupted, run the INSTALL program and select "Volume Options." If the volume cannot be fixed, delete the volume and re-create it.

Note: If you delete the volume, all data will be destroyed. You will have to restore the data from a backup.

Volume has no volume name.

Source OS, INSTALL

Explanation The MOUNT or DISMOUNT command was issued, but the volume name was not specified.

Action Specify a volume name.

Volume Manager Error.

Source OS

Explanation An error prevented the volume from being mounted.

Action Run VREPAIR. If the problem persists, make sure you have a backup of the volume. Delete the volume, re-create it using INSTALL, and restore the data from the backup.

Volume name *<name>* is too short.

Source OS, INSTALL

Explanation A volume name must be at least two characters long.

Action Make sure that you typed a valid volume name in the MOUNT console command, and that you spelled it correctly.

Volume segment entry *<number>* on *<disk label>* is invalid: *<description>*.

Source INSTALL

Explanation A segment of a volume is corrupted.

Action See "General Disk I/O Errors" on page 438 in Appendix A, "Troubleshooting." You may need to re-create the volume.

Volume SYS: can not be mounted with write protected device

Source OS

Explanation Since NetWare must be able to make changes to the files on the volume SYS:, it cannot reside on a write-protected disk drive.

Action Remove write protection from the disk drive, or reinstall NetWare placing SYS: on another disk drive. (Make sure that you back up all data on the affected server before you reinstall NetWare.)

WARNING: Adjacent disk segments do not line up.

Source INSTALL

Explanation An internal system error has occurred.

Action Try again. If the problem persists, contact your Novell Authorized Reseller.

WARNING: Byte value greater than 255 was truncated

Source IPXODI, Shell

Explanation An IPX or SPX parameter specified in the NET.CFG file was set to a value greater than 255. The actual value used will be 255 (which is the maximum configurable value).

Action Change the NET.CFG file so that the IPX or SPX parameter has a valid value.

WARNING: Commercial power detected off during UPS installation. Check commercial power lines or the UPS.

Source UPS

Explanation When the UPS module was loaded, the module detected that commercial power was off. If this message occurs during first-time installation, the online jumper has been configured incorrectly.

Action If this warning occurs during a first-time installation, check the online configuration setting on the UPS controller board.

WARNING: Directory name "*<old directory name>*" will be renamed to "*<new directory name>*".

Source 2XUPGRADE

Explanation An illegal directory name was found. NetWare v2.1*x* allowed for directory names up to 14 characters long. NetWare v3.*x* shortened the length to 11 characters to conform to DOS's eight character name, three character extension format.

With the 8.3 format, directories can have up to 8 characters before the period (.) and up to 3 characters after the period. If a name conflict occurs, the directory will be given a numbered extension starting with ".001."

Action Make note of the new directory name.

WARNING: Error *<number>* reading from *<disk label>*. NetWare Partition sector *<number>*. *<description>*.

Source INSTALL

Explanation INSTALL could not read from the disk.

Action See "General Disk I/O Errors" on page 438 in Appendix A, "Troubleshooting."

WARNING: Error *<number>* writing to *<disk label>* sector *<number>*.

Source INSTALL

Explanation The disk could not be written to. The driver or disk may not be configured correctly, or a hardware failure may have occurred.

Action See "General Disk I/O Errors" on page 438 in Appendix A, "Troubleshooting."

WARNING: Error registering Protocol = *<name>*, PID = *<number>*, Frame = *<type>*

Source MLID

Explanation The MLID was unable to register the specified Protocol ID.

- *<name>*The name of the protocol.
- *<number>*The value of the Protocol ID used to register the Protocol ID.
- *<type>*The frame type for which the Protocol ID was registered.

Action Verify the protocol information in the NET.CFG file.

WARNING: File name "*<old file name>*" will be renamed to "*<new file name>*".

Source 2XUPGRADE

Explanation An illegal file name was found. NetWare v2.1*x* allowed for file names up to 14 characters long. NetWare v3.*x* shortened the length to 11 characters to conform to DOS's eight character name, three character extension format.

With the 8.3 format, files can have up to 8 characters before the period (.) and up to 3 characters after the period. If a name conflict occurs, the file will be given a numbered extension starting with ".001."

Action Make note of the new filename.

WARNING: Invalid LOOK AHEAD SIZE value, will be set to maximum (128 bytes).

Source MLID

Explanation The "LOOK AHEAD SIZE" option was specified in the NET.CFG for an MLID. The value specified was greater than 128 bytes. The MLID will use 128 bytes for its look ahead size.

Action Change the "LOOK AHEAD SIZE" option in the NET.CFG file to a valid value.

WARNING: MLID does not support Frame *<type>*—Protocol keyword ignored.

Source MLID

Explanation The "PROTOCOL" option was specified in the NET.CFG for an MLID. The specified frame type is not supported by the MLID.

Action Check the "PROTOCOL" line in the NET.CFG file for possible misspellings or omissions of required dashes and underscores. Check the MLID documentation for supported frame types.

Warning, More than one sync entry exists for volume *<name>*.

Source INSTALL

Explanation Multiple disk devices are online devices that contain volumes with the same name. Two volumes on the same server cannot have the same name.

Action Bring the disks that contain these volumes online one at a time, rather than at the same time. If one of the volumes is old and no longer needed, delete it to avoid the problem in the future.

Warning: Ncopy will NOT copy the resource fork for Macintosh directories.

Source NCOPY

Explanation NCOPY can copy both the resource fork and the data fork for Macintosh files, but it can only copy the data fork for a directory.

Action Log in from a Macintosh workstation and copy the directory (folder).

WARNING: NET.CFG ignored—file length must be less than 4097 bytes.

Source IPXODI

Explanation The NET.CFG file is larger than 4,096 bytes in length. IPX still loads, but it ignores the information in the NET.CFG file.

Action Reduce the size of the NET.CFG file.

WARNING: NET.CFG ignored—file length must be less than 4097 bytes.

Source LSL

Explanation The NET.CFG file is larger than 4,096 bytes in length. The LSL still loads, but it ignores the information in the NET.CFG file.

Action Reduce the size of the NET.CFG file.

WARNING: NET.CFG ignored—file length must be less than 4097 bytes.

Source MLID

Explanation The NET.CFG file is larger than 4,096 bytes. The MLID still loads, but it ignores the information in the NET.CFG file.

Action Reduce the size of the NET.CFG file.

WARNING: NET.CFG ignored—MLID name cannot be more than 8 characters long.

Source IPXODI

Explanation The "BIND MLID" option in the NET.CFG file specified an MLID with a name longer than eight characters.

Action Refer to the MLID's documentation for more information on the name.

WARNING: No room in the LSL for another board. Board *<number>* will not be activated.

Source MLID

Explanation The maximum number of boards has been registered with the Link Support Layer. The DOS ODI LSL can support up to eight boards.

Action Reduce the number of active boards in the system by unloading a board.

WARNING: Node Address override not supported. Specify override when loading IBM LAN Support Software.

Source LANSUP.COM

Explanation A node address was specified in the NET.CFG file for the LANSUP.COM driver. The node override must be specified when loading the IBM LAN Support software.

Action Refer to the IBM LAN Support documentation for instructions.

WARNING: Overlapping segment entry found starting at sector *<number>* on *<name>* for volume *<name>* segment *<number>*.

Source INSTALL

Explanation Disk data may be corrupted, or an internal error may have occurred.

Action See "General Disk I/O Errors" on page 438 in Appendix A, "Troubleshooting." If these actions fail, contact your Novell Authorized Reseller.

WARNING: Protocol keyword must have a frame type—entry ignored.

Source MLID

Explanation The "PROTOCOL" option was specified in the NET.CFG for an MLID. The entry failed to specify the associated frame type for the protocol ID addition. An entry in the NET.CFG file for the "PROTOCOL" option should look similar to the following:

```
LINK DRIVER NE1000
PROTOCOL IPX 8137 ETHERNET_II
```

Action Specify a frame type with the "PROTOCOL" option.

WARNING: Specified MAX PACKET SIZE too big for this adapter, max size used.

Source LANSUP.COM

Explanation The specified maximum packet size in the NET.CFG file was too large for the network board installed in the workstation. The maximum packet size for the network board was used.

Action Modify the maximum packet size in the NET.CFG file.

WARNING: The file NEW.PWD in the SYS:SYSTEM directory already exists. It has been renamed to "*<new name>*". Random passwords for this upgrade session will still be written to NEW.PWD.

Source 2XUPGRADE

Explanation The file name used to store user's random passwords already exists. Other NetWare utilities which create NEW.PWD are NetWare Name Service (NNS) and the Across-The-Wire Migration utility. The old NEW.PWD file will be renamed to NEWPWD.*xxx*, where *xxx* is a numbered extension starting with ".001".

Action Take note of the name change so the old file can be deleted if it is no longer needed.

Warning: There are no more redirection blocks.

Source OS Media Manager

Explanation The partition has used all its redirection blocks. Future I/O errors cannot be redirected to Hot Fix.

Action See "General Disk I/O Errors" on page 438 in Appendix A, "Troubleshooting."

Warning: There are only *<number>* redirection blocks left.

Source OS Media Manager

Explanation The partition is running out of redirection blocks. If the Hot Fix redirection area is not increased, the disk will not be able to use Hot Fix to correct future I/O errors.

Action See "General Disk I/O Errors" on page 438 in Appendix A, "Troubleshooting."

Warning: Unable to create bindery files

Source OS

Explanation The system could not open and was unable to create the necessary bindery files. Since access to the bindery files is not possible, users cannot log in.

This condition can be caused by missing bindery files, a full disk, a full directory, or any combination of the three. The condition can also be caused by a poorly written NLM or a malfunctioning backup system.

Because one or more of the bindery files (NET$OBJ.SYS, NET$PROP.SYS, and NET$VAL.SYS) are missing, and both the disk and directory entries (at least in the SYS:SYSTEM directory) are full, attempts to log in will fail.

Action There are two possibilities for system recovery. First, run the VREPAIR utility. This utility might be able to reclaim some disk space which would then allow the creation of the bindery files.

The second (and more drastic) of the possible solutions is to run the INSTALL utility and reinitialize volume SYS:. After reinitialization, restore from a current backup (including security) to create a working file server.

Warning, Unable to lock the disk; it is currently being used by another process. A mounted volume may be using it. The Partition Table cannot be modified at this time.

Source INSTALL

Explanation The disk cannot be locked because it is currently being used by another process. A mounted volume may be using it.

Action See "Locked Device Errors" on page 440 in Appendix A, "Troubleshooting."

WARNING: UPS battery is low. Repair or replace battery.

Source UPS

Explanation During installation, the UPS check routine detected a low battery condition.

Action — Check the low battery configuration setting on the UPS controller board. Make sure the battery is connected properly. Test the battery's condition with a battery tester. If the battery is bad, replace it.

WARNING: UPS hardware configuration error was detected. Check for errors in your UPS hardware configuration settings.

Source — UPS

Explanation — UPS installation failed due to a hardware configuration error. Both the online and low battery configurations are wrong.

Action — Change the online and low battery configuration settings on the UPS controller board; then try again.

Warning, volume <*name*> has multiple sync definitions. All definitions except <*number*> have been discarded.

Source — INSTALL

Explanation — More than one volume with the same name was found. All definitions but one were removed from memory. The volumes are still intact on disk.

Action — Since a given server may have only one volume with the same name, you must take one of the physical disks offline. You may delete one of the volumes and then bring the disks online simultaneously.

WARNING: volume <*name*> has multiple sync entries. It can not be deleted at this time.

Source — INSTALL

Explanation — Multiple disk devices are online devices that contain volumes with the same name. Two volumes on the same server cannot have the same name.

Action — Bring the disks that contain these volumes online one at a time, rather than at the same time. If one of the volumes is old and no longer needed, delete it to avoid the problem in the future.

Warning, volume *<name>* is missing segment *<number>*.

Source INSTALL

Explanation An incomplete volume has been discovered. A segment is missing.

Action Make sure that all segments of the volume are online. See "General Disk I/O Errors" on page 438 in Appendix A, "Troubleshooting."

Wild cards not allowed.

Source SETPASS

Explanation Wildcard characters (* and ?) are not allowed in passwords.

Action Retype your password.

Wrong sequence number in FAT block during redirection of bad block.

Source INSTALL

Explanation An internal system error has occurred. The installation process has terminated prematurely, and INSTALL will be unloaded.

Action Try again. If the problem persists, contact your Novell Authorized Reseller.

XMS Error during Free High Memory Area

Source: Shell

Explanation: The extended memory (HMA) used by the resident shell could not be released. The XMS driver must be in an unpredictable state; therefore, the shell cannot be unloaded.

Action: Check the state of the XMS driver. (See the vendor's documentation.) Make sure the copy of the shell being used to unload the shell is identical to the one used to load the shell.

XMS Shell Error: A20 Error Occurred.

Source: Extended memory shell

Explanation: The XMS driver could not enable or disable the A20 line in the workstation's CPU. The shell could not determine whether the problem is an XMS driver problem or a problem with the CPU.

Action: Check the XMS driver to ensure that it is working properly. Check with the vendor of the workstation to ensure that the XMS driver you are using is compatible with the workstation. Check the workstation's extended memory for problems.

XMS Shell Error: Function Not Implemented.

Source: Extended memory shell

Explanation: The extended memory shell uses the XMS driver to enable and disable the A20 line in the CPU. These functions have not been implemented in the installed XMS driver. (The functions are Local Enable A20 or Local Disable A20.)

Action: Either install an XMS driver with the functions specified above, or do not use the extended memory shell.

XMS Shell Error: VDISK Detected.

Source — Extended memory shell

Explanation — The XMS driver detected a virtual disk driver (VDISK.SYS) in use; the XMS driver is not compatible with the VDISK.SYS driver. The VDISK.SYS currently distributed by IBM is not compatible with Microsoft's HIMEM.SYS (XMS v2.0 driver).

Action — Use a VDISK.SYS driver and an XMS v2.0 driver that are compatible.

Y

You are attached to the server *<servername>* but not logged in.

Source NPRINT

Explanation You are attached to the server you are trying to print from, but you have not established an account by declaring a username.

Action Log out of the specified server, then use either LOGIN or ATTACH to access a user account on the server.

You are being logged out of all servers.

Source Shell

Explanation Before the resident shell can be unloaded, it must log you out of all servers.

Action None. This message is for information only.

You are not an authorized user of the print queue *<queuename>*.

Source NPRINT, CAPTURE

Explanation You are not an authorized print queue user in the specified queue.

Action Have the network supervisor use PCONSOLE to make you a print queue user.

You are not attached to any server matching the pattern *<pattern>*.

Source USERLIST

Explanation You specified either a file server that does not exist or a file server that your workstation is not attached to.

Action Use ATTACH to attach to the file server. Then try again.

You are not attached to server *<servername>*

Source FLAGDIR, SYSTIME, USERLIST, VOLINFO, WHOAMI

Explanation You specified either a file server that does not exist or a file server that your workstation is not attached to.

Action Use ATTACH to attach to the file server. Then try again.

You are not attached to specified server.

Source CHKDIR

Explanation You specified either a file server that does not exist or a file server that your workstation is not attached to.

Action Use ATTACH to attach to the file server. Then try again.

You are not attached to the source server *<servername>*.

Source NPRINT

Explanation You specified either a file server that does not exist or a file server that your workstation is not attached to.

Action Use ATTACH to attach to the file server. Then try again.

You are not connected to any file server.

Source LOGOUT

Explanation This message may appear if you are not logged in to any file servers and you execute the LOGOUT command from a local disk drive.

Action None. This message is for information only.

You are not connected to any file servers. The shell will try to connect to a file server whenever the current default drive is changed to an invalid drive.

Source Shell

Explanation The shell has lost its connection with the network; the default drive is a network drive. This error is probably caused by one of the following:

- A cable has been disconnected.

- The connection to all file servers on the internetwork, including your default server, has been lost.

Action — Check the cables. Change the default drive to a local drive. Then try changing to a drive that could be a network drive (usually drive F: or above). The shell will try to attach the workstation to the first available file server. If the shell fails, this message will appear again. See the "Troubleshooting Guide" in *System Administration*.

You are not connected to file server *<servername>*.

Source — SETPASS

Explanation — You tried to execute a command on a file server (other than your default file server), but you are not attached to that file server.

Action — You do not need to *log in* to the other file server; you only need to *attach* to the file server.

If you *log in* to another file server, the connection to your current default file server (and any connections you may have to other file servers) will be lost. If you *attach* to an additional file server, you will retain all your current connections, and you will be able to execute commands successfully on that file server.

You are not logged in to file server *<servername>*.

Source — SETPASS

Explanation — You tried to execute a command on a file server (other than your default file server), but you are not attached to that file server.

Action — You do not need to *log in* to the other file server; you only need to *attach* to the file server.

If you *log in* to another file server, the connection to your current default file server (and any connections you may have to other file servers) will be lost. If you *attach* to an additional file server, you will retain all your current connections, and you will be able to execute commands successfully on that file server.

You are not logged in to the server *<servername>*.

Source NPRINT

Explanation You tried to execute a command on a file server (other than your default file server), but you are not attached to that file server.

Action You do not need to *log in* to the other file server; you only need to *attach* to the file server.

If you *log in* to another file server, the connection to your current default file server (and any connections you may have to other file servers) will be lost. If you *attach* to an additional file server, you will retain all your current connections, and you will be able to execute commands successfully on that file server.

You can not copy files to themselves.

Source NCOPY

Explanation You tried to copy a file to itself.

Action Change the destination file.

You can not copy multiple files to a single file.

Source NCOPY

Explanation You specified source files with a wildcard (* or ?). You also specified a destination file, but you did not use a wildcard with your destination filename.

Action If you use a wildcard with your source filename, you do not need to specify a destination filename unless you do one of the following:

- Specify different names for the destination files.
- Copy the destination files to the same directory that the source files reside in.

If you use a wildcard in your source file and you specify a destination filename, you must use a corresponding wildcard to specify your destination file.

You do not have access rights to queue *<queuename>*.

Source CAPTURE

Explanation You are not an authorized user for the specified print queue.

Action Have the network supervisor use PCONSOLE to make you a print queue user.

You do not have an account balance. This server charges for file services.

Source ATTACH, LOGIN, MAP

Explanation Your account balance is zero. You cannot use this file server until your account has a higher balance.

Action See your network supervisor.

You do not have rights to copy from the specified directory.

Source NCOPY

Explanation You tried to copy files from a directory in which you do not have sufficient rights. You must have at least Read and File Scan rights in a directory to copy files from that directory.

Action Have the network supervisor or a user with Access Control rights in the directory assign you the appropriate rights.

You do not have rights to copy to the specified directory.

Source NCOPY

Explanation You tried to copy files to a directory in which you do not have sufficient rights. You must have the Create right in a directory to copy files to that directory.

Action Have the network supervisor or a user with Access Control rights in the directory assign you the appropriate rights.

You do not have rights to see the trustee list for this directory.

Source TLIST

Explanation You must have the Access Control right to view the trustees in a particular directory.

Action Ask the network supervisor to grant you the Access Control right to the directory.

You do not have the Search right on client service.

Source TSA

Explanation The TSA could not scan the client file system because of a rights violation.

Action Try one or more of the following:

- Change to another server or volume where you have the Search right.
- Log in as another user that does have Search rights.
- Grant the user appropriate access rights.

You don't have the right to use the print queue.

Source NPRINT, CAPTURE

Explanation You are not an authorized print queue user in the specified queue.

Action Have the network supervisor use PCONSOLE to make you a print queue user.

You exceeded your outstanding NCP directory search limit.

Source OS

Explanation You cannot search directories beyond a certain depth.

Action No action is necessary. Increase the search limit if this error appears often.

You have exceeded your credit limit for this server.

Source ATTACH, LOGIN, MAP

Explanation Your account balance is below zero. You cannot use this account until your account balance is above zero.

Action See your network supervisor.

You have inserted the wrong media cartridge into the storage device. Remove the media cartridge and insert the correct media cartridge.

Source SBACKUP

Explanation The requested media does not match the media in the device.

Action Place correct media in the device, and try again.

You have no rights to alter trustee assignments for the specified directory.

Source REVOKE

Explanation You tried to revoke a trustee of a directory, but you do not have Access Control rights in that directory.

Action If you need to revoke a trustee from a directory, ask your network supervisor to either give you Access Control rights or revoke the trustee for you.

You have no rights to grant trustee assignments for that directory.

Source GRANT

Explanation You tried to assign a user as a trustee of a directory, but you do not have Access Control or Supervisory rights in that directory.

Action If you need to assign a trustee to a directory in which you have no Access Control or Supervisory rights, you will need to ask your network supervisor or a user who has Access Control or Supervisory rights to assign the trustee.

You have no rights to print files from this directory.

Source NPRINT

Explanation You tried to print files from a directory in which you do not have sufficient rights. You must have at least Read and File Scan rights in a directory to print files from that directory.

Action Have the network supervisor or a user with Access Control rights in the directory assign you the appropriate rights. (The network supervisor can also change the directory's rights mask.)

You have no rights to remove trustees.

Source REMOVE

Explanation You tried to remove a trustee of a directory, but you do not have Access Control rights in that directory.

Action If you need to remove a trustee from a directory, ask your network supervisor to either give you Access Control rights or remove the trustee.

You have reached the limit for file server connections. Unable to attach to file server *<servername>*.

Source PSERVER (.EXE, .NLM, or .VAP)

Explanation PSERVER can attach to eight file servers. You cannot attach to more than the specified limit.

Action None. This message is for information only.

You have reached the maximum number of server attachments.

Source ATTACH, LOGIN, MAP

Explanation You are already attached to the maximum number of file servers. A workstation can be attached to no more than eight file servers at any one time.

Action If you need to log in to another file server, log out of a file server to which you are currently attached.

You must be a user on printer server *<print server>* to issue this command.

Source PSC

Explanation To view the status of the printers, you must be defined as a user of *<print server>* and attached to the file server that authorizes you to be a print server user.

Action Have the network supervisor or your Workgroup Manager define you as a user of the print server. If you are a user of the print server, make sure you are attached to the file server that authorizes you to be a print server user.

You must be an operator on print server *<print server>* to issue this command.

Source PSC

Explanation To issue any command other than "Status," you must be a print server operator and attached to the file server that authorizes you to be a print server operator.

Action Have a print server operator issue the command. If you are a print server operator, make sure you are attached to the file server that authorizes you to be a print server operator.

You must have Supervisor Rights to grant Supervisor privilege.

Source GRANT

Explanation You do not have the Supervisory right; therefore, you cannot grant the Supervisory right to anyone else.

Action None. This message is for information only.

You must specify the form number.

Source PSC

Explanation You used the MOUNT option, but you did not specify the form number.

Action Specify a form number with the MOUNT option.

You must specify the print server name.

Source PSC

Explanation You did not specify a print server with PSC.

Action Specify the print server with PSC, or set a default print server with the SET PSC command.

You only have rights to see trustee assignments that relate to you.

Source TLIST

Explanation You must have Access Control rights to view the trustees in a particular directory.

Action Ask the network supervisor to grant you Access Control rights to the directory.

Your password was not changed.

Source SETPASS

Explanation The file server returned a condition that the utility has not accounted for. Your password could not be changed.

Action Make sure the file server is still running; then try again.

Your station is not attached to server "*<servername>*".

Source FLAGDIR, NCOPY, REMOVE, REVOKE, SEND, TLIST

Explanation You specified a file server name with the command, but you are not attached to that file server.

Action Use the ATTACH command to attach to the file server; then try again.

Your station is not attached to specified server.

Source GRANT

Explanation You specified a file server name with the command, but you are not attached to that file server.

Action Use the ATTACH command to attach to the file server; then try again.

Your station is unapproved to be attached to server *<servername>* using the specified user account.

Source CAPTURE, NPRINT

Explanation You tried to access an account on the file server *<servername>* from an unauthorized workstation. A network supervisor can restrict an account on a file server to one or more workstations from which users can access the account.

Action Use only authorized workstations to access this account.

chapter **2** *Server Abend Messages*

Overview of Server Abend Messages

The NetWare v3.1*x* operating system is very resilient, but errors can and will arise. Serious problems are usually accompanied by abend (abnormal end) messages.

Abend messages are usually caused by consistency check errors, but they also can be caused by insufficient memory, DMA (Direct Memory Access) conflicts, or hardware and software interrupts.

A list of the abend messages that can occur in NetWare v3.1*x* begins on page 328.

Consistency Check Errors

Consistency check errors are internal tests placed in the NetWare operating system by Novell software engineers. The primary function of consistency checks is to ensure the stability and integrity of internal operating system data. Numerous consistency checks are interlaced throughout NetWare to validate critical disk, memory, and communications processes.

Consistency check errors might be caused by a corrupted operating system file, by corrupted or outdated drivers and NetWare Loadable Modules (NLMs), or by hardware failure. These errors can also be associated with defective memory chips, static discharges, faulty power supplies, or power surges or spikes.

What to Do When You Get an Abend

If an abend occurs, try one or more of the following:

- Reboot the file server.
- Check the memory using MONITOR, and add more if needed.
- Check the system board, memory chips, power supplies, and power conditioning equipment. Replace any faulty hardware.
- Make sure that you have the latest drivers and NLMs. Update everything that is not current.
- If new hardware has been recently installed in the file server, remove the hardware. If the error does not reoccur, run diagnostics on the removed hardware. Check for conflicts (interrupts, memory addresses, I/O ports, DMA) between the hardware in the computer and the new hardware.
- If your hardware is good, unload individual NLMs, reboot, and repeat the procedures that created the original abend. You may be able to isolate an NLM that is causing the problem.
- Reinstall the operating system, drivers, or NLMs from the master diskettes. If you get a serialization error, reinstall SERVER.EXE from the master diskettes. Make sure that the copy of NetWare you are using is a correct, legal (nonpirated) original.

If none of these remedies resolves the problem, record all the hardware installed on the file server and all actions you have taken to correct the problem. Then contact your Novell Authorized Reseller for technical support.

Preparing a Core Dump

Upon contacting your reseller, you may be asked for a "core dump" to be analyzed in Novell's diagnostic laboratory. A core dump is a "snapshot" of your server's RAM at the time it abended. Often, though not always, Novell's technicians can diagnose your problem by analyzing the core dump. In essence, they can duplicate your server on an identical machine in Novell's diagnostic laboratory.

If you are asked to prepare a core dump, be sure you have sufficient diskettes on hand to copy all of your machine's RAM. For example, to copy 12 MB of RAM, you would need nine 3.5-inch high-density (1.44MB) diskettes.

Also, if you can re-create the problem and describe exactly what steps led up to the abend, please record this information and send it in along with your diskettes.

If Novell's staff is able to correct the problem, and if the problem has been caused by a software bug, they can debug the program and send you a patch for the problem.

List of Abends in NetWare v3.12 Operating System

The following abends can occur in NetWare v3.12. Most represent internal consistency check errors; refer to the troubleshooting procedures described earlier.

<Process> **Process did not relinquish control frequently. ActivateIOScreenRequest called with a screen that is not mine.**

Explanation See "Overview of Server Abend Messages" on page 325.

ActivateIOScreenRequest called with a screen that was already active.

Explanation See "Overview of Server Abend Messages" on page 325.

ActivateIOScreenRequest called with invalid screen ID.

Explanation See "Overview of Server Abend Messages" on page 325.

ActivatePopUpScreen called with a screen which is not a pop up screen.

Explanation See "Overview of Server Abend Messages" on page 325.

ActivatePopUpScreenRequest called with a screen which is not a pop up screen.

Explanation See "Overview of Server Abend Messages" on page 325.

ActivatePopUpScreen called with invalid screen ID.

Explanation See "Overview of Server Abend Messages" on page 325.

ActivatePopUpScreenRequest called with invalid screen ID.

Explanation See "Overview of Server Abend Messages" on page 325.

ActivatePopUpScreenRequest found count non-zero but screen not active.

Explanation See "Overview of Server Abend Messages" on page 325.

ActivatePopUpScreen found count non-zero but screen not active.

Explanation See "Overview of Server Abend Messages" on page 325.

ActivateScreen called with a pop up screen.

Explanation See "Overview of Server Abend Messages" on page 325.

ActivateScreen called with a screen that has already been closed.

Explanation See "Overview of Server Abend Messages" on page 325.

ActivateScreen called with invalid screen ID.

Explanation See "Overview of Server Abend Messages" on page 325.

ActivateScreenEvent called with flag indicating FSEngine was not holding hardware.

Explanation See "Overview of Server Abend Messages" on page 325.

ActivateScreenEvent called with invalid screen ID.

Explanation See "Overview of Server Abend Messages" on page 325.

AddFile called with directory entry with invalid first disk block.

Explanation See "Overview of Server Abend Messages" on page 325.

AddNameSpace found invalid name list.

Explanation See "Overview of Server Abend Messages" on page 325.

AddSubdirectory was called with a directory entry not in memory.

Explanation See "Overview of Server Abend Messages" on page 325.

AddToDeletedBlockList found an invalid DeletedBlockList.

Explanation See "Overview of Server Abend Messages" on page 325.

AddToHash was called with a directory entry not in memory.

Explanation See "Overview of Server Abend Messages" on page 325.

AddToHashUnlockAndMarkDirectory called with a directory that was already unlocked.

Explanation See "Overview of Server Abend Messages" on page 325.

Alloc Block Header does not contain proper structure tag.

Explanation See "Overview of Server Abend Messages" on page 325.

Alloc called with invalid resource tag.

Explanation See "Overview of Server Abend Messages" on page 325.

Alloc Cleanup Procedure called with invalid resource tag.

Explanation See "Overview of Server Abend Messages" on page 325.

Alloc Node Header does not contain proper structure tag.

Explanation See "Overview of Server Abend Messages" on page 325.

Alloc Short Term Memory allocator is out of memory.

Explanation See "Overview of Server Abend Messages" on page 325.

Alloc Short Term Memory allocator requests exceeded the configuration limit.

Explanation See "Overview of Server Abend Messages" on page 325.

AllocateBlock found an invalid cache buffer.

Explanation See "Overview of Server Abend Messages" on page 325.

AllocateDiskBlock allocated a block that was not really available.

Explanation See "Overview of Server Abend Messages" on page 325.

AllocateDiskBlock called and freed a file with blocks already returned.

Explanation See "Overview of Server Abend Messages" on page 325.

AllocateDiskBlock given a FAT chain that started with zero.

Explanation   See "Overview of Server Abend Messages" on page 325.

AllocateDiskBlock was given an invalid FAT chain.

Explanation   See "Overview of Server Abend Messages" on page 325.

AllocateNonMovableReturnableMemory discovered invalid memory block segment.

Explanation   See "Overview of Server Abend Messages" on page 325.

AllocatePermanentMemory called at interrupt time.

Explanation   See "Overview of Server Abend Messages" on page 325.

AllocatePermanentMemory discovered invalid memory block segment.

Explanation   See "Overview of Server Abend Messages" on page 325.

AllocatePhysicalPages invalid cache segment/cache block list.

Explanation   See "Overview of Server Abend Messages" on page 325.

AllocateReturnableMemory called with invalid resource tag.

Explanation   See "Overview of Server Abend Messages" on page 325.

AllocateWaitNode found an invalid wait node on the avail list.

Explanation   See "Overview of Server Abend Messages" on page 325.

AllocBufferBelow16Meg was given an invalid resource tag.

Explanation   See "Overview of Server Abend Messages" on page 325.

AllocMovableCacheMemory could not allocate a page when it should be available.

Explanation   See "Overview of Server Abend Messages" on page 325.

AllocMovableCacheMemory found invalid cache segment/cache block list.

Explanation See "Overview of Server Abend Messages" on page 325.

AllocNonMovable couldnt get a page when one should have been available.

Explanation See "Overview of Server Abend Messages" on page 325.

AllocNonMovableCacheMemory called with invalid resource tag.

Explanation See "Overview of Server Abend Messages" on page 325.

AllocNonMovableCacheMemory did a bad calculation.

Explanation See "Overview of Server Abend Messages" on page 325.

AllocNonMovableMemory found invalid cache segment/cache block list.

Explanation See "Overview of Server Abend Messages" on page 325.

AllocPermMemory got an invalid resource tag.

Explanation See "Overview of Server Abend Messages" on page 325.

AllocRealModeSemiPermMemory got an invalid resource tag.

Explanation See "Overview of Server Abend Messages" on page 325.

AllocSemiPermMemory got an invalid resource tag.

Explanation See "Overview of Server Abend Messages" on page 325.

Already being used on SetBeingUsed in disk cache.

Explanation See "Overview of Server Abend Messages" on page 325.

AskForIOScreenStateRequest called with invalid screen ID.

Explanation See "Overview of Server Abend Messages" on page 325.

Attempt to mount SYS volume while volume 0 is already used.

Explanation See "Overview of Server Abend Messages" on page 325.

Attempt to use Free with an invalid pointer.

Explanation See "Overview of Server Abend Messages" on page 325.

Bad drive given to the disk procedures.

Explanation See "Overview of Server Abend Messages" on page 325.

Bad page directory address passed to SetNewCR3.

Explanation See "Overview of Server Abend Messages" on page 325.

Bad protocol control handler called.

Explanation See "Overview of Server Abend Messages" on page 325.

Bad Resource Tag Address detected in LSL AES Routines.

Explanation See "Overview of Server Abend Messages" on page 325.

Bad Resource Tag Address detected in AES Process Routines.

Explanation See "Overview of Server Abend Messages" on page 325.

Bad Resource Tag passed to LSLFastRcvECB.

Explanation See "Overview of Server Abend Messages" on page 325.

Bad Resource Tag passed to LSLGetECB.

Explanation See "Overview of Server Abend Messages" on page 325.

Bad Resource Tag passed to LSLHoldPacket.

Explanation See "Overview of Server Abend Messages" on page 325.

Bad Resource Tag passed to LSLHoldRcvECB.

Explanation See "Overview of Server Abend Messages" on page 325.

Bad Resource Tag passed to LSLReturnRcvECB.

Explanation See "Overview of Server Abend Messages" on page 325.

Bad Resource Tag Pointer detected in call to IPXOpenSocket.

Explanation See "Overview of Server Abend Messages" on page 325.

Bad structure link detected. Pointer in eax.

Explanation See "Overview of Server Abend Messages" on page 325.

BadGetExtendedInfo bad name space.

Explanation See "Overview of Server Abend Messages" on page 325.

Cache buffer being removed from drive index not found in disk cache.

Explanation See "Overview of Server Abend Messages" on page 325.

Cache buffer not found in drive table or avail list by AllocateReturnableMemory.

Explanation See "Overview of Server Abend Messages" on page 325.

Cache buffer not found in drive table or avail list by AllocateNonMovableReturnableMemory.

Explanation See "Overview of Server Abend Messages" on page 325.

Cache Buffer was lost.

Explanation See "Overview of Server Abend Messages" on page 325.

Cache Memory Manager found invalid cache segment.

Explanation See "Overview of Server Abend Messages" on page 325.

Cache Memory Manager found invalid cache block on collapse.

Explanation See "Overview of Server Abend Messages" on page 325.

Cache Memory Manager found invalid memory node.

Explanation See "Overview of Server Abend Messages" on page 325.

Cache Memory Manager had an invalid cache control avail list.

Explanation See "Overview of Server Abend Messages" on page 325.

Cache Memory Manager had error collapsing memory nodes.

Explanation See "Overview of Server Abend Messages" on page 325.

Cache Memory Manager had error collapsing cache control nodes.

Explanation See "Overview of Server Abend Messages" on page 325.

CacheNonMovableMemoryCleanUp detected lost memory segment.

Explanation See "Overview of Server Abend Messages" on page 325.

Call to CreateProcess failed.

Explanation See "Overview of Server Abend Messages" on page 325.

Call to MakeProcess failed.

Explanation See "Overview of Server Abend Messages" on page 325.

Call to MakeProcess to create the Poll Process failed.

Explanation See "Overview of Server Abend Messages" on page 325.

CFindLoadModuleHandle could not find loaded NLM in address range.

Explanation See "Overview of Server Abend Messages" on page 325.

ChangeActiveScreen found a screen with an invalid active count.

Explanation See "Overview of Server Abend Messages" on page 325.

ChangeActiveScreen found the cursor bit not set on the new screen.

Explanation See "Overview of Server Abend Messages" on page 325.

ChangeActiveScreen found the cursor or title bar bit still set on the old screen.

Explanation See "Overview of Server Abend Messages" on page 325.

ChangeDataStream bad stream number.

Explanation See "Overview of Server Abend Messages" on page 325.

ChangeDirectory called with the root.

Explanation See "Overview of Server Abend Messages" on page 325.

ChangeDirectory found an invalid directory entry.

Explanation See "Overview of Server Abend Messages" on page 325.

ChangeDirNumber called with new directory number with indirected bit already set.

Explanation See "Overview of Server Abend Messages" on page 325.

ChangeDirNumber called with old directory number not on the hash.

Explanation See "Overview of Server Abend Messages" on page 325.

ChangeFATChainToLimbo called with invalid OwnerID.

Explanation See "Overview of Server Abend Messages" on page 325.

ChangeHandleTNode was given an invalid handle.

Explanation See "Overview of Server Abend Messages" on page 325.

ChangeLockDir called with existing destination.

Explanation See "Overview of Server Abend Messages" on page 325.

ChangeOpenFileTrustee called with non-defined trustee.

Explanation See "Overview of Server Abend Messages" on page 325..

ChangeStreamsToLimbo bad name space.

Explanation See "Overview of Server Abend Messages" on page 325.

ChangeTitleBarEvent called with invalid screen ID.

Explanation See "Overview of Server Abend Messages" on page 325.

ChangeToPhantom bad name space.

Explanation See "Overview of Server Abend Messages" on page 325.

CheckAndAddHardware could not allocate a resource tag.

Explanation See "Overview of Server Abend Messages" on page 325.

CheckAndAddMemory detected an inconsistency between cache memory and the memory lists.

Explanation See "Overview of Server Abend Messages" on page 325.

CheckAndConvertName bad name space.

Explanation See "Overview of Server Abend Messages" on page 325.

CheckCache cache buffer counters inconsistent.

Explanation See "Overview of Server Abend Messages" on page 325.

CheckCache cache buffer counts inconsistent.

Explanation See "Overview of Server Abend Messages" on page 325.

CheckCache cache control with invalid cache buffer address.

Explanation See "Overview of Server Abend Messages" on page 325.

CheckCache cache control with invalid signature.

Explanation See "Overview of Server Abend Messages" on page 325.

CheckCache cache segment invalid cache block list.

Explanation See "Overview of Server Abend Messages" on page 325.

CheckCache cache segment links inconsistent.

Explanation See "Overview of Server Abend Messages" on page 325.

CheckCache check segment invalid cache control list tail.

Explanation See "Overview of Server Abend Messages" on page 325.

CheckCache check segment invalid cache control list head.

Explanation See "Overview of Server Abend Messages" on page 325.

CheckCache found inconsistant movable memory list.

Explanation See "Overview of Server Abend Messages" on page 325.

CheckCache found inconsistant non-movable memory list.

Explanation See "Overview of Server Abend Messages" on page 325.

CheckCache found invalid cache control avail node.

Explanation See "Overview of Server Abend Messages" on page 325.

CheckCache found invalid cache control node.

Explanation See "Overview of Server Abend Messages" on page 325.

CheckCache found invalid cache segment.

Explanation See "Overview of Server Abend Messages" on page 325.

CheckCache found invalid memory node avail node.

Explanation See "Overview of Server Abend Messages" on page 325.

CheckCache found invalid memory node.

Explanation See "Overview of Server Abend Messages" on page 325.

CheckCache found movable memory already claimed.

Explanation See "Overview of Server Abend Messages" on page 325.

CheckCache found non-movable memory already claimed.

Explanation See "Overview of Server Abend Messages" on page 325.

CheckCache found not contiguous movable memory.

Explanation See "Overview of Server Abend Messages" on page 325.

CheckCache found two non-contiguous cache buffers.

Explanation See "Overview of Server Abend Messages" on page 325.

CheckCache inconsistant avail count.

Explanation See "Overview of Server Abend Messages" on page 325.

CheckCache inconsistant below 16 meg cache lists.

Explanation See "Overview of Server Abend Messages" on page 325.

CheckCache inconsistant cache segment size.

Explanation See "Overview of Server Abend Messages" on page 325.

CheckCache inconsistant memory node avail count.

Explanation See "Overview of Server Abend Messages" on page 325.

CheckCache inconsistant movable memory counts.

Explanation See "Overview of Server Abend Messages" on page 325.

CheckCache inconsistant node page count.

Explanation See "Overview of Server Abend Messages" on page 325.

CheckCache inconsistant non-movable memory counts.

Explanation See "Overview of Server Abend Messages" on page 325.

CheckCache invalid cache block avail entry.

Explanation See "Overview of Server Abend Messages" on page 325.

CheckCache invalid cache block entry.

Explanation See "Overview of Server Abend Messages" on page 325.

CheckCache invalid cache control list.

Explanation See "Overview of Server Abend Messages" on page 325.

CheckCache invalid cache segment entry.

Explanation See "Overview of Server Abend Messages" on page 325.

CheckCache invalid cache segment flag.

Explanation See "Overview of Server Abend Messages" on page 325.

CheckCache invalid cache segment list head.

Explanation See "Overview of Server Abend Messages" on page 325.

CheckCache invalid list segment list end.

Explanation See "Overview of Server Abend Messages" on page 325.

CheckCache invalid memory node avail entry.

Explanation See "Overview of Server Abend Messages" on page 325.

CheckCache invalid memory node entry.

Explanation See "Overview of Server Abend Messages" on page 325.

CheckCache invalid movable memory list head.

Explanation See "Overview of Server Abend Messages" on page 325.

CheckCache invalid movable memory list tail.

Explanation See "Overview of Server Abend Messages" on page 325.

CheckCache invalid movable memory node memory address.

Explanation See "Overview of Server Abend Messages" on page 325.

CheckCache invalid movable memory node.

Explanation See "Overview of Server Abend Messages" on page 325.

CheckCache invalid node page list.

Explanation See "Overview of Server Abend Messages" on page 325.

CheckCache invalid non-movable memory list head.

Explanation See "Overview of Server Abend Messages" on page 325.

CheckCache invalid non-movable memory node memory address.

Explanation See "Overview of Server Abend Messages" on page 325.

CheckCache invalid non-movable memory node.

Explanation See "Overview of Server Abend Messages" on page 325.

CheckCache page node already used.

Explanation See "Overview of Server Abend Messages" on page 325.

CheckCache too long movable memory segment.

Explanation See "Overview of Server Abend Messages" on page 325.

CheckCache too long non-movable memory segment.

Explanation See "Overview of Server Abend Messages" on page 325.

CheckCache two cache buffers claim the same memory.

Explanation See "Overview of Server Abend Messages" on page 325.

CheckCacheBlockControl could not locate the cache node.

Explanation See "Overview of Server Abend Messages" on page 325.

CheckIfCountedAsFreeableLimbo received a directory not in a deleted block.

Explanation See "Overview of Server Abend Messages" on page 325.

CheckIfScreenActive called with invalid screen ID.

Explanation See "Overview of Server Abend Messages" on page 325.

CheckKeyStatus called with invalid screen ID.

Explanation See "Overview of Server Abend Messages" on page 325.

CheckMemory first block fragment not pointing to the Header.

Explanation See "Overview of Server Abend Messages" on page 325.

CheckMemory found a available fragment not on the avail list.

Explanation See "Overview of Server Abend Messages" on page 325.

CheckMemory found a block that ended with an available last fragment.

Explanation See "Overview of Server Abend Messages" on page 325.

CheckMemory found a block that ended incorrectly.

Explanation See "Overview of Server Abend Messages" on page 325.

CheckMemory found a fragment with an invalid node length.

Explanation See "Overview of Server Abend Messages" on page 325.

CheckMemory found contiguous fragments not pointing to each other.

Explanation See "Overview of Server Abend Messages" on page 325.

CheckMemory found that LastNodePointer was invalid.

Explanation See "Overview of Server Abend Messages" on page 325.

CheckMemory found that the avail list ends improperly.

Explanation See "Overview of Server Abend Messages" on page 325.

CheckMemory found two nodes on the Avail list that do not point to each other.

Explanation See "Overview of Server Abend Messages" on page 325.

CheckNameIgnoreLocks bad name space.

Explanation See "Overview of Server Abend Messages" on page 325.

CheckOff found it on the LR list.

Explanation See "Overview of Server Abend Messages" on page 325.

CheckOn didnt find it on the LR list.

Explanation See "Overview of Server Abend Messages" on page 325.

CleanUpScreensRequest called with an invalid resource tag.

Explanation See "Overview of Server Abend Messages" on page 325.

ClearPhantom called with not primary directory number.

Explanation See "Overview of Server Abend Messages" on page 325.

ClearPhantom found invalid name list.

Explanation See "Overview of Server Abend Messages" on page 325.

ClientHandle not Found on Active EA list.

Explanation See "Overview of Server Abend Messages" on page 325.

ClonePoll should never be called.

Explanation See "Overview of Server Abend Messages" on page 325.

CloseScreen called with a screen that is still being used.

Explanation See "Overview of Server Abend Messages" on page 325.

CloseScreen called with invalid screen ID.

Explanation See "Overview of Server Abend Messages" on page 325.

CloseScreen called with system console.

Explanation See "Overview of Server Abend Messages" on page 325.

CloseScreenRequest called with a screen that did not belong to the file server engine.

Explanation See "Overview of Server Abend Messages" on page 325.

CloseScreenRequest called with file server engine not active.

Explanation See "Overview of Server Abend Messages" on page 325.

CloseScreenRequest called with invalid screen ID.

Explanation See "Overview of Server Abend Messages" on page 325.

CompareFileNames bad name space.

Explanation See "Overview of Server Abend Messages" on page 325.

ConnectionTasksCleanupProcedure could not find all the tasks.

Explanation See "Overview of Server Abend Messages" on page 325.

ConnectionTasksCleanupProcedure found an invalid resource count.

Explanation See "Overview of Server Abend Messages" on page 325.

CopyDeviceInfoAck was call with invalid parameter.

Explanation See "Overview of Server Abend Messages" on page 325.

CopyDeviceInfoAckCallBack was called with invalid disk id.

Explanation See "Overview of Server Abend Messages" on page 325.

CopySystemInfoAck was call with invalid parameter.

Explanation See "Overview of Server Abend Messages" on page 325.

CopySystemInfoAckCallBack was called with invalid system id.

Explanation See "Overview of Server Abend Messages" on page 325.

Could not cleanup hooked NCP verbs.

Explanation See "Overview of Server Abend Messages" on page 325.

Could not find block with redirection bit set in UpdateRequest.

Explanation See "Overview of Server Abend Messages" on page 325.

Could not find block with redirection bit set.

Explanation See "Overview of Server Abend Messages" on page 325.

Could not find block with redirection bit set in RedirectThisBlock.

Explanation See "Overview of Server Abend Messages" on page 325.

Could not get Alloc space to register a page for an NLM.

Explanation See "Overview of Server Abend Messages" on page 325.

CreateFile found invalid name space list.

Explanation See "Overview of Server Abend Messages" on page 325.

CreateFile found invalid phantom list.

Explanation See "Overview of Server Abend Messages" on page 325.

CScheduleDelayedWorkToDo was called with work to do already enqueued.

Explanation See "Overview of Server Abend Messages" on page 325.

CScheduleWorkToDo passed invalid resource tag.

Explanation See "Overview of Server Abend Messages" on page 325.

CScheduleWorkToDo was called with work to do already enqueued.

Explanation See "Overview of Server Abend Messages" on page 325.

Dangling TNode found backing up the deleted file list.

Explanation See "Overview of Server Abend Messages" on page 325.

DeactivateIOScreenRequest called with a screen that was not active.

Explanation See "Overview of Server Abend Messages" on page 325.

DeactivateIOScreenRequest called with a screen that is not mine.

Explanation See "Overview of Server Abend Messages" on page 325.

DeactivateIOScreenRequest called with invalid screen ID.

Explanation See "Overview of Server Abend Messages" on page 325.

DeactivatePopUpScreenRequest called with a non-active pop up screen.

Explanation See "Overview of Server Abend Messages" on page 325.

DeactivateScreenEvent called with FSEngine already holding the hardware.

Explanation See "Overview of Server Abend Messages" on page 325.

DeactivateScreenEvent called with invalid screen ID.

Explanation See "Overview of Server Abend Messages" on page 325.

DeAllocate semaphore attempted on active semaphore in kernel.

Explanation See "Overview of Server Abend Messages" on page 325.

Delay Between Watchdog Packets.

Explanation See "Overview of Server Abend Messages" on page 325.

Delay had a problem allocating a resource tag for a NLM.

Explanation See "Overview of Server Abend Messages" on page 325.

DeleteHardLinkedFile has Invalid List or Already Been Deleted.

Explanation See "Overview of Server Abend Messages" on page 325.

Deleted file is a Subdirectory.

Explanation See "Overview of Server Abend Messages" on page 325.

DeleteDirectory found bad name list.

Explanation See "Overview of Server Abend Messages" on page 325.

DeleteDirectory found invalid phantom list.

Explanation See "Overview of Server Abend Messages" on page 325.

DeleteDirectory found invalid UNIX hard link info...bad master link.

Explanation See "Overview of Server Abend Messages" on page 325.

DeleteDirectory found invalid UNIX hard link info.

Explanation See "Overview of Server Abend Messages" on page 325.

DeleteDirNumber called with bad internal number.

Explanation See "Overview of Server Abend Messages" on page 325.

DeleteDirNumber found bad external number.

Explanation See "Overview of Server Abend Messages" on page 325.

DeleteDirNumber found external number without bit vector set.

Explanation See "Overview of Server Abend Messages" on page 325.

DeleteFileCompletely file is already deleted.

Explanation See "Overview of Server Abend Messages" on page 325.

DeleteFileCompletely found an invalid name list.

Explanation See "Overview of Server Abend Messages" on page 325.

DeleteFileCompletely found an invalid TNode.

Explanation See "Overview of Server Abend Messages" on page 325.

DeleteFileToLimbo file is already deleted.

Explanation See "Overview of Server Abend Messages" on page 325.

DeleteFileToLimbo found an invalid name list.

Explanation See "Overview of Server Abend Messages" on page 325.

DeleteFileToLimbo found an invalid TNode.

Explanation See "Overview of Server Abend Messages" on page 325.

DeleteFromHash was called with a directory entry number not on the Hash Search List.

Explanation See "Overview of Server Abend Messages" on page 325.

DeleteFromHash was called with a directory entry not in memory.

Explanation See "Overview of Server Abend Messages" on page 325.

DeleteFromTrusteeList could not find the trustee node.

Explanation See "Overview of Server Abend Messages" on page 325.

DeleteHardLinkedDirectory found a hard linked directory with trustees.

Explanation See "Overview of Server Abend Messages" on page 325.

DeleteHardLinkedDirectory found a hard linked directory with something in it.

Explanation See "Overview of Server Abend Messages" on page 325.

DeleteHardLinkedDirectory found a hard linked directory with extended attributes.

Explanation See "Overview of Server Abend Messages" on page 325.

DeleteHardLinkedDirectory found a hard linked directory with deleted files in it.

Explanation See "Overview of Server Abend Messages" on page 325.

DeleteHardLinkedDirectory found bad name list.

Explanation See "Overview of Server Abend Messages" on page 325.

DeleteHardLinkedFile called with file with extended attributes.

Explanation See "Overview of Server Abend Messages" on page 325.

DeleteHardLinkedFile called with file with trustees.

Explanation See "Overview of Server Abend Messages" on page 325.

DeleteHardLinkedFile found hard link file with disk space.

Explanation See "Overview of Server Abend Messages" on page 325.

DeleteLimboFile bad name space.

Explanation See "Overview of Server Abend Messages" on page 325.

DeleteTrustee to a file with FileHasTrustee bit cleared.

Explanation See "Overview of Server Abend Messages" on page 325.

DelFRoot called with invalid TNode value.

Explanation See "Overview of Server Abend Messages" on page 325.

DeRegisterHardwareOptions passed invalid pointer.

Explanation See "Overview of Server Abend Messages" on page 325.

DeRegisterMLID did not find protocol node on ProtocolList.

Explanation See "Overview of Server Abend Messages" on page 325.

DeRegisterNCPExtension called with invalid Resource Tag Pointer.

Explanation See "Overview of Server Abend Messages" on page 325.

DeRegisterStack did not find the node on the board list.

Explanation See "Overview of Server Abend Messages" on page 325.

DestroyProcess called with invalid process ID in kernel.

Explanation See "Overview of Server Abend Messages" on page 325.

DestroyProcess called with process ID not found on delayed list in kernel.

Explanation See "Overview of Server Abend Messages" on page 325.

DestroyProcess could not find the process on the active list.

Explanation See "Overview of Server Abend Messages" on page 325.

DestroyUserDiskRestriction had a trustee list.

Explanation See "Overview of Server Abend Messages" on page 325.

DetachFile called with invalid file handle.

Explanation See "Overview of Server Abend Messages" on page 325.

DetachStation was called multiple times to clear the same connection number.

Explanation See "Overview of Server Abend Messages" on page 325.

Device handle was not found on resource list.

Explanation See "Overview of Server Abend Messages" on page 325.

Directory buffer with no dirty bits set was encountered on the dirty list.

Explanation See "Overview of Server Abend Messages" on page 325.

Directory entry contains an invalid file name.

Explanation See "Overview of Server Abend Messages" on page 325.

DisableInputCursor called with invalid screen ID.

Explanation See "Overview of Server Abend Messages" on page 325.

DiskRead invalid use count.

Explanation See "Overview of Server Abend Messages" on page 325.

DiskRelease invalid use count.

Explanation See "Overview of Server Abend Messages" on page 325.

DiskWrite invalid use count.

Explanation See "Overview of Server Abend Messages" on page 325.

DOSGenerateUniqueName tried over 100000000 names and couldn't get a unique one.

Explanation See "Overview of Server Abend Messages" on page 325.

DOSGetName called with a non-DOS directory entry.

Explanation See "Overview of Server Abend Messages" on page 325.

EAEndOfTask Handle Table looped back to itself.

Explanation See "Overview of Server Abend Messages" on page 325.

EnableInputCursor called with invalid screen ID.

Explanation See "Overview of Server Abend Messages" on page 325.

End of FAT chain found on zero fill during WriteFile.

Explanation See "Overview of Server Abend Messages" on page 325.

EndPopUpScreen called with a pop up screen that was not properly activated.

Explanation See "Overview of Server Abend Messages" on page 325.

EndPopUpScreen called with a screen which is not a pop up screen.

Explanation See "Overview of Server Abend Messages" on page 325.

EndPopUpScreen called with invalid screen ID.

Explanation See "Overview of Server Abend Messages" on page 325.

EraseFile found a hard linked file being used.

Explanation See "Overview of Server Abend Messages" on page 325.

EraseFile found invalid UNIX hard link info...bad master link.

Explanation See “Overview of Server Abend Messages” on page 325.

EraseFile found invalid UNIX hard link info.

Explanation See “Overview of Server Abend Messages” on page 325.

EraseFile should have changed something.

Explanation See “Overview of Server Abend Messages” on page 325.

Error getting broadcast alloc resource tag.

Explanation See “Overview of Server Abend Messages” on page 325.

Error getting directory handles alloc resource tag.

Explanation See “Overview of Server Abend Messages” on page 325.

Error getting file lock alloc resource tag.

Explanation See “Overview of Server Abend Messages” on page 325.

Error getting memory for disk cacheing.

Explanation See “Overview of Server Abend Messages” on page 325.

Error getting NCP tables alloc resource tag.

Explanation See “Overview of Server Abend Messages” on page 325.

Error getting queue system alloc resource tag.

Explanation See “Overview of Server Abend Messages” on page 325.

Error getting record lock alloc resource tag.

Explanation See “Overview of Server Abend Messages” on page 325.

Error getting router tables alloc signature tag.

Explanation See “Overview of Server Abend Messages” on page 325.

Error getting server tables alloc resource tag.

Explanation See "Overview of Server Abend Messages" on page 325.

Error getting user tracking alloc resource tag.

Explanation See "Overview of Server Abend Messages" on page 325.

Error registering file server network number.

Explanation See "Overview of Server Abend Messages" on page 325.

ErrorLog invalid use count.

Explanation See "Overview of Server Abend Messages" on page 325.

ErrorLog invalid write error count.

Explanation See "Overview of Server Abend Messages" on page 325.

ExhumeLimboFile bad name space.

Explanation See "Overview of Server Abend Messages" on page 325.

ExpandMemory discovered an invalid memory block segment.

Explanation See "Overview of Server Abend Messages" on page 325.

ExpandMemory was given an invalid memory block.

Explanation See "Overview of Server Abend Messages" on page 325.

ExpandMovableCacheMemory passed invalid memory address.

Explanation See "Overview of Server Abend Messages" on page 325.

FAT Control request not found on FATBeingUpdatedVector after FAT write.

Explanation See "Overview of Server Abend Messages" on page 325.

FAT sector to be written had its bit not set.

Explanation See "Overview of Server Abend Messages" on page 325.

FAT Update Process could not find the dirty bit.

Explanation See "Overview of Server Abend Messages" on page 325.

FATToUpdateCount is larger than the DirtyFATWaitingCount.

Explanation See "Overview of Server Abend Messages" on page 325.

FATToUpdateCount was just set larger than DirtyFATWaitingCount.

Explanation See "Overview of Server Abend Messages" on page 325.

FATUpdateProcess writing beyond end FAT chain.

Explanation See "Overview of Server Abend Messages" on page 325.

FindDirectoryEntry bad name space.

Explanation See "Overview of Server Abend Messages" on page 325.

FindDirectoryEntryOrPhantom bad name space.

Explanation See "Overview of Server Abend Messages" on page 325.

FinishRemoveScreenRequest called with removeOtherEngineScreenID set to 0.

Explanation See "Overview of Server Abend Messages" on page 325.

FinishRemoveScreenRequest could not find the indicated screen.

Explanation See "Overview of Server Abend Messages" on page 325.

Free called with a memory block that has an invalid resource tag.

Explanation See "Overview of Server Abend Messages" on page 325.

Free detected modified memory beyond the end of the cell being returned.

Explanation See "Overview of Server Abend Messages" on page 325.

FreeableProcedure found an invalid deleted file block.

Explanation See "Overview of Server Abend Messages" on page 325.

FreeableProcedure found an invalid deleted file.

Explanation See "Overview of Server Abend Messages" on page 325.

FreeableProcedure found invalid name space list.

Explanation See "Overview of Server Abend Messages" on page 325.

FreeALimboFile detected a problem with the deleted file block list.

Explanation See "Overview of Server Abend Messages" on page 325.

FreeALimboFile found an invalid block on the deleted file list.

Explanation See "Overview of Server Abend Messages" on page 325.

FreeALimboFile found an invalid deleted block on the delete list.

Explanation See "Overview of Server Abend Messages" on page 325.

FreeALimboFile found an invalid name list.

Explanation See "Overview of Server Abend Messages" on page 325.

FreeALimboFile found an invalid name list.

Explanation See "Overview of Server Abend Messages" on page 325.

FreeALimboFile had a error synchonrizing on deleted file list.

Explanation See "Overview of Server Abend Messages" on page 325.

FreeDirectoryEntry was called with a directory block not on the block list.

Explanation See "Overview of Server Abend Messages" on page 325.

FreeDirectoryEntry was called with a directory entry not in memory.

Explanation See "Overview of Server Abend Messages" on page 325.

FreeMovableCacheMemory found an invalid memory list.

Explanation See "Overview of Server Abend Messages" on page 325.

FreeMovableCacheMemory given invalid memory.

Explanation See "Overview of Server Abend Messages" on page 325.

FreeNonMovableMemory found an invalid memory list.

Explanation See "Overview of Server Abend Messages" on page 325.

FreeUpProcessFromSemaphore called with invalid process ID.

Explanation See "Overview of Server Abend Messages" on page 325.

FreeUpProcessFromSemaphore could not find the semaphore.

Explanation See "Overview of Server Abend Messages" on page 325.

FreeUpProcessFromSpecificSemaphore the process was not waiting on the specific semaphore.

Explanation See "Overview of Server Abend Messages" on page 325.

GenerateDirectoryHandled called with directory entry that was unlocked.

Explanation See "Overview of Server Abend Messages" on page 325.

GenerateTurboFAT found a bad turbo FAT search list.

Explanation See "Overview of Server Abend Messages" on page 325.

GenerateUniqueName bad name space.

Explanation See "Overview of Server Abend Messages" on page 325.

GetAccessRightsFromID given an invalid tree.

Explanation See "Overview of Server Abend Messages" on page 325.

GetActualFileLength found invalid name space list.

Explanation See "Overview of Server Abend Messages" on page 325.

GetDataStream bad stream number.

Explanation See "Overview of Server Abend Messages" on page 325.

GetDataStreamLengthsFromPathStringBase found invalid name space list.

Explanation See "Overview of Server Abend Messages" on page 325.

GetDirectoryEntry called with invalid directory entry number.

Explanation See "Overview of Server Abend Messages" on page 325.

GetDirectoryHandle bad name space.

Explanation See "Overview of Server Abend Messages" on page 325.

GetEntryFromPathStringBase found invalid name space list.

Explanation See "Overview of Server Abend Messages" on page 325.

GetFATEntry called with an invalid parameter.

Explanation See "Overview of Server Abend Messages" on page 325.

GetFileAccessRights cannot find directory buffer.

Explanation See "Overview of Server Abend Messages" on page 325.

GetKey called when another process is already using the keyboard.

Explanation See "Overview of Server Abend Messages" on page 325.

GetKey called with invalid screen ID.

Explanation See "Overview of Server Abend Messages" on page 325.

GetKey called with too large a value in lines to protect.

Explanation See "Overview of Server Abend Messages" on page 325.

GetName bad name space.

Explanation See "Overview of Server Abend Messages" on page 325.

GetNodePage found invalid last cache segment.

Explanation See “Overview of Server Abend Messages” on page 325.

GetNodePage invalid cache segment/cache block list.

Explanation See “Overview of Server Abend Messages” on page 325.

GetOpenCount called with invalid file handle.

Explanation See “Overview of Server Abend Messages” on page 325.

GetOtherNameSpaceEntry found invalid name space list.

Explanation See “Overview of Server Abend Messages” on page 325.

GetPath bad name space.

Explanation See “Overview of Server Abend Messages” on page 325.

GetRequest was called with invalid device handle.

Explanation See “Overview of Server Abend Messages” on page 325.

GetSpaceUtilized bad name space.

Explanation See “Overview of Server Abend Messages” on page 325.

GiveMaximumPacketSize out of sync with other server.

Explanation See “Overview of Server Abend Messages” on page 325.

Hole between file entries found backing up the deleted file list.

Explanation See “Overview of Server Abend Messages” on page 325.

Hole between TNode and file entry found backing up the deleted file list.

Explanation See “Overview of Server Abend Messages” on page 325.

InitializeIPXProtocol had an ERROR.

Explanation See “Overview of Server Abend Messages” on page 325.

InitializeKernel error allocating memory.

Explanation See "Overview of Server Abend Messages" on page 325.

InitializeTTS could not do 100 different renames of a backup file.

Explanation See "Overview of Server Abend Messages" on page 325.

InputFromKeyboard called with default string longer than buffer.

Explanation See "Overview of Server Abend Messages" on page 325.

InputFromKeyboard called with invalid screen ID.

Explanation See "Overview of Server Abend Messages" on page 325.

InputFromKeyboard called with too large a value in lines to protect.

Explanation See "Overview of Server Abend Messages" on page 325.

InputFromKeyboard was called when another process is already using the keyboard.

Explanation See "Overview of Server Abend Messages" on page 325.

Insufficient memory available to allocate enough receive buffers.

Explanation See "Overview of Server Abend Messages" on page 325.

Insufficient memory to allocate initial memory test block.

Explanation See "Overview of Server Abend Messages" on page 325.

Insufficient memory to allocate process stacks.

Explanation See "Overview of Server Abend Messages" on page 325.

Insufficient memory to setup first load search path entry.

Explanation See "Overview of Server Abend Messages" on page 325.

InternalAllocatePhysicalPages found invalid last cache segment.

Explanation See "Overview of Server Abend Messages" on page 325.

InternalDiskGet invalid use count.

Explanation See "Overview of Server Abend Messages" on page 325.

InternalDiskRelease invalid use count.

Explanation See "Overview of Server Abend Messages" on page 325.

InternalDiskUpdate invalid use count.

Explanation See "Overview of Server Abend Messages" on page 325.

InternalSendPacket got a ECB that was already being sent.

Explanation See "Overview of Server Abend Messages" on page 325.

InternalSendPacket got a ECB that was already being sent.

Explanation See "Overview of Server Abend Messages" on page 325.

Invalid cache buffer handle used.

Explanation See "Overview of Server Abend Messages" on page 325.

Invalid Connection Number or Type passed to ReturnAConnectionNumber.

Explanation See "Overview of Server Abend Messages" on page 325.

Invalid deleted file found backing up the deleted file list.

Explanation See "Overview of Server Abend Messages" on page 325.

Invalid DeletedBlockList.

Explanation See "Overview of Server Abend Messages" on page 325.

Invalid device handle in DiskDeviceCleanUpRoutine.

Explanation See "Overview of Server Abend Messages" on page 325.

Invalid device number passed to LogicalParitionRequest.

Explanation See "Overview of Server Abend Messages" on page 325.

Invalid device used by request in PhysicalRequest.

Explanation See "Overview of Server Abend Messages" on page 325.

Invalid directory FAT chain.

Explanation See "Overview of Server Abend Messages" on page 325.

Invalid directory number code.

Explanation See "Overview of Server Abend Messages" on page 325.

Invalid directory space restriction on charge node detected by ReturnDirectorySpaceRestriction.

Explanation See "Overview of Server Abend Messages" on page 325.

Invalid directory space restriction tree detected by ReturnDirectorySpaceRestriction.

Explanation See "Overview of Server Abend Messages" on page 325.

Invalid disk passed to DiskDeleteEvent.

Explanation See "Overview of Server Abend Messages" on page 325.

Invalid disk passed to DiskFailureEvent.

Explanation See "Overview of Server Abend Messages" on page 325.

Invalid disk passed to DiskLostServerEvent.

Explanation See "Overview of Server Abend Messages" on page 325.

Invalid disk passed to DiskMessageEvent.

Explanation See "Overview of Server Abend Messages" on page 325.

Invalid disk passed to DiskUnloadEvent.

Explanation See "Overview of Server Abend Messages" on page 325.

Invalid disk request on DiskRequestAvailList.

Explanation See "Overview of Server Abend Messages" on page 325.

Invalid disk request passed to ReturnDiskRequest.

Explanation See "Overview of Server Abend Messages" on page 325.

Invalid drive passed to DiskIO.

Explanation See "Overview of Server Abend Messages" on page 325.

Invalid entry found on deleted file list during backup.

Explanation See "Overview of Server Abend Messages" on page 325.

Invalid In Use Count for directory cache buffer.

Explanation See "Overview of Server Abend Messages" on page 325.

Invalid initial semaphore value passed to AllocateSemaphore.

Explanation See "Overview of Server Abend Messages" on page 325.

Invalid logical partition handle in DiskLogicalPartitionCleanUpRoutine.

Explanation See "Overview of Server Abend Messages" on page 325.

Invalid memory block given to AllocateAddMemory.

Explanation See "Overview of Server Abend Messages" on page 325.

Invalid module load handle passed to CFindResourceTag.

Explanation See "Overview of Server Abend Messages" on page 325.

Invalid partition handle in DiskPartitionCleanUpRoutine.

Explanation See "Overview of Server Abend Messages" on page 325.

Invalid partition number return at ReturnDeviceNumber.

Explanation See "Overview of Server Abend Messages" on page 325.

Invalid partition number return at ReturnHandleNumber.

Explanation See "Overview of Server Abend Messages" on page 325.

Invalid partition number return at ReturnLogicalPartitionNumber.

Explanation See "Overview of Server Abend Messages" on page 325.

Invalid partition number return at ReturnPartitionNumber.

Explanation See "Overview of Server Abend Messages" on page 325.

Invalid partition number return at ReturnSystemNumber.

Explanation See "Overview of Server Abend Messages" on page 325.

Invalid process id passed by interrupt procedure to kernel.

Explanation See "Overview of Server Abend Messages" on page 325.

Invalid request returned NPutIOCTL.

Explanation See "Overview of Server Abend Messages" on page 325.

Invalid resource tag passed to AddDiskSystem.

Explanation See "Overview of Server Abend Messages" on page 325.

Invalid resource tag passed to AllocateSemaphore.

Explanation See "Overview of Server Abend Messages" on page 325.

Invalid resource tag passed to CreateProcess.

Explanation See "Overview of Server Abend Messages" on page 325.

Invalid resource tag passed to DeviceLock.

Explanation See "Overview of Server Abend Messages" on page 325.

Invalid resource tag passed to LogicalPartitionLock.

Explanation See "Overview of Server Abend Messages" on page 325.

Invalid resource tag passed to ParseDriverParameters.

Explanation See "Overview of Server Abend Messages" on page 325.

Invalid resource tag passed to PartitionLock.

Explanation See "Overview of Server Abend Messages" on page 325.

Invalid resource tag passed to ScheduleInterruptTimeCallBack.

Explanation See "Overview of Server Abend Messages" on page 325.

Invalid resource tag passed to SystemLock.

Explanation See "Overview of Server Abend Messages" on page 325.

Invalid screen ID passed to screen manager.

Explanation See "Overview of Server Abend Messages" on page 325.

Invalid semaphore number passed to kernel.

Explanation See "Overview of Server Abend Messages" on page 325.

Invalid send status *<status>* **returned by LAN board** *<number>*.

Explanation See "Overview of Server Abend Messages" on page 325.

Invalid send status %02x returned by LAN board *<number>*.

Explanation See "Overview of Server Abend Messages" on page 325.

Invalid starting extant number passed to ClaimExtendedDirectorySpace.

Explanation See "Overview of Server Abend Messages" on page 325.

Invalid system handle in DiskSystemCleanUpRoutine.

Explanation See "Overview of Server Abend Messages" on page 325.

Invalid system id passed to GetIOCTL.

Explanation See "Overview of Server Abend Messages" on page 325.

Invalid system id passed to NPutIOCTL.

Explanation See "Overview of Server Abend Messages" on page 325.

Invalid system passed to SystemMessageEvent.

Explanation See "Overview of Server Abend Messages" on page 325.

Invalid TNode found by AddTrusteeRights.

Explanation See "Overview of Server Abend Messages" on page 325.

Invalid TNode found by DeleteTrusteeRights.

Explanation See "Overview of Server Abend Messages" on page 325.

Invalid user restriction list.

Explanation See "Overview of Server Abend Messages" on page 325.

Invalid user restriction node list found by AddUserRestriction.

Explanation See "Overview of Server Abend Messages" on page 325.

Invalid user restriction node list found by DeleteUserRestriction.

Explanation See "Overview of Server Abend Messages" on page 325.

Invalid user restriction node...too many trustees.

Explanation See "Overview of Server Abend Messages" on page 325.

Invalid volume segment not found in disk segment list.

Explanation See "Overview of Server Abend Messages" on page 325.

INWMountVolume called without volume semaphore.

Explanation See "Overview of Server Abend Messages" on page 325.

IPX Protocol Receive Stack got a receive buffer with a bad resource tag.

Explanation See "Overview of Server Abend Messages" on page 325.

Kernel detected a process switch during interrupt time.

Explanation See "Overview of Server Abend Messages" on page 325.

Kernel detected process going to sleep when it was not allowed.

Explanation See "Overview of Server Abend Messages" on page 325.

Kernel detected unmatched call to EndSleepNotAllowed.

Explanation See "Overview of Server Abend Messages" on page 325.

LinkHandle returned an error.

Explanation See "Overview of Server Abend Messages" on page 325.

LockDirectoryEntry called with entry already locked.

Explanation See "Overview of Server Abend Messages" on page 325.

LSLGetInfoRequest made after the file server is mirrored.

Explanation See "Overview of Server Abend Messages" on page 325.

LSLGetInfoRequest made after the file server is mirrored.

Explanation See "Overview of Server Abend Messages" on page 325.

MapExternalToInternalDirNumber did not find the entry.

Explanation See "Overview of Server Abend Messages" on page 325.

MapInternalToExternalDirNumber did not find the entry.

Explanation See "Overview of Server Abend Messages" on page 325.

MapSubdirectoryToDirectory could not find the subdirectory.

Explanation See "Overview of Server Abend Messages" on page 325.

MarkDirectoryChanged was called with a non-subdirectory number.

Explanation See “Overview of Server Abend Messages” on page 325.

MarkDirectoryChanged was called with an invalid subdirectory number.

Explanation See “Overview of Server Abend Messages” on page 325.

MarkDirectoryEntryChanged was called with a directory entry not in memory.

Explanation See “Overview of Server Abend Messages” on page 325.

MatchAttributes bad name space.

Explanation See “Overview of Server Abend Messages” on page 325.

Memory allocation error initializing volume manager tables.

Explanation See “Overview of Server Abend Messages” on page 325.

MMU page initialization failed.

Explanation See “Overview of Server Abend Messages” on page 325.

ModifyDirectoryFields bad name space.

Explanation See “Overview of Server Abend Messages” on page 325.

ModifyEntry found an invalid name list.

Explanation See “Overview of Server Abend Messages” on page 325.

MoveCacheNode could not locate the cache node.

Explanation See “Overview of Server Abend Messages” on page 325.

MoveDeletedFiles called with the root.

Explanation See “Overview of Server Abend Messages” on page 325.

MoveDeletedFiles didn-t find a entry on the block list.

Explanation See “Overview of Server Abend Messages” on page 325.

MoveDeletedFiles found an invalid DeletedFileList.

Explanation See "Overview of Server Abend Messages" on page 325.

Multi-packeted read called with invalid re-transmit fragment list.

Explanation See "Overview of Server Abend Messages" on page 325.

Multi-packeted write could not find control node.

Explanation See "Overview of Server Abend Messages" on page 325.

Multi-packeted write generated too large ACK fragment count.

Explanation See "Overview of Server Abend Messages" on page 325.

NCP Packet Burst had an error opening a screen.

Explanation See "Overview of Server Abend Messages" on page 325.

NCP Packet Burst had an error allocating a screen resouce tag.

Explanation See "Overview of Server Abend Messages" on page 325.

NCP Packet Burst had an error allocating a AESProc resource tag.

Explanation See "Overview of Server Abend Messages" on page 325.

NCP Packet Burst had an error allocating memory resource tag.

Explanation See "Overview of Server Abend Messages" on page 325.

New NCP Lock Waits could not find corresponding wait node.

Explanation See "Overview of Server Abend Messages" on page 325.

NLM Polling Procedure.

Explanation See "Overview of Server Abend Messages" on page 325.

NLM unloaded without deleting all its processes.

Explanation See "Overview of Server Abend Messages" on page 325.

NLM unloaded without deleting all its semaphores.

Explanation See "Overview of Server Abend Messages" on page 325.

NM VMCB Consistency Check failed in nmincupd.386.

Explanation See "Overview of Server Abend Messages" on page 325.

No dirty bits found in cache buffer on dirty list in disk cache.

Explanation See "Overview of Server Abend Messages" on page 325.

No memory for Disk IO Request nodes.

Explanation See "Overview of Server Abend Messages" on page 325.

No semaphores available in kernel.

Explanation See "Overview of Server Abend Messages" on page 325.

NULL string pointer was passed to the output formatter.

Explanation See "Overview of Server Abend Messages" on page 325.

Object not found for inform in disk cache.

Explanation See "Overview of Server Abend Messages" on page 325.

OpenFileSyncCheck found a open file on this task.

Explanation See "Overview of Server Abend Messages" on page 325.

OpenScreenRequest called with invalid screen ID.

Explanation See "Overview of Server Abend Messages" on page 325.

Out of memory allocating diskrequest.

Explanation See "Overview of Server Abend Messages" on page 325.

Packet to be sent to invalid LAN board.

Explanation See "Overview of Server Abend Messages" on page 325.

PhysicalRequest returned an error in HotfixBlockingIO.

Explanation See "Overview of Server Abend Messages" on page 325.

Pop up screen with a count of zero was marked switchable.

Explanation See "Overview of Server Abend Messages" on page 325.

PositionInputCursor called with invalid column.

Explanation See "Overview of Server Abend Messages" on page 325.

PositionInputCursor called with invalid row.

Explanation See "Overview of Server Abend Messages" on page 325.

PositionInputCursor called with invalid screen ID.

Explanation See "Overview of Server Abend Messages" on page 325.

PositionOutputCursor called with invalid column.

Explanation See "Overview of Server Abend Messages" on page 325.

PositionOutputCursor called with invalid row.

Explanation See "Overview of Server Abend Messages" on page 325.

PositionOutputCursor called with invalid screen ID.

Explanation See "Overview of Server Abend Messages" on page 325.

Process waiting for disk I/O to complete was awakened prematurely.

Explanation See "Overview of Server Abend Messages" on page 325.

PurgeLimboFile could not find the deleted file on the deleted file list.

Explanation See "Overview of Server Abend Messages" on page 325.

PurgeLimboFile detected a problem with the deleted file block list.

Explanation See "Overview of Server Abend Messages" on page 325.

PurgeLimboFile found an invalid deleted block on the delete list.

Explanation See "Overview of Server Abend Messages" on page 325.

PurgeTrustee found an entry it couldn't deal with.

Explanation See "Overview of Server Abend Messages" on page 325.

PurgeTrustee found invalid name list.

Explanation See "Overview of Server Abend Messages" on page 325.

ReadExistingFile invalid use count.

Explanation See "Overview of Server Abend Messages" on page 325.

ReadFile called with file with non-zero file length but no disk blocks.

Explanation See "Overview of Server Abend Messages" on page 325.

ReAttachFile called with invalid file handle.

Explanation See "Overview of Server Abend Messages" on page 325.

RegisterNCPExtension called with invalid Resource Tag Pointer.

Explanation See "Overview of Server Abend Messages" on page 325.

RegisterScreenInputRoutine called with invalid screen ID.

Explanation See "Overview of Server Abend Messages" on page 325.

RegisterScreenInputRoutine called with too large a value in lines to protect.

Explanation See "Overview of Server Abend Messages" on page 325.

Registration of MIT root failed.

Explanation See "Overview of Server Abend Messages" on page 325.

RemoveCacheNode could not locate the cache node.

Explanation See "Overview of Server Abend Messages" on page 325.

RemoveCacheSegment found invalid cache list.

Explanation See "Overview of Server Abend Messages" on page 325.

RemoveEntry found an invalid subdirectory space node search list.

Explanation See "Overview of Server Abend Messages" on page 325.

RemoveEntryName bad name space.

Explanation See "Overview of Server Abend Messages" on page 325.

RemoveFile called with file to be truncated with blocks already returned.

Explanation See "Overview of Server Abend Messages" on page 325.

RemoveFile called with invalid file handle.

Explanation See "Overview of Server Abend Messages" on page 325.

RemoveHardwareOptions called with invalid pointer.

Explanation See "Overview of Server Abend Messages" on page 325.

RemoveHardwareOptions passed invalid pointer.

Explanation See "Overview of Server Abend Messages" on page 325.

RemoveInfoFromLimboFile bad name space.

Explanation See "Overview of Server Abend Messages" on page 325.

RemoveOtherInfo bad name space.

Explanation See "Overview of Server Abend Messages" on page 325.

RemovePollingProcedure found invalid DelayedWorkToDoLis.

Explanation See "Overview of Server Abend Messages" on page 325.

RemoveStation could not find FCB on the station list.

Explanation See "Overview of Server Abend Messages" on page 325.

RemoveStation could not find the FCB on the open file list.

Explanation   See "Overview of Server Abend Messages" on page 325.

RemoveSubdirectory cannot find a subdirectories location in the space restriction list.

Explanation   See "Overview of Server Abend Messages" on page 325.

RemoveSubdirectory was called with a directory entry not in memory.

Explanation   See "Overview of Server Abend Messages" on page 325.

RenameEntry found invalid name list.

Explanation   See "Overview of Server Abend Messages" on page 325.

RenameEntry found invalid UNIX hard link info.

Explanation   See "Overview of Server Abend Messages" on page 325.

RenameEntry found invalid UNIX hard link info...bad master link.

Explanation   See "Overview of Server Abend Messages" on page 325.

RenameEntry got a unanticipated OpenLock failure.

Explanation   See "Overview of Server Abend Messages" on page 325.

RenameEntryName bad name space.

Explanation   See "Overview of Server Abend Messages" on page 325.

Reply was called with non-matching sequence numbers.

Explanation   See "Overview of Server Abend Messages" on page 325.

ReplyKeep was called with data too large to keep.

Explanation   See "Overview of Server Abend Messages" on page 325.

ReplyKeepBufferFilledOut was called with data too large to keep.

Explanation See "Overview of Server Abend Messages" on page 325.

Request not on list in DiskIOCTLSendDataAckRoutine.

Explanation See "Overview of Server Abend Messages" on page 325.

Request not on list in DiskIOSendDataAckRoutine.

Explanation See "Overview of Server Abend Messages" on page 325.

ReRead error on TTS backout file.

Explanation See "Overview of Server Abend Messages" on page 325.

Resource Signature could not be created in InitSignatures.

Explanation See "Overview of Server Abend Messages" on page 325.

Resource tag link error detected in NCompleteRequest.

Explanation See "Overview of Server Abend Messages" on page 325.

Resource tag link error detected in PutIOCTL.

Explanation See "Overview of Server Abend Messages" on page 325.

Resource Tag could not be allocated in InitSignatures.

Explanation See "Overview of Server Abend Messages" on page 325.

ReturnAllLeftOverResources called with LoadRecord not on the scan list.

Explanation See "Overview of Server Abend Messages" on page 325.

ReturnAllLeftOverResources couldn't find the resource signature node for the resource tag.

Explanation See "Overview of Server Abend Messages" on page 325.

ReturnAllLeftOverResources did not return all tracked resources on the scan list.

Explanation See "Overview of Server Abend Messages" on page 325.

ReturnAllocResourceTag caught a resource tag out of sync with memory.

Explanation See "Overview of Server Abend Messages" on page 325.

ReturnAllocResourceTag was given an invalid resource tag.

Explanation See "Overview of Server Abend Messages" on page 325.

ReturnControlBlock called with invalid control handle.

Explanation See "Overview of Server Abend Messages" on page 325.

ReturnMemory discovered an invalid memory block segment.

Explanation See "Overview of Server Abend Messages" on page 325.

ReturnMemory was given an invalid memory block.

Explanation See "Overview of Server Abend Messages" on page 325.

ReturnNonMovableMemory called with invalid return segment.

Explanation See "Overview of Server Abend Messages" on page 325.

ReturnPermanentMemory called at interrupt time.

Explanation See "Overview of Server Abend Messages" on page 325.

ReturnPermanentMemory couldnt find the block on the resource list.

Explanation See "Overview of Server Abend Messages" on page 325.

ReturnPermanentMemory received an invalid memory block.

Explanation See "Overview of Server Abend Messages" on page 325.

ReturnResourceTag called with a resource tag that didn't have a signature node.

Explanation See "Overview of Server Abend Messages" on page 325.

ReturnWaitNode was given an un-allocated wait node.

Explanation See "Overview of Server Abend Messages" on page 325.

SalvageLimboFile could not find the deleted file on the deleted file list.

Explanation See "Overview of Server Abend Messages" on page 325.

SalvageLimboFile detected a problem with the deleted file block list.

Explanation See "Overview of Server Abend Messages" on page 325.

SalvageLimboFile found an invalid deleted block on the delete list.

Explanation See "Overview of Server Abend Messages" on page 325.

SalvageLimboFile found an invalid name list.

Explanation See "Overview of Server Abend Messages" on page 325.

SalvageLimboFile found invalid deleted file block.

Explanation See "Overview of Server Abend Messages" on page 325.

SalvageLimboFile found invalid TNode.

Explanation See "Overview of Server Abend Messages" on page 325.

ScanLimboFilesInDirectory found an invalid deleted file.

Explanation See "Overview of Server Abend Messages" on page 325.

ScanTree found a too large subdirectory tree.

Explanation See "Overview of Server Abend Messages" on page 325.

ScanTree found an invalid name lis.

Explanation See "Overview of Server Abend Messages" on page 325.

ScanTrusteeRights found non-TNode on TNode list.

Explanation See "Overview of Server Abend Messages" on page 325.

ScreenBufferReleasedRequest called with unexpected releasing screenID.

Explanation See "Overview of Server Abend Messages" on page 325.

ScreenBufferReleasedRequest was called with no pending active screen.

Explanation See "Overview of Server Abend Messages" on page 325.

ScreenCleanupCompletedEvent called with a resource tag with a non-zero count.

Explanation See "Overview of Server Abend Messages" on page 325.

ScreenCleanupCompletedEvent called with an invalid resource tag.

Explanation See "Overview of Server Abend Messages" on page 325.

ScreenInputCleanUpProcedure could not find all the input routines.

Explanation See "Overview of Server Abend Messages" on page 325.

ScreenWasClosedEvent called with invalid screen ID.

Explanation See "Overview of Server Abend Messages" on page 325.

SecondaryHasFinishedClose called with a non-file server screen.

Explanation See "Overview of Server Abend Messages" on page 325.

SecondaryHasFinishedClose called with invalid screen ID.

Explanation See "Overview of Server Abend Messages" on page 325.

Semaphored directory buffer was encountered on the dirty list.

Explanation See "Overview of Server Abend Messages" on page 325.

SemiPermanentMemory clean up procedure found an incorrect resource block list.

Explanation See "Overview of Server Abend Messages" on page 325.

Server process awakened incorrectly.

Explanation See "Overview of Server Abend Messages" on page 325.

SetDeletedFileEntryName bad name space.

Explanation See "Overview of Server Abend Messages" on page 325.

SetFileName bad name space.

Explanation See "Overview of Server Abend Messages" on page 325.

SetInputToOutputCursorPosition called with invalid screen ID.

Explanation See "Overview of Server Abend Messages" on page 325.

SetInputToOutputCursorPosition was called when another process is already using the keyboard.

Explanation See "Overview of Server Abend Messages" on page 325.

SetOpenCountToOne called with invalid file handle.

Explanation See "Overview of Server Abend Messages" on page 325.

SetRestOfFileEntry bad name space.

Explanation See "Overview of Server Abend Messages" on page 325.

SetRestOfSubDirEntry bad name space.

Explanation See "Overview of Server Abend Messages" on page 325.

SetThreadHandicapAmount called with invalid process ID in kernel.

Explanation See "Overview of Server Abend Messages" on page 325.

ShrinkMovableCacheMemory passed invalid memory block or size.

Explanation See "Overview of Server Abend Messages" on page 325.

Sleeping process was prematurely awakened during Delay.

Explanation See "Overview of Server Abend Messages" on page 325.

SPXInit had a memory allocation ERROR.

Explanation See "Overview of Server Abend Messages" on page 325.

Stack overflow detected by kernel.

Explanation See "Overview of Server Abend Messages" on page 325.

StartDirectoryHandles called with not new station.

Explanation See "Overview of Server Abend Messages" on page 325.

StartNameSpaceAddition bad name space.

Explanation See "Overview of Server Abend Messages" on page 325.

String with too long a length was passed to the output formatter.

Explanation See "Overview of Server Abend Messages" on page 325.

Subdirectory was deleted during FindDirectoryEntry.

Explanation See "Overview of Server Abend Messages" on page 325.

The FAT table was hit.

Explanation See "Overview of Server Abend Messages" on page 325.

Timer node passed to timer call back with signature but not on the list.

Explanation See "Overview of Server Abend Messages" on page 325.

TNode changed during volume mount.

Explanation See "Overview of Server Abend Messages" on page 325.

Total sprintf string length was too long.

Explanation See "Overview of Server Abend Messages" on page 325.

Total sprintf string length was too long.

Explanation See "Overview of Server Abend Messages" on page 325.

TransferFileNameAndInfoToLimbo bad name space.

Explanation See "Overview of Server Abend Messages" on page 325.

TransferInfo bad name space.

Explanation See "Overview of Server Abend Messages" on page 325.

TransferLimboInfoToFile bad name space.

Explanation See "Overview of Server Abend Messages" on page 325.

TransferOnlyInfoToLimbo bad name space.

Explanation See "Overview of Server Abend Messages" on page 325.

TTS invalid use count.

Explanation See "Overview of Server Abend Messages" on page 325.

TTSAbortTransaction detected a bad TTS file.

Explanation See "Overview of Server Abend Messages" on page 325.

TTSAbortTransaction found a bad transaction backout list.

Explanation See "Overview of Server Abend Messages" on page 325.

TTSGetFileHandle could not find the file handle.

Explanation See "Overview of Server Abend Messages" on page 325.

TTSGuaranteeWait was passed an invalid wait node.

Explanation See "Overview of Server Abend Messages" on page 325.

TTSInformOnVolumeDismount found an invalid transaction header.

Explanation See "Overview of Server Abend Messages" on page 325.

TTSSetTransaction was given an invalid file handle.

Explanation See "Overview of Server Abend Messages" on page 325.

Unable to allocate a process resource tag in CCreateProcess.

Explanation See "Overview of Server Abend Messages" on page 325.

Unable to allocate a semaphore resource tag in CAllocateSemaphore.

Explanation See "Overview of Server Abend Messages" on page 325.

Unable to allocate a timer resource tag in InitializeTimer.

Explanation See "Overview of Server Abend Messages" on page 325.

Unable to allocate an alloc resource tag in InitializeMemory.

Explanation See "Overview of Server Abend Messages" on page 325.

Unable to allocate an alloc resource tag in InitializeMemory.

Explanation See "Overview of Server Abend Messages" on page 325.

Unable to allocate memory to initialize screen manager.

Explanation See "Overview of Server Abend Messages" on page 325.

Unable to allocate resource tag during screen manager init.

Explanation See "Overview of Server Abend Messages" on page 325.

Unable to find EA handle in RemoveHandleFromStation.

Explanation See "Overview of Server Abend Messages" on page 325.

UnbindStack did not find the node on the protocol list.

Explanation See "Overview of Server Abend Messages" on page 325.

UnConvertName bad name space.

Explanation See "Overview of Server Abend Messages" on page 325.

UnLockDirectoryEntry called with entry that was already unlocked.

Explanation See "Overview of Server Abend Messages" on page 325.

UpdateIOScreenCursor request could not find the indicated screen.

Explanation See "Overview of Server Abend Messages" on page 325.

UpdateIOScreenImage request could not find the indicated screen.

Explanation See "Overview of Server Abend Messages" on page 325.

UpdateIOScreenState request could not find the indicated screen.

Explanation See "Overview of Server Abend Messages" on page 325.

UpdateScreenTitleBar called when title bar flag was not set.

Explanation See "Overview of Server Abend Messages" on page 325.

UpdateScreenTitleBar detected invalid screen list state.

Explanation See "Overview of Server Abend Messages" on page 325.

UpdateScreenTitleBar detected invalid server mirror state.

Explanation See "Overview of Server Abend Messages" on page 325.

Volume with invalid starting sector passed to DiskIO.

Explanation See "Overview of Server Abend Messages" on page 325.

Wait node was lost by the TTS support code.

Explanation See "Overview of Server Abend Messages" on page 325.

WildReplace bad name space.

Explanation See "Overview of Server Abend Messages" on page 325.

WildSearchDirectoryFromInfo bad name space.

Explanation See "Overview of Server Abend Messages" on page 325.

WildSearchDirectory bad name space.

Explanation See "Overview of Server Abend Messages" on page 325.

WriteFile was called with file that had a non-zero first cluster.

Explanation See "Overview of Server Abend Messages" on page 325.

chapter **3** *Across-the-Wire Migration Error Messages*

Overview of Migration Error Messages

Error messages originating in the Across-the Wire Migration utility are accompanied by a three-part prefix as follows:

```
MIGRATE-4.0-001: The program cannot update an
  account balance.
```

The following messages are listed by prefix number.

Numerical List of Migration Error Messages

001: The program cannot update an account balance.

Explanation The program was unable to update a user or print server's account balance property.

Action Make sure that the workstation running the migration still has a valid connection to the network, and that the destination server's bindery is not locked.

002: The program cannot set up an account server.

Explanation While setting up accounting services for either the destination file server or one of the migrated print servers, the program was unable to write to the bindery.

Action Make sure that the workstation running the migration still has a valid connection to the network, and that the destination server's bindery is not locked.

003: The program could not allocate *<number>* bytes of memory.

Explanation: The program was unable to allocate memory, and failed.

Action: See "Insufficient Workstation Memory Errors" on page 442 in Appendix A, "Troubleshooting."

004: The program cannot add a trustee to a directory.

Explanation: This error can occur during two phases of the migration: while creating print servers, and while writing trustee assignments to the destination server. In both cases, the program was unable to write trustee information to the destination server.

Action: Make sure that the workstation running the migration still has a valid connection to the network, and that the destination server's bindery is not locked.

006: The program cannot give console operator privileges to a user or group.

Explanation: The program was unable to access the bindery in order to make a user or group a console operator.

Action: Make sure that the workstation running the migration still has a valid connection to the network, and that the destination server's bindery is not locked.

007: The program cannot create a directory on the destination server.

Explanation: The program was unable to create either a user's home directory or a print server's working directory on the destination server.

Action: Make sure that the workstation running the migration still has a valid connection to the network, and that the destination server's bindery is not locked. Also, check whether the named directory path already exists on the destination, and whether you have rights to access that directory path.

008: The program cannot create a file.

Explanation — The program was unable to create a login script file by accessing DOS services.

Action — Make sure that the workstation running the migration still has a valid connection to the network, and that the destination server's bindery is not locked. Also check whether or not the named file exists, and whether you have access rights to that file.

009: The program cannot create an object.

Explanation — The program was unable to create an object in the destination server's bindery.

Action — Make sure that the workstation running the migration still has a valid connection to the network, and that the destination server's bindery is not locked. Also, make sure that the destination server has enough disk space on volume SYS: to allow creation of more bindery objects.

010: The program cannot create a bindery property.

Explanation — The program was unable to create a bindery property for a bindery object (such as user, group, print server, or print queue).

Action — Make sure that the workstation running the migration still has a valid connection to the network, and that the destination server's bindery is not locked. Also, make sure that the destination server has enough disk space on volume SYS: to allow the bindery to expand.

012: The program cannot delete a bindery property.

Explanation — This message may occur in the following circumstances:

- Intruder detection is being turned off on the destination server.
- Accounting services is being installed on the destination server by the program.
- Accounting services is being deleted from the destination server by the program.

- The program has finished writing all users, groups, etc., and is cleaning up after itself. The program adds an extra property to each object it creates on the destination server to keep track of which objects have been migrated and which have not.

  As a final operation before copying data files and setting up trustee assignments, this property is deleted from the migrated objects.

Action — Make sure that the workstation running the migration still has a valid connection to the network, and that the destination server's bindery is not locked.

013: The program cannot update the full name of a user, group, or print server.

Explanation — The program could not write the full name of the object to the bindery.

Action — Make sure that the workstation running the migration still has a valid connection to the network, and that the destination server's bindery is not locked. Also, make sure that the bindery object being updated has not been modified or deleted by another user on the network.

014: The program cannot obtain the target server's name.

Explanation — The program queries the destination server to obtain its name before proceeding with the migration. In this case, the query failed.

Action — Make sure that the workstation running the migration still has a valid connection to the network, and that the destination server's bindery is not locked.

015: The program cannot obtain an object's bindery ID.

Explanation — In order to make a trustee assignment on the destination server, the program must first obtain the bindery object ID of the trustee. The attempt to obtain this ID has failed.

Action — Make sure that the workstation running the migration still has a valid connection to the network, and that the destination server's bindery is not locked. Also, make sure that the bindery object being given trustee rights has not been modified or deleted by another user on the network.

016: The program cannot obtain the NetWare server's date and time.

Explanation — The program queries the destination server to obtain the date and time before proceeding with the migration. In this case, the query failed.

Action — Make sure that the workstation running the migration still has a valid connection to the network, and that the destination server's bindery is not locked.

017: The program cannot obtain file server information.

Explanation — The program queries the destination server to obtain its NetWare version information before proceeding with the migration. In this case, the query failed.

Action — Make sure that the workstation running the migration still has a valid connection to the network, and that the destination server's bindery is not locked.

018: The program cannot read migration information from the intermediate file.

Explanation — This error occurs whenever the program cannot access the intermediate file (in the working directory).

Action — If the working directory is on the network, make sure that the workstation still has a valid connection to the file server where the working directory is located; also make sure that the intermediate file has not been locked or deleted by another network user.

If the working directory is on the workstation's hard disk, check the integrity of the hard disk.

019: The program cannot add a user to a group.

Explanation — When users are created on the destination server, they are automatically added to group EVERYONE. Later, users are added to other groups to which they belonged on the source server.

This message indicates that the program could not access the destination server's bindery to add a user to a group.

Action — Make sure that the workstation running the migration still has a valid connection to the network, and that the destination server's bindery is not locked. Also, make sure that the named user and group being updated have not been modified or deleted by another user on the network.

020: The program cannot add a group to a user's list of groups.

Explanation: Each user's bindery object contains a property that lists the names of groups to which the user belongs. An attempt by the program to update this list in the bindery has failed.

Action: Make sure that the workstation running the migration still has a valid connection to the network, and that the destination server's bindery is not locked. Also, make sure that the named user and group being updated have not been modified or deleted by another user on the network.

021: The program cannot install accounting on the target server.

Explanation: This error occurs when accounting charge rates are migrated from a source server that has accounting services installed to a destination server that does not have accounting services installed.

In this scenario, the program attempts to install accounting on the destination server by adding a bindery property to the destination server's bindery.

This message indicates that the attempt to add that property failed.

Action: Make sure that the workstation running the migration still has a valid connection to the network, and that the destination server's bindery is not locked.

022: The program cannot give a user or group account manager privileges for another user or group.

Explanation: In order to give a user or group manager rights for another bindery object, the program must write to the destination server's bindery. This message indicates that this attempt to access the bindery failed.

Action: Make sure that the workstation running the migration still has a valid connection to the network, and that the destination server's bindery is not locked. Also, make sure that the bindery object being updated has not been modified or deleted by another user on the network.

023: An internal error has occurred. The program cannot convert a NetWare-style path to a UNC path.

Explanation
In order to access files on the destination server, the program must convert NetWare paths so that DOS can interpret them. The naming convention that DOS understands is called the Universal Naming Convention (UNC), and has the following format:

```
\\<server>\<volume>\<directory>\<directory>
```

While trying to convert a name from the NetWare naming convention to the UNC naming convention, the program failed.

Action
Exit the utility, ensure the integrity of the workstation's memory, and run the utility again.

024: The program cannot open a file.

Explanation
The program accesses DOS services to open files on the destination server. This message indicates that the call to DOS has failed.

Action
Make sure that the workstation's CONFIG.SYS file allows a sufficient number of files to be opened (for example: "FILES=20").

025: The program cannot designate a user or group as an operator of a print queue or print server.

Explanation
In order to designate a user or group as the operator of a print queue or print server, the program must write to the destination server's bindery. This message indicates that this bindery access has failed.

Action
Make sure that the workstation running the migration still has a valid connection to the network, and that the destination server's bindery is not locked. Also, make sure that the bindery object being updated has not been modified or deleted by another user on the network.

026: The program cannot read the value of a bindery property.

Explanation The program could not read a bindery property from the destination server.

Action Make sure that the workstation running the migration still has a valid connection to the network, and that the destination server's bindery is not locked. Also, make sure that the bindery object being read from has not been modified or deleted by another user on the network.

027: The program cannot find an object in the bindery.

Explanation This error can occur whenever the program turns accounting services off for the destination server, or when the program is cleaning up bindery objects it has created during the migration.

This message indicates that the program could not read an object in the bindery.

Action Make sure that the workstation running the migration still has a valid connection to the network, and that the destination server's bindery is not locked. Also, make sure that the bindery object being updated has not been modified or deleted by another user on the network.

028: The program cannot find a bindery property.

Explanation The program could not find a property for an object in the bindery.

Action Make sure that the workstation running the migration still has a valid connection to the network, and that the destination server's bindery is not locked. Also, make sure that the bindery object being updated has not been modified or deleted by another user on the network.

029: The program cannot make a user security equivalent to another user or group.

Explanation In order to make a user security-equivalent to another user or group, the program must modify properties in the destination server's bindery. This message is displayed whenever the program's attempt to modify those properties fails.

Action — Make sure that the workstation running the migration still has a valid connection to the network, and that the destination server's bindery is not locked. Also, make sure that the bindery object being updated has not been modified or deleted by another user on the network.

030: The program cannot designate a print server to service a print queue.

Explanation — In order to designate a print server to service a print queue, the program must modify properties in the destination server's bindery. This message indicates that the attempted access failed.

Action — Make sure that the workstation running the migration still has a valid connection to the network, and that the destination server's bindery is not locked. Also, make sure that the bindery object being updated has not been modified or deleted by another user on the network.

031: An internal error has occurred. The program cannot translate a path on the source server to its corresponding path on the destination server.

Explanation — In order to translate directory path names from the source server to their corresponding location on the destination server, the program must use information supplied in the destination volume's table of the destination configuration form.

This message indicates that a source path could not be translated, given the information in the destination volume's table.

Action — Return to the configuration form, and make sure that the destination volume's table is properly configured.

032: The program cannot designate a user or group as the user of a print queue or print server.

Explanation — In order to designate a user of a print queue or print server, the program must modify properties in the destination server's bindery. This message indicates that the attempt to modify those properties failed.

Action — Make sure that the workstation running the migration still has a valid connection to the network, and that the destination server's bindery is not locked. Also, make sure that the bindery object being updated has not been modified or deleted by another user on the network.

033: The program cannot give workgroup manager privileges to a user or group.

Explanation: In order to give Workgroup Manager privileges to a user or group, the program must modify properties in the destination server's bindery. This message indicates that the program was unable to modify those properties.

Action: Make sure that the workstation running the migration still has a valid connection to the network, and that the destination server's bindery is not locked. Also, make sure that the bindery object being updated has not been modified or deleted by another user on the network.

034: The program cannot write a value to a bindery property.

Explanation: In order to properly set up objects created in the destination server's bindery, the program must read properties from those objects, modify them, and write them back to the bindery.

This message indicates that the program was unable to write a modified property back to the destination server's bindery.

Action: Make sure that the workstation running the migration still has a valid connection to the network, and that the destination server's bindery is not locked. Also, make sure that the bindery object being updated has not been modified or deleted by another user on the network.

035: The program cannot write to a file.

Explanation: This error can occur whenever the program is writing a file (for example, a user login script, the NEW.PWD file, printer definition files, or print server files) to the destination server. The program relies on DOS services for its file access.

This message indicates that the DOS request to write to a file failed.

Action: Check the integrity of the workstation's memory.

036: The program cannot write a user's login control property to the bindery.

Explanation: Each user's account restrictions are contained in what is known as the login control property. This property is modified when users are created and again when user restrictions are migrated to the destination server.

This message indicates that the program was unable to write the modified login control property to the destination server.

Action Make sure that the workstation running the migration still has a valid connection to the network, and that the destination server's bindery is not locked. Also, make sure that the bindery object being updated has not been modified or deleted by another user on the network.

037: The program cannot read a user's login control property from the bindery.

Explanation Each user's account restrictions are contained in what is known as the login control property. This property is modified when users are created and again when user restrictions are migrated to the destination server.

This message indicates that the program was unable to read a user's login control property from the destination server.

Action Make sure that the workstation running the migration still has a valid connection to the network, and that the destination server's bindery is not locked. Also, make sure that the bindery object being updated has not been modified or deleted by another user on the network.

038: A random password was generated for the following object, but could not be set. The password has not been recorded in the NEW.PWD file. This object will be able to login to the network without a password.

Explanation The program must modify a property in the bindery in order to change a user or print server's password. This message indicates that the attempt to modify the bindery property failed.

Action After the migration, the network supervisor can set a password for the named bindery object either through SYSCON (for users) or PCONSOLE (for print servers).

039: An internal error has occurred. The program cannot compress an accounting charge rate.

Explanation Accounting charge rates are stored in the bindery in compressed form. While attempting to compress an accounting charge rate table, the program failed.

Action After the migration, the network supervisor may need to manually set up the named charge rate on the destination server.

045: The program cannot create a user's mail directory.

Explanation — The program relies upon the services of DOS for its directory services. This message indicates that an attempt to create a mail directory on the destination server failed.

Action — Check the mail directory of the destination server to make sure that all mail directories of deleted users have been deleted. The failure to create the directory may have occurred because a directory by the same name already exists, in which case a new directory could not be created.

046: The program cannot give a user rights to his mail directory.

Explanation — Whenever the program creates a mail directory for a user, it grants the user a default set of trustee rights to that directory. This message indicates that the attempt to assign those rights failed.

Action — After the migration, the network supervisor can manually assign rights to the named user in the named directory.

047: The program cannot obtain trustee information from the target server.

Explanation — For each trustee assignment migrated from the source server, the program reads any existing trustee rights on the destination server for the translated directory path.

If any trustee assignment has already been made, the program combines the existing assignment with the migrated assignment to ensure that no trustee rights are lost on the destination server.

This message indicates that the attempt to read existing trustee assignments from the destination server failed.

Action — The previous trustee assignment will be lost if the migrated trustee rights are successfully set up on the destination server. If this occurs, the network supervisor will need to manually examine the named directory to evaluate whether or not to grant additional rights to the named user.

048: The following user's account has been disabled, so a random password could not be set. When the account is enabled, the user will be able to login without a password.

Explanation — The bindery will not allow a password to be changed for a user whose account has been disabled. This message is displayed if a migrated user is given a random password on the destination server, but his or her account is disabled (because it was disabled on the source server).

Action — Since the account is disabled, the user will not be able to log in, and the account is secure. However, as soon as the network supervisor enables the account, he or she must manually assign a password to the account in order to maintain proper security.

049: The program cannot set the status of the print queue.

Explanation — The server returned an unexpected error while attempting to set the status of the print queue.

Action — After the migration, the network supervisor can use PCONSOLE to manually set the printer queue status on the destination server.

050: An invalid NetWare object name was used.

Explanation — This error is probably the result of an extended ASCII character in the object name, especially if you are migrating from a LAN Server or PCLP.

Action — Rename objects with names that conform to the NetWare file server naming convention.

100: The program attempted to access LAN Server network information, but the network failed to process the request. LAN Server error code: *<number>*.

Explanation — An unexpected error has occurred on the LAN Server network, and the program is unable to complete the current operation.

Action — Refer to the LAN Server documentation for the meaning of the error code.

102: You must specify a working directory before proceeding.

Explanation — Either you failed to specify a working directory, or the path you entered is invalid. This message reappears until a valid directory is specified.

Action — Specify a valid path and directory name.

103: An internal error has occurred. The NWParsePath() function failed with *<path>*.

Explanation — This indicates a problem with a directory path or with the connection to the server that a path is pointing to. This usually happens when a connection has developed a problem or has been lost.

Action — Restart the Migration utility.

105: A memory allocation failure has occurred. Restart this utility after configuring DOS for more memory.

Explanation — You need to free more memory before migration can run.

Action — See "Insufficient Workstation Memory Errors" on page 442 in Appendix A, "Troubleshooting."

106: You cannot create more than 999 migration reports. Delete some reports and try again.

Explanation — The report file uses a 3-digit number in the report filename. This number is incremented with each new report, so the maximum is 999.

Action — Delete some report files. (Copy them elsewhere if needed.)

107: The report file cannot be opened.

Explanation — You may not have appropriate rights to write or modify the report file.

Action — Make sure you have access rights to the file.

108: The report file cannot be written to.

Explanation You may not have appropriate rights to write or modify the report file.

Action Make sure that you have access rights to the file. If this is not the problem, contact your Novell Authorized Reseller.

109: No report file names could be read from the working directory.

Explanation The working directory name you specified is invalid.

Action Make sure that the working directory exists and that you specified the correct name for the directory.

110: The report file, *<name>*, cannot be deleted.

Explanation You may not have the Delete right to the report file.

Action Obtain the Delete right. If this is not the problem, contact your Novell Authorized Reseller.

111: You do not have enough memory to create a screen portal.

Explanation You do not have enough memory to complete this operation.

Action See "Insufficient Workstation Memory Errors" on page 442 in Appendix A, "Troubleshooting."

113: An internal error occurred during an attempt to display text.

Explanation The scrolling function used for the report file has encountered an error.

Action Try again. If the problem persists, contact your Novell Authorized Reseller.

114: An internal error occurred during an attempt to read the report file.

Explanation The report file is probably corrupted.

Action Review the report file with an ASCII text editor.

117: The program cannot create the intermediate file.

Explanation The database file for your migration cannot be created.

Action Make sure that you have the Create right in the working directory. If this is not the problem, contact your Novell Authorized Reseller.

118: The program cannot write to the destination bindery.

Explanation The write portion of the migration has had a general failure. This could have happened because the correct message file was not found, or because the intermediate file is corrupted.

Action Make sure that the message file is current and located in SYS:PUBLIC. Reboot the workstation and try again. If the problem persists, contact your Novell Authorized Reseller.

119: The migration report cannot be opened.

Explanation The report file cannot be opened, perhaps because you do not have appropriate file rights or because an invalid path to the working directory was specified.

Action Make sure that you have sufficient file rights to the current report file. Also make sure that the working directory path exists and was specified correctly.

120: The intermediate file (MIGRATE.GMF) could not be opened.

Explanation The report file cannot be opened, perhaps because you do not have appropriate access rights or because an invalid path to the working directory was specified.

Action Check your access rights on the current report file. Also, make sure that the working directory path exists and was specified correctly.

121: The program cannot get the connection ID for the destination server.

Explanation The shell has lost its connection to the destination server, and the connection needs to be reestablished.

Action Go back into the configuration form and reestablish a connection to the destination server.

122: The directory *<path>* cannot be created.

Explanation — The program attempted to create a directory, but the specified directory could not be created. This may occur while specifying the program's working directory, or while specifying destination directories for data files migrated from the source server.

Action — If the path is on a file server, check your rights in each directory in the path. You will need the Create right in order to create subdirectories. If this is not the problem, reboot the workstation and try again.

If the problem persists, contact your Novell Authorized Reseller.

123: An internal error has occurred. The program cannot get the current working directory.

Explanation — This is an internal DOS error. DOS cannot get the working directory string.

Action — Reboot the workstation and try again. If the problem persists, contact your Novell Authorized Reseller.

124: An internal error has occurred. The drives cannot be changed.

Explanation — This is an internal DOS error. The drive indicated in the working directory cannot be made the current drive.

Action — Reboot the workstation and try again. If the problem persists, contact your Novell Authorized Reseller.

125: An internal error has occurred. The directories cannot be changed.

Explanation — An internal DOS error has occurred preventing you from changing to the working directory.

Action — Reboot the workstation and try again. If the problem persists, contact your Novell Authorized Reseller.

126: An internal error has occurred. The program cannot get your effective rights.

Explanation — An internal system error has occurred. The program could not get an Effective Rights Mask from the server for the working directory.

Action — Reboot the workstation and try again. If the problem persists, contact your Novell Authorized Reseller.

127: An internal error has occurred. The program cannot get NetWare server information.

Explanation An internal system error has occurred. Version information could not be read from the file server.

Action Reboot the workstation and try again. If the problem persists, contact your Novell Authorized Reseller.

128: An internal error has occurred. Could not expand path fragment—<*fragment*>.

Explanation An internal system error has occurred. The path fragment shown in the message could not be expanded to a full path.

Action Reboot the workstation and try again. If the problem persists, contact your Novell Authorized Reseller.

129: An internal error has occurred. The program cannot make directory <*name*>.

Explanation The directory cannot be created.

Action Make sure that the path string is correct. If this is not the problem, reboot the workstation and try again. If the problem persists, contact your Novell Authorized Reseller.

130: The program could not allocate memory while migrating to the destination LAN.

Explanation Your computer does not have enough available RAM to continue migration.

Action See "Insufficient Workstation Memory Errors" on page 442 in Appendix A, "Troubleshooting."

131: The program could not allocate memory while migrating from the source LAN.

Explanation Your computer does not have enough available RAM to continue migration.

Action See "Insufficient Workstation Memory Errors" on page 442 in Appendix A, "Troubleshooting."

132: An internal error has occurred. The source bindery could not be read.

Explanation The import part of the migration failed because the bindery information could not be read.

Action Make sure that the workstation running the migration still has a valid connection to the network, and that the destination server's bindery is not locked.

133: A directory specified in the path was longer than the 8.3 DOS standard.

Explanation All directory names and filenames must conform to the DOS 8-character filename and 3-character extension standard.

Action Rename files or directories that do not conform to the standard.

135: The specified path points to a file, not a directory.

Explanation The last element in the path was a file when a directory was needed.

Action Enter a valid directory path.

137: You must have the Administrative privilege in the LAN Server domain to access LAN Server network information.

Explanation Your LAN Server user is not of the appropriate type to perform this task.

Action Exit the Migration utility; log on to the LAN Server domain as a user that has Administrative privileges, and run the utility again.

138: You are not logged on to the LAN Server domain. Please logon to the LAN Server domain as a user with administrative privileges, and try again.

Explanation Your workstation is not logged on to the LAN Server domain.

Action Exit the Migration utility; log on to the LAN Server domain as a user that has Administrative privileges, and run the utility again.

140: The requester service has not been started.

Explanation: Either the DOS LAN Requester has not been started, or it has been started with an incorrect setting for the /NMS parameter.

Action: Make sure that the NET START command has been used to start the requester at your workstation. Also, make sure that this command has been issued with a nonzero setting for the /NMS parameter, either on the command line itself, or in the file DOSLAN.INI.

For further information, refer to the DOS LAN Requester documentation.

150: LAN Server network access is denied.

Explanation: The LAN Server network refused access to the program.

Action: Make sure that the workstation is logged in to the LAN Server network as a user that has Administrative privileges. Also make sure that the servers in the domain are still up and operational.

151: No domain controller was found on this domain.

Explanation: The program could not locate a domain controller for the domain that the workstation is logged on to.

Action: Make sure that the domain's domain controller is operational. Refer to the LAN Server documentation.

152: The server is not configured for transactions.

Explanation: The LAN Server domain controller has not been configured to allow programs to access network information.

Action: Reconfigure the server to allow the IPC resource to be shared. Refer to the LAN Server documentation.

153: OS/2: sufficient memory is not available.

Explanation: The LAN Server server does not have enough memory to complete the requested operation.

Action: Refer to the LAN Server and OS/2 documentation to determine how to free more memory on the LAN Server server.

154: The LAN Server network device driver has not been started on the workstation.

Explanation — The LAN Server device driver must be loaded on the workstation in order to perform the migration.

Action — Start the DOS LAN Requester on the workstation. Refer to the LAN Server and DOS LAN Requester documentation for more information.

157: The Requester service has not been started.

Explanation — The Requester service must be started on all domain servers and on the client workstation in order to access LAN Server network resources.

Action — Make sure that the Requester service has been started on all servers in the LAN Server domain, and that the service is not paused. Also make sure that the DOS LAN Requester has been properly started on the client workstation. Refer to the LAN Server and DOS LAN Requester documentation for more information.

158: The server service has not been started.

Explanation — The server service must be started on all LAN Server servers in the domain before migration can proceed.

Action — Make sure that the server service is started and not paused on all servers in the LAN Server domain. Refer to the LAN Server documentation for more information.

159: An Across the Wire migration cannot be performed from a server to itself.

Explanation — You have specified the same server name for both the source and destination servers.

Action — Be sure that the destination server name is different from the source server name.

201: An internal error has occurred. The program cannot obtain the name of a bindery object.

Explanation This error can occur while the program is reading relationships among objects in the bindery (for example, security equivalences, group membership, and managed users). Whenever the error occurs, the relationship between the bindery objects is lost on the destination server.

(Note that the source server's bindery object ID of the object whose name could not be obtained is displayed with this error.)

Action After the migration, you can restore the relationships by identifying the object whose name could not be read on the source server, then manually setting up the relationship on the destination server.

For example, assume that this error occurred while the program was reading the names of members of the group TOP_SECRET from the source server. This means that the user whose object ID is displayed would not appear as a member of TOP_SECRET on the destination server.

Also assume that the migration ran to completion in such a way that group TOP_SECRET was successfully created on the destination server.

To make sure that the destination server's TOP_SECRET group had the missing user added as a member, the migrator could run SYSCON on the source server and look at the "Other Information" field of each defined user to determine which user's object ID was displayed with the error message.

Then, taking the name of the user that was left out of group TOP_SECRET, the migrator could change to the destination server and add the missing user to group TOP_SECRET.

Note that object IDs for users and groups can be viewed with SYSCON, while object IDs for print queues and print servers can be viewed with PCONSOLE.

202: The program cannot obtain the NetWare server's date and time.

Explanation The program was unable to obtain the date and time from the source file server.

Action Make sure that the workstation still has a connection to the source server and that the bindery is not locked.

203: The program cannot obtain NetWare server information.

Explanation Prior to reading trustee assignments from the source server, the program was unable to obtain the version information from the source file server. As a result, the program is unable to translate trustee rights masks.

Action Make sure that the workstation still has a connection to the source server and that the bindery is not locked.

204: The program cannot obtain the name of the NetWare server.

Explanation While preparing to read information from the source file server, the program could not obtain the name of the server.

Action Make sure that the workstation still has a connection to the source server and that the bindery is not locked.

205: The program cannot get a volume's number.

Explanation In order to obtain trustee rights masks from a volume, the program must first obtain NetWare's ID number for that volume. The attempt to obtain the volume's number has failed.

Action Make sure that the volume is mounted and that the workstation still has a connection to the source server.

206: The program cannot read a user's account balance.

Explanation The program was unable to read the user's account balance property from the source server's bindery.

Action Make sure that the workstation still has a connection to the source server, that the bindery is not locked, and that the user still exists. Also, make sure that the accounting feature was not removed from the server by another user during the migration.

207: The program cannot read a user's account restrictions from the bindery.

Explanation In order to get a user's account restrictions, the program must read the user's login control property from the source server's bindery. The attempt to read that property has failed.

Action Make sure that the workstation still has a connection to the source server and that the bindery is not locked. Also, make sure that the user was not deleted by another user during the migration.

208: The program cannot read an accounting charge rate from the bindery.

Explanation In order to get the accounting charge rates from the source server, the program must read a series of properties from the source server object in the bindery. The program failed to read one of these properties.

Action Make sure that the workstation still has a connection to the source server and that the bindery is not locked. Also, make sure that the accounting feature was not deleted by another user during the migration.

209: The program cannot read the default user restrictions.

Explanation In order to obtain default user restrictions from the source server, the program must read the user defaults property from the SUPERVISOR object in the bindery. The attempt to read this property failed.

Action Make sure that the workstation still has a connection to the source server and that the bindery is not locked.

210: The program cannot read an object's full name from the bindery.

Explanation The program was unable to read the object's identification property from the bindery.

Action Make sure that the workstation still has a connection to the source server and that the bindery is not locked. Also, make sure that the object was not deleted by another user during the migration.

211: The program cannot read the default home directory.

Explanation The home directory path is obtained from the home directory property of the Supervisor user in the source server's bindery. The program was unable to read this property.

Action Make sure that the workstation still has a connection to the source server and that the bindery is not locked.

212: The program cannot read the value from a bindery property.

Explanation The program failed to read the named property from the source server's bindery.

Action Make sure that the workstation still has a connection to the source server and that the bindery is not locked.

213: The program cannot read security equivalences for a user.

Explanation Security equivalences have been defined for the given user on the source server, but the program was unable to read the bindery property that contains those equivalences.

Action Make sure that the workstation still has a connection to the source server and that the bindery is not locked. Also, make sure that the named user was not deleted by another user during the migration.

214: The program cannot read a user's station restrictions.

Explanation Each user's station restrictions are contained in the bindery, in the node control property which is associated with the given user object. The program failed to read this property from the bindery.

Action Make sure that the workstation still has a connection to the source server and that the bindery is not locked. Also, make sure that the user's account was not deleted by another user during the migration process.

216: The program cannot read the next group name from the bindery.

Explanation While reading groups from the source server, the program was unable to obtain the name of a group from the bindery.

Action Make sure that the workstation still has a connection to the source server and that the bindery is not locked.

217: The program cannot read the next print queue name from the bindery.

Explanation While reading print queues from the source server, the program was unable to obtain the name of a print queue from the bindery.

Action Make sure that the workstation still has a connection to the source server and that the bindery is not locked.

218: The program cannot read the next print server name from the bindery.

Explanation While reading print servers from the source server, the program was unable to obtain the name of a print server from the bindery.

Action Make sure that the workstation still has a connection to the source server and that the bindery is not locked.

219: The program cannot find an object's property from the bindery.

Explanation The program scanned the named object to determine whether it had the given property, but was unable to read from the bindery.

Action Make sure that the workstation still has a connection to the source server and that the bindery is not locked.

220: The program cannot read the next user name from the bindery.

Explanation While reading users from the source server, the program was unable to obtain the name of a user from the bindery.

Action Make sure that the workstation still has a connection to the source server and that the bindery is not locked.

221: The program cannot update the intermediate file.

Explanation The program was unable to write information to the intermediate file.

Action Make sure that the workstation still has access to the working directory.

222: An attempt to allocate *<number>* bytes of memory failed.

Explanation The program was unable to allocate memory, and failed.

Action See "Insufficient Workstation Memory Errors" on page 442 in Appendix A, "Troubleshooting."

223: An internal error has occurred. A NetWare-style path could not be converted to a UNC path.

Explanation In order to access files on the destination server, the program must convert NetWare paths so that DOS can interpret them. The naming convention that DOS understands is called the Universal Naming Convention (UNC), and has the following format:

```
\\<server>\<volume>\<directory>\<directory>
```

While trying to convert a name from the NetWare naming convention to the UNC naming convention, the program failed.

Action Exit the utility, ensure the integrity of the workstation's memory, and run the utility again.

224: The program cannot obtain the size of a file.

Explanation When reading login scripts, printer definition files, and print server setup files, the program tries to determine the size of the file by issuing a call to DOS. When this error message is displayed, the call to DOS has failed.

Action Make sure that the workstation still has a connection to the source server and that the workstation's memory has not been corrupted. Otherwise, consult your DOS manuals.

225: The program cannot read from a file.

Explanation The file may not exist or it may be locked by another user. A DOS error also may have occurred.

Action Make sure that the file has not been deleted and that it is not locked by another user. Otherwise, consult your DOS manuals.

226: The program cannot verify an object's password.

Explanation While determining whether a user or print server has a password, the utility could not access the bindery.

Action Make sure that the workstation still has a connection to the source server and that the bindery is not locked. Also, make sure that the user or print server has not been deleted from the bindery by another user.

227: An internal error has occurred. The program cannot add a field to a record.

Explanation The program has run out of memory on the client workstation, preventing the program from assembling a record before writing it to the intermediate file.

Action See "Insufficient Workstation Memory Errors" on page 442 in Appendix A, "Troubleshooting."

228: The program could not read intruder detection information from the source server's bindery.

Explanation The program tried to access the source server's bindery in order to read intruder detection information, but the attempt resulted in a network error.

Action Make sure that the workstation running the migration still has a valid connection to the NetWare network, that the source server is still operational, and that the source server's bindery is not locked.

229: The program could not read the status of a print queue from the source server.

Explanation A call to the file server returned an unexpected error.

Action After migration, the network supervisor can manually set the print queue status on the destination server using PCONSOLE.

230: The program could not read a file or directory's trustee information from the source server.

Explanation The program failed in its attempt to read trustee information of a file or directory on the source server.

Action After migration, the trustee information will have to be set up manually on the destination server using RIGHTS. The required trustee information can be obtained from the source server using RIGHTS.

231: The program could not obtain an object's type from the source server.

Explanation The program failed in its attempt to read trustee information of a file or directory on the source server.

Action After migration, the trustee information will have to be set up manually on the destination server using the RIGHTS utility. The required trustee information can be obtained from the source server using the RIGHTS utility.

302: The program cannot get the specified volume's number.

Explanation In order to copy files to or from a file server, the program must first obtain NetWare's ID number for the volumes being affected by the copy. The attempt to obtain the volume's number has failed.

Action Make sure that the volume is mounted and that the workstation still has a valid connection to the file server.

303: The program cannot get the destination file's long name.

Explanation If the source server supports long names, the program attempts to create and read long names for files that it copies from the source server. This error occurs when the program knows there is a long name associated with a file on the source server, but is unable to read it.

Action Make sure that the source server supports long names, and try again. If the problem persists, contact your Novell Authorized Reseller.

305: An invalid path was specified.

Explanation This is an internal error. The path was invalid.

Action Try again. If the problem persists, contact your Novell Authorized Reseller.

308: The maximum number of directory levels has been exceeded. MIGRATE supports a maximum of 25 subdirectory levels.

Explanation: The Migration utility cannot support more than 25 levels in a directory tree. Files and directories farther from the root than level 25 will not be copied.

Action: Decrease the number of levels in the directory structure on the source server before attempting to copy data files to the destination server.

317: The program cannot create the destination directory.

Explanation: The program attempted to create a directory, but failed.

Action: Reboot the workstation and try again. If the problem persists, contact your Novell Authorized Reseller.

318: A destination Macintosh file already exists. This file cannot be copied.

Explanation: The Migration utility will not copy over files that already exist in the destination directory.

Action: Try renaming the file in the destination directory.

319: A destination file already exists. This file cannot be copied.

Explanation: The Migration utility will not copy over files that already exist in the destination directory.

Action: Try renaming the file in the destination directory.

322: An unexpected error has occurred.

Explanation: This message can indicate a variety of possible errors.

Action: If you cannot continue, try rebooting the workstation and try the migration again. If the problem persists, contact your Novell Authorized Reseller.

324: DOS has denied access to the file.

Explanation: This error is returned by DOS. No other information is available.

Action: Consult your DOS manual.

325: The file cannot be created because a file with the same name exists in the destination directory that DOS cannot delete.

Explanation The Migration utility will not copy over existing files.

Action Try renaming the file in the destination directory; then retry the copy.

328: The file cannot be copied.

Explanation An internal error has occurred while copying files.

Action Reboot the workstation and try again. If the problem persists, contact your Novell Authorized Reseller.

329: The file cannot be created.

Explanation An internal error has occurred.

Action Reboot the workstation and try again. If the problem persists, contact your Novell Authorized Reseller.

330: The program cannot obtain an AFP entry ID.

Explanation An internal error has occurred.

Action Reboot the workstation and try again. If the problem persists, contact your Novell Authorized Reseller.

331: The destination file cannot be opened.

Explanation An internal error has occurred.

Action Reboot the workstation and try again. If the problem persists, contact your Novell Authorized Reseller.

332: The source file cannot be opened.

Explanation An internal error has occurred.

Action Reboot the workstation and try again. If the problem persists, contact your Novell Authorized Reseller.

333: The file cannot be read.

Explanation An internal error has occurred.

Action Reboot the workstation and try again. If the problem persists, contact your Novell Authorized Reseller.

334: File information could not be scanned on the destination file.

Explanation An internal error has occurred.

Action Reboot the workstation and try again. If the problem persists, contact your Novell Authorized Reseller.

335: File information could not be scanned on the source file.

Explanation An internal error has occurred.

Action Reboot the workstation and try again. If the problem persists, contact your Novell Authorized Reseller.

336: File information cannot be set.

Explanation An internal error has occurred.

Action Reboot the workstation and try again. If the problem persists, contact your Novell Authorized Reseller.

337: The specified file cannot be written to the disk.

Explanation An internal error has occurred.

Action Reboot the workstation and try again. If the problem persists, contact your Novell Authorized Reseller.

338: An application error has detached this file.

Explanation An internal error has occurred.

Action Reboot the workstation and try again. If the problem persists, contact your Novell Authorized Reseller.

339: The specified file is already being used by another workstation.

Explanation You cannot copy a file that is in use.

Action Wait until the file is no longer in use; then try the copy again.

340: FTAM name space is not supported on the destination volume. Only the data will be copied.

Explanation FTAM name space is not loaded. Only file data can be transferred.

Action If FTAM information is needed, load the name space functionality and restart migration.

341: A bad sector was found on the hard disk for the destination volume.

Explanation This error indicates a bad sector on the destination server's hard disk.

Action Either choose a different hard disk as your destination, or reformat the destination disk and try again.

343: This operation cannot be completed due to insufficient memory.

Explanation Your workstation does not have enough available RAM.

Action See "Insufficient Workstation Memory Errors" on page 442 in Appendix A, "Troubleshooting."

344: The specified file handle is invalid.

Explanation An internal error has occurred.

Action Reboot the workstation and try again. If the problem persists, contact your Novell Authorized Reseller.

345: The specified file name is invalid.

Explanation An internal error has occurred.

Action Reboot the workstation and try again. If the problem persists, contact your Novell Authorized Reseller.

346: The specified file contains a record that is currently locked.

Explanation An internal error has occurred.

Action Reboot the workstation and try again. If the problem persists, contact your Novell Authorized Reseller.

347: Macintosh name space is not supported on the destination volume. Only the data fork will be copied.

Explanation An internal error has occurred, indicating that the Macintosh name space is not loaded on the destination volume.

Action If Macintosh files are to be copied, you must load the Macintosh name space.

348: No more file handles are available on the network.

Explanation An internal error has occurred.

Action Reboot the workstation and try again. If the problem persists, contact your Novell Authorized Reseller.

349: You do not have Create/Erase rights on the destination directory.

Explanation NetWare security rights control what users can do with directories, files, or objects. Create and erase operations can be done only if you have been granted the rights to perform them.

Action Make sure that you have the necessary rights.

350: You do not have Create rights necessary to create this file.

Explanation NetWare security rights control what users can do with directories, files, or objects. Create and erase operations can be done only if you have been granted the rights to perform them.

Action Make sure that you have the necessary rights.

351: You do not have Erase rights on the destination directory.

Explanation NetWare security rights control what users can do with directories, files, or objects. Create and erase operations can be done only if you have been granted the rights to perform them.

Action Make sure that you have the necessary rights.

352: No such DOS file or directory exists.

Explanation The file or directory may exist on a different path, or the file or directory may have been deleted somehow. Another possibility is that an internal system error occurred.

Action Make sure that you specified a valid filename or directory name, that the path is correct, and that the file or directory exists. If none of these is the problem, reboot the workstation and try again. If the problem persists, contact your Novell Authorized Reseller.

353: You do not have Modify rights on the destination directory.

Explanation Novell's security determines what users can do with files and directories. Security rights are assigned by the network supervisor. You must have the Modify right to the destination directory in order to complete this procedure.

Action Make sure that you have the necessary rights.

354: You do not have Open rights necessary to open this file.

Explanation Novell's security determines what users can do with files and directories. Security rights are assigned by the network supervisor. You must have the Open right to the file in order to complete this procedure.

Action Make sure that you have the necessary rights.

355: You do not have Read rights on the destination directory.

Explanation Novell's security determines what users can do with files and directories. Security rights are assigned by the network supervisor. You must have the Read right to the destination directory in order to complete this procedure.

Action Make sure that you have the necessary rights.

356: You do not have Rename rights on the destination directory.

Explanation Novell's security determines what users can do with files and directories. Security rights are assigned by the network supervisor. You must have the Rename right to the destination directory in order to complete this procedure.

Action Make sure that you have the necessary rights.

357: You do not have Search rights on the destination directory.

Explanation — Novell's security determines what users can do with files and directories. Security rights are assigned by the network supervisor. You must have the Search right to the destination directory in order to complete this procedure.

Action — Make sure that you have the necessary rights.

358: You do not have Write rights on the destination directory.

Explanation — Novell's security determines what users can do with files and directories. Security rights are assigned by the network supervisor. You must have the Write right to the destination directory in order to complete this procedure.

Action — Make sure that you have the necessary rights.

359: The destination file is flagged Read Only.

Explanation — The Migration utility does not allow you to copy over an existing file.

Action — Try renaming the source file so that it has a unique name.

360: The OS/2 name space is not supported on the destination volume. Only the data will be copied.

Explanation — As with all name spaces, OS/2 name space support must be loaded if it is to be used.

Action — Load OS/2 name space support.

361: The server is out of directory entries.

Explanation — Only a set percentage of a hard disk is set aside for directory information. This percentage has been exceeded.

Action — If all directories are to be migrated, you will probably need a larger hard disk.

362: No more disk space exists in the destination directory.

Explanation — Your destination directory's disk drive does not have sufficient capacity to hold all migrated data.

Action — If all data is to be migrated, you will probably need a larger hard disk.

363: The server has run out of dynamic memory.

Explanation — This message is self-explanatory.

Action — See "Insufficient Server Memory Errors" on page 440 in Appendix A, "Troubleshooting."

364: The server does not have enough disk space for spool files.

Explanation — This message is self-explanatory.

Action — See "Insufficient Server Memory Errors" on page 440 in Appendix A, "Troubleshooting."

365: You cannot rename across volumes or servers.

Explanation — The Migration utility does not allow you to rename files or directories.

Action — No action is necessary. The file or directory will not be renamed.

366: The specified subdirectory is in use by another workstation.

Explanation — You cannot migrate until all users are logged off.

Action — Wait until all users are logged off; then try again.

367: The specified subdirectory is not empty.

Explanation — This message may appear if the a failure occurs while the Migration utility is copying files. This message can also appear if you attempt to delete a directory that is not empty.

Action — Try copying the files again. If the problem persists, contact your Novell Authorized Reseller.

368: The UNIX name space is not supported on the destination volume. Only the data will be copied.

Explanation: As with all name spaces, UNIX name space support must be loaded if it is to be used.

Action: Load UNIX name space support.

369: The specified volume does not exist.

Explanation: You cannot migrate to a volume that does not exist.

Action: Make sure that the volume you want to migrate to is mounted, and that you have spelled the volume's name correctly; then try again.

370: The resource fork for Macintosh directories cannot be copied.

Explanation: The source volume supports Macintosh name space, but the destination volume does not.

Action: Load Macintosh name space support on the destination server.

372: No more file handles are available on the workstation.

Explanation: The workstation has used all the file handles specified in its CONFIG.SYS file.

Action: Increase the number of file handles in the CONFIG.SYS file, reboot the workstation, and run the migration again.

373: The source directory's name space information cannot be copied to the destination volume.

Explanation: Name space information may exist on the source that will not be copied to the destination, because the destination lacks support for that name space.

Action: Load the correct name space support on the destination server.

375: The source file's name space information cannot be copied to the destination volume.

Explanation: Name space information may exist on the source that will not be copied to the destination because the destination lacks support for that name space.

Action: Load the correct name space support on the destination server.

376: The connection to the source server has been lost.

Explanation — The connection to the source server may have been lost due to one of the following:

- Heavy network traffic.
- A large number of routing links between the source server and the destination server (where the utility is running).
- The source server may be down.
- Physical connection may be broken to either the source server or the destination server.

Action — Depending on the cause of the error, stop migration and then do one of the following:

- Go back to the configuration screen and edit the "Source Server" field to reestablish the source server connection.
- Make sure that the source server is up and running.
- Check the physical network connections on the source server and the destination server.

Then retry the migration.

377: The connection to the destination server has been lost.

Explanation — The connection to the destination server may have been lost due to one of the following:

- Heavy network traffic.
- A large number of routing links between the source server and the destination server.
- The destination server may be down.
- Physical connection may be broken to either the source server or the destination server.

Action — Depending on the cause of the error, stop migration and then do one of the following:

- Go back to the configuration screen and edit the "Destination Server" field to reestablish the destination server connection.
- Make sure that the destination server is up and running.
- Check the physical network connections on the source server and the destination server.

Then retry the migration.

378: The program could not read the source file's extended attributes.

Explanation — The source file has corrupted extended attributes that cannot be read, so the file was not copied.

Action — After migration, use NCOPY to manually copy the file from the source server.

379: The program could not write an extended attribute to the destination directory.

Explanation — The program failed in its attempt to write extended attributes to a file or directory on the destination server.

Action — After migration, use NCOPY to manually copy the files or directories to the destination server.

380: The program could not read an extended attribute from the source directory.

Explanation — The program failed in its attempt to read extended attributes of a file or directory on the source server.

Action — After migration, use NCOPY to manually copy the files or directories from the source server.

381: An extended attribute could not be copied from the source server to the destination server.

Explanation — The program failed in its attempt to copy extended attributes to a file or directory on the destination server.

Action — After migration, use NCOPY to manually copy the files or directories to the destination server.

382: An error occurred while writing an extended attribute to the destination server.

Explanation — The program failed in its attempt to write extended attributes to a file or directory on the destination server.

Action — After migration, use NCOPY to manually copy the files or directories to the destination server.

383: The program could not locate an extended attribute for a file or directory on the source server.

Explanation — There are extended attributes for the source file or directory, but they could not be found.

Action — After migration, use NCOPY to manually copy the files or directories to the destination server.

400: The program could not read the number of groups in the domain.

Explanation — The program was unable to determine the number of groups to read from the LAN Server domain controller.

Action — Make sure that the workstation running the migration still has a valid connection to the LAN Server network, and that the domain controller is still running and available.

401: The program could not read the number of users in the domain.

Explanation — The program was unable to determine the number of users to read from the LAN Server domain controller.

Action — Make sure that the workstation running the migration still has a valid connection to the LAN Server network, and that the domain controller is still running and available.

402: The program could not obtain the date and time from the domain controller.

Explanation — The program was unable to access the domain controller to retrieve the date and time.

Action — Make sure that the workstation running the migration still has a valid connection to the LAN Server network, and that the domain controller is still running and available.

Also, make sure that the LAN Server object being read has not been modified or deleted by another user on the network.

405: The program could not read group information. No groups will be read from the domain controller.

Explanation A network error occurred while the program was reading group information from the domain controller of the LAN Server network.

Action Make sure that the workstation running the migration still has a valid connection to the LAN Server network, and that the domain controller is still running and available.

406: An internal error has occurred. The program could not allocate a record for the intermediate file.

Explanation Your workstation does not have enough memory.

Action See "Insufficient Workstation Memory Errors" on page 442 in Appendix A, "Troubleshooting."

407: An internal error has occurred. The program could not add a data field to a record.

Explanation Your workstation does not have enough memory.

Action See "Insufficient Workstation Memory Errors" on page 442 in Appendix A, "Troubleshooting."

408: The program could not read the number of members in a group.

Explanation The program received an error from the LAN Server network while attempting to read the number of members in a group.

Action Make sure that the workstation running the migration still has a valid connection to the LAN Server network, and that the domain controller is still running and available.

Also, make sure that the LAN Server group being read has not been modified or deleted by another user on the network.

409: The program could not read the members of a group from the domain controller.

Explanation The program received an error from the LAN Server network while reading the names of the members of a group.

Action Make sure that the workstation running the migration still has a valid connection to the LAN Server network, and that the domain controller is still running and available.

Also, make sure that the LAN Server group whose members are being read has not been modified or deleted by another user on the network.

410: The program could not read the number of aliases in the domain. No aliases will be read from the domain controller.

Explanation Most likely, the program was unable to read the number of aliases defined on the LAN Server domain controller. This can also occur while the program is reading printers.

Action Make sure that the workstation running the migration still has a valid connection to the LAN Server network, and that the domain controller is still running and available.

411: The program could not read alias information.

Explanation Most likely, the program was unable to read alias names from the LAN Server domain controller. This error can also occur while the program is reading printers.

Action Make sure that the workstation running the migration still has a valid connection to the LAN Server network, and that the domain controller is still running and available.

412: The program could not read user modal information.

Explanation The program was unable to read LAN Server user modal information (data that affects all users in the domain) from the domain controller.

Action Make sure that the workstation running the migration still has a valid connection to the LAN Server network, and that the domain controller is still running and available.

413: The program could not read user information.

Explanation — The program was unable to read the list of all usernames, or all information for an individual user.

Action — Make sure that the workstation running the migration still has a valid connection to the LAN Server network, and that the domain controller is still running and available.

Also, make sure that the LAN Server user being read has not been modified or deleted by another user on the network.

414: The program could not read printer queue information.

Explanation — The program was unable to read information about a printer from the LAN Server domain controller.

Action — Make sure that the workstation running the migration still has a valid connection to the LAN Server network, and that the domain controller is still running and available.

Also, make sure that the LAN Server printer being read has not been modified or deleted by another user on the network.

416: The program could not obtain the number of LAN Server servers in the domain.

Explanation — In order to read all access control assignments from the domain, the program needs to determine how many servers are in the domain and what their names are. An error occurred during the program's attempt to read the number of servers in the LAN Server domain.

Action — Make sure that the workstation running the migration still has a valid connection to the LAN Server network, and that the domain controller is still running and available.

417: The program could not obtain workstation information.

Explanation — The program was unable to obtain the name of the domain that the workstation is logged on to.

Action — Make sure that the workstation running the migration still has a valid connection to the LAN Server network, and that the domain controller is still running and available.

421: The program could not update the intermediate file.

Explanation — The program was unable to write migration information to the intermediate file.

Action — If the intermediate file is located on the network, make sure that the workstation still has access to the file. If the file is on the workstation's hard disk, check the integrity of the hard disk and the intermediate file (MIGRATE.GMF).

422: The program could not allocate <*number*> bytes of memory.

Explanation — Your workstation does not have enough memory.

Action — See "Insufficient Workstation Memory Errors" on page 442 in Appendix A, "Troubleshooting."

426: The program could not read the number of access control entries for a resource.

Explanation — The program was unable to obtain the number of access control records for a resource.

Action — Make sure that the workstation running the migration still has a valid connection to the LAN Server network, and that the domain controller is still running and available.

Also, make sure that the LAN Server resource whose access control is being read has not been deleted by another user on the network.

427: The program could not read access permission records for a path.

Explanation — The program was unable to obtain access control information for the named directory path.

Action — Make sure that the workstation running the migration still has a valid connection to the LAN Server network, and that the domain controller is still running and available.

428: The program could not read the size of an access control list.

Explanation — The program was unable to determine the size of buffer needed to hold access control information.

Action — Make sure that the workstation running the migration still has a valid connection to the LAN Server network, and that the domain controller is still running and available.

429: The program could not read an access control list.

Explanation The program was unable to obtain access control information for a network resource.

Action Make sure that the workstation running the migration still has a valid connection to the LAN Server network, and that the domain controller is still running and available.

430: The program could not read the names of the domain's servers.

Explanation The program was unable to obtain the names of all servers in the domain.

Action Make sure that the workstation running the migration still has a valid connection to the LAN Server network, and that the domain controller is still running and available.

431: The program could not read the list of hard drives for a server on the network.

Explanation The program was unable to read the list of hard drives available on the named server.

Action Make sure that the workstation running the migration still has a valid connection to the LAN Server network, and that the domain controller is still running and available.

Also, make sure that the named LAN Server is still functioning properly.

432: The program could not obtain the size of a buffer for holding LAN Server information.

Explanation The program was unable to determine the memory requirements for retrieving information.

Action Make sure that the workstation running the migration still has a valid connection to the LAN Server network, and that the domain controller is still running and available.

433: An internal error has occurred. The program could not extract the server name from a UNC path.

Explanation: In order to access files on the destination server, the program must convert NetWare paths so that DOS can interpret them. The naming convention that DOS understands is called the Universal Naming Convention (UNC), and has the following format:

```
\\<server>\<volume>\<directory>\<directory>
```

While attempting to obtain access control information, the program was unable to determine the server name from the given UNC path.

Action: Exit the utility and ensure the integrity of the LAN Server connection. Then retry the utility.

501: An attempt to allocate memory for writing to the intermediate file failed.

Explanation: The program has run out of memory.

Action: See "Insufficient Workstation Memory Errors" on page 442 in Appendix A, "Troubleshooting."

502: An internal error has occurred. An attempt to add a data field to a record failed.

Explanation: The program has run out of memory.

Action: See "Insufficient Workstation Memory Errors" on page 442 in Appendix A, "Troubleshooting."

503: An attempt to write to the intermediate file failed.

Explanation: The program was unable to write information to the intermediate file.

Action: If the intermediate file is located on the network, make sure that the workstation still has access to the file. If the file is on the workstation's hard disk, check the integrity of the hard disk and the intermediate file (MIGRATE.GMF).

504: An attempt to read this group's list of users from the DCDB file failed.

Explanation: The program could not read the list of users that belong to the group currently being read from the DCDB file. The DCDB file has probably been corrupted.

Action: Run the Migration utility again. If the problem persists, contact your Novell Authorized Reseller.

505: An attempt to read a group from the DCDB file failed.

Explanation: The program had trouble reading a group record from the DCDB file. The DCDB file has probably been corrupted.

Action: Run the Migration utility again. If the problem persists, contact your Novell Authorized Reseller.

506: An attempt to read this group's description from the DCDB file failed.

Explanation: The program had trouble reading the description for the group currently being read from the DCDB file. The DCDB file has probably been corrupted.

Action: Run the Migration utility again. If the problem persists, contact your Novell Authorized Reseller.

507: An attempt to read a print queue from the DCDB file failed.

Explanation: The program had trouble reading a print queue record from the DCDB file. The DCDB file has probably been corrupted.

Action: Run the Migration utility again. If the problem persists, contact your Novell Authorized Reseller.

508: An attempt to read this print queue's description from the DCDB file failed.

Explanation: The program had trouble reading the description for the print queue currently being read from the DCDB file. The DCDB file has probably been corrupted.

Action: Run the migration again. If the problem persists, contact your Novell Authorized Reseller.

509: An attempt to read a user from the DCDB file failed.

Explanation: The program had trouble reading a user record from the DCDB file. The DCDB file has probably been corrupted.

Action: Run the Migration utility again. If the problem persists, contact your Novell Authorized Reseller.

510: An attempt to read this user's description from the DCDB file failed.

Explanation: The program had trouble reading the description for the user currently being read from the DCDB file. The DCDB file has probably been corrupted.

Action: Run the Migration utility again. If the problem persists, contact your Novell Authorized Reseller.

511: An attempt to read this user's administrator privilege flag from the DCDB file failed.

Explanation: The program had trouble reading the Supervisor Equivalent Flag for the user currently being read from the DCDB file. The DCDB file has probably been corrupted.

Action: Run the Migration utility again. If the problem persists, contact your Novell Authorized Reseller.

512: An attempt to read this user's password required flag from the DCDB file failed.

Explanation: The program had trouble reading the Password Required Flag for the user currently being read from the DCDB file. The DCDB file has probably been corrupted.

Action: Run the Migration utility again. If the problem persists, contact your Novell Authorized Reseller.

513: An attempt to read this user's logon revoked flag from the DCDB file failed.

Explanation: The program had trouble reading the Logon Revoked Flag for the user currently being read from the DCDB file. The DCDB file has probably been corrupted.

Action: Run the Migration utility again. If the problem persists, contact your Novell Authorized Reseller.

514: An attempt to read an access control profile's server from the DCDB file failed.

Explanation: The program had trouble reading the server name for the access control profile currently being read from the DCDB file. The DCDB file has probably been corrupted.

Action: Run the Migration utility again. If the problem persists, contact your Novell Authorized Reseller.

515: An attempt to read an access control profile's resource name from the DCDB file failed.

Explanation: The program had trouble reading the resource name for the access control profile currently being read from the DCDB file. The DCDB file has probably been corrupted.

Action: Run the Migration utility again. If the problem persists, contact your Novell Authorized Reseller.

516: An attempt to read an access control profile's user entry from the DCDB file failed.

Explanation: The program had trouble reading the user entry list for the access control profile currently being read from the DCDB file. The DCDB file has probably been corrupted.

Action: Run the Migration utility again. If the problem persists, contact your Novell Authorized Reseller.

517: An attempt to read this user's server from the DCDB file failed.

Explanation: The program had trouble reading the user's server from the DCDB file. The DCDB file has probably been corrupted.

Action: Run the Migration utility again. If the problem persists, contact your Novell Authorized Reseller.

518: An attempt to read this printer's server from the DCDB file failed.

Explanation: The program had trouble reading the printer's server from the DCDB file. The DCDB file has probably been corrupted.

Action: Run the Migration utility again. If the problem persists, contact your Novell Authorized Reseller.

appendix

A Troubleshooting

General Hardware and Network Troubleshooting

Hardware Errors

To resolve hardware errors on a dedicated file server, try the following troubleshooting suggestions. Before you begin, notify users that they may lose data, and do a complete system backup if possible. Then try to reboot the server.

Check all newly installed hardware

- If new hardware has been recently installed in the file server, remove the hardware.
- If the error does not reoccur, run diagnostics on the removed hardware. Check for conflicts (interrupts, memory addresses, I/O ports, DMA) between the hardware in the computer and the new hardware.

Check all cabling

- Be sure cable segments are properly terminated on both ends. One end should have a grounded terminator. (If you are using an Ethernet board, do not use a grounded terminator on both ends.)
- Check for cable breaks. Use a Time Delay Reflectometer (TDR), a LANalyzer, or a Volt-Ohm Meter (VOM) to test cabling for breaks in the cable conductor or shield.

- Test terminators and inline cable connectors with a VOM. If you are not sure whether a terminator or connector is working properly, replace it with one you are sure of. If the new components work properly, discard the old ones.

- Make sure that your cable segment lengths do not exceed those recommended for the topology you are using (such as Ethernet).

- Make sure that cabling is routed away from flourescent lights, microwaves, radar, X rays, and copy machines.

Check your power supply

See "Power Supply Errors" on page 437.

Run LAN diagnostic tools

Check the system board, memory board, memory chips, and hard disk. The following tools provide LAN diagnostic capabilities:

- LANalyzer

- MONITOR.NLM

- Manufacturer's diagnostic programs

Make sure configuration settings and network addresses are correct

- Create a binder in which you list all workstation and server configuration settings. Include a printout of all current configuration files in this binder.

- Maintain an error log recording all previous errors and problems experienced by the servers and workstations on the network. Also get a screen dump when errors occur, whenever possible.

- Make sure that the servers and workstations are using the same packet frame type (such as Ethernet II).

- Make sure that each node address is unique and that all network addresses are the same.
- Make sure that each network segment has a unique network address.

Power Supply Errors

An inconsistent power source is the most common cause of hardware problems. It also produces the most devastating results.

Power outages cause workstations, file servers, print servers, and backup devices to reboot. When this happens, all information stored in RAM is lost, and sometimes hardware is damaged.

Power spikes and "brownouts" also can cause a variety of hardware errors.

You can have reliable network performance only if you plan for power outages and fluctuations, and protect against them. The following tips can help you do this:

- Add a dedicated power feed and ground line from your breaker box to critical equipment. Make sure that the ground line connects to earth ground.
- Install an uninterruptible power supply (UPS) or a standby power system (SPS) to provide power to critical equipment for 15 minutes after a power outage. The capacity of such power supplies is limited, so you may not want to plug nonvital hardware (such as monitors) into the UPS or SPS line.
- Train users to save data and log out of the network when the lights go out. Then you can bring down the file server in an orderly fashion without forcing users off the system while the server is running on UPS or SPS power.
- Install a surge suppressor or power conditioner on all power lines that are used by computers. Many UPS and SPS devices already have this feature.

- Do not allow anyone to plug fans, printers, copy machines, or other motor-driven appliances into the dedicated line or into any power line with computers. Insert dummy plugs into open outlets to prevent people from plugging such appliances as vacuum cleaners into computer power sources.

Server Troubleshooting

General Disk I/O Errors

To resolve a general disk I/O error, try one or more of the following remedies:

- Check the disk subsystems to make certain power is on and the cables are correctly connected between the controller and the subsystems.
- Make sure that the subsystem cables are terminated correctly.
- Make sure that the disks are installed correctly.
- Make sure that you have a current v3.12-certified driver loaded for the disk device or devices. Many drivers can be found on the NetWare CD-ROM or on the master diskettes.
- Make sure that the interrupt parameters, I/O port settings, slot settings, etc. for the driver match those for the hardware. Also, make sure custom parameters have been set correctly for your hardware.
- At the server console, type "scan for new devices." This causes the operating system to request controller information about all devices.
- Load INSTALL, selecting "Selective Install/Maintain," "Disk Options," and then "Modify Disk Partitions and Hot Fix." Make sure that the device is visible and has a valid partition.

- Increase the Hot Fix redirection area using INSTALL.NLM. To change the Hot Fix on a drive, back up all the data on the partition, delete the volumes on the partition, and delete the partition; then re-create it. Assign the partition a different percentage to Hot Fix; then re-create the volumes and restore the data.

If you have tried all the above without success, contact your Novell Authorized Reseller or hard disk manufacturer.

Insufficient Disk Space Errors

To resolve an insufficient disk space error, do one or more of the following:

- Delete unnecessary files from the volume.
- Change the SET server utility's "File Delete Wait Time" parameter so that files can be purged immediately, rather than being retained in a salvageable state on the volume.
- Use FILER to purge deleted files if they cannot be purged automatically. (They are using up directory table space.)
- Delete NLMs you no longer use.
- Increase the size of the volume.
- Add more disks to the volume.
- Delete files or increase the percent of disk space that can be used by a directory. For more information, see "Memory Maintenance" in *System Administration* and "SET?" in *Utilities Reference*.
- If the disk or volume has space available, check the disk drives and channel to see if a failure has occurred.

Insufficient Server Memory Errors

To resolve an insufficient memory error, you should, if possible, add more memory to the server. To free up memory temporarily, do one or more of the following:

- Delete unused files and directories on the specified volume.
- Change the SET server utility's "Minimum File Delete Wait Time" parameter so that files can be purged immediately, rather than being retained in a salvageable state on the volume.
- Use FILER to purge deleted files on the specified directory that cannot be purged automatically. (They are using up directory table space.)
- Use REMOVE DOS or SECURE CONSOLE to free the memory in the server that has been reserved for DOS.
- Unload some loadable modules, such as INSTALL or MONITOR, that are not currently needed.
- Dismount any volumes that are not being used.

For more information, see "Memory Maintenance" in *System Administration*.

Locked Device Errors

To resolve a locked device error, try one or more of the following actions:

- Wait for a while. The task in process may reach completion and free the device.
- Retry the action that resulted in the error.
- Load MONITOR, delete all user connections, and disable logins.
- Unload other NLMs that may be using the disk. Dismount all volumes on this disk.

If you have tried all of the above without success, contact your Novell Authorized Reseller or the hard disk manufacturer.

File I/O Errors

To resolve a file I/O error, try one or more of the following actions:

- Check to see that the volume is mounted (especially volume SYS:). You may do this by switching to the system console and typing "VOLUMES."
- If the volume is out of disk space, error messages will have appeared on the console screen, indicating that the volume is almost out of disk space. Check the console screen.
- Type "DIR" from a DOS workstation to see how much space remains.

To increase the amount of free space, do one or more of the following:

- Delete extraneous files (if you can log in from a workstation).
- Type "SET IMMEDIATE PURGE OF DELETED FILES= ON" from the console and retry the action.
- If you have an additional disk, increase the size of the volume by creating an additional segment of the volume on the disk.
- See "Volume I/O Errors."

Volume I/O Errors

To resolve a volume I/O error, try one or more of the following actions:

- See "General Disk I/O Errors" and make sure that *all* devices that contain the volume are online. (Volumes may span multiple devices.)
- Load and execute VREPAIR.

- Load INSTALL and select "Volume Options." Make sure that the volume is visible.

If you have tried all of the above without success, contact your Novell Authorized Reseller or the hard disk manufacturer.

Workstation Troubleshooting

Insufficient Workstation Memory Errors

To resolve an insufficient workstation memory error, you should, if possible, add more memory. To free up memory temporarily, do one or more of the following:

- Unload any unneeded TSR (terminate-and-stay-resident) programs.
- Optimize memory usage by loading DOS and other programs into high memory.
- Modify the CONFIG.SYS file to reduce the number of files that can be open at the same time, the number of buffers allocated for disk drives, and the memory size allocated by the shell for your DOS environment (the /E option).

  The following settings are sufficient for normal workstation operation, but the values can be reduced further until problems occur:

  ```
  FILES=20
  BUFFERS=20
  SHELL=C:\COMMAND.COM /E:640 /P
  ```

  Be sure to reboot your machine after modifying the CONFIG.SYS file.

appendix **B** *Error Codes*

Error Codes in NetWare v3.12

Table 2-1
Error Code Table

Decimal	Hex	Description
000	00h	Server not in use.
000	00h	Shell version too old.
000	00h	TTS not available.
001	01h	Semaphore overflow.
001	01h	Server in use.
001	01h	TTS available.
128	80h	File in use error.
129	81h	No more file handles.
130	82h	No open privileges.
131	83h	I/O error on network disk.
132	84h	No create privileges.
133	85h	No create or delete privileges.
134	86h	Create file exists read-only.
135	87h	Wildcards in create file name.
136	88h	Invalid file handle.
137	89h	No search privileges.

Table 2-1 *continued*

Error Code Table

Decimal	Hex	Description
138	8Ah	No delete privileges.
139	8Bh	No rename privileges.
140	8Ch	No modify privileges.
141	8Dh	Some files affected in use.
142	8Eh	No files affected in use.
143	8Fh	Some files affected read-only.
144	90h	No files affected read-only.
145	91h	Some files renamed name exists.
146	92h	No files renamed name exists.
147	93h	No read privileges.
148	94h	No write privileges or read-only.
149	95h	File detached.
150	96h	Server out of memory.
151	97h	No disk space for spool file.
152	98h	Volume does not exist.
153	99h	Directory full.
154	9Ah	Renaming across volumes.
155	9Bh	Bad directory handle.
156	9Ch	Invalid path.
156	9Ch	No more trustees.
157	9Dh	No more directory handles.
158	9Eh	Invalid filename.
159	9Fh	Directory active.

Table 2-1 *continued*
Error Code Table

Decimal	Hex	Description
160	A0h	Directory not emtpy.
161	A1h	Directory I/O error.
162	A2h	Attempt to read file with record locked.
176	B0h	Search drive vector full.
177	B1h	Drive is not mapped.
178	B2h	Can't map local drive.
179	B3h	Invalid map type.
180	B4h	Invalid drive letter.
181	B5h	No drive available.
182	B6h	Workstation out of memory.
183	B7h	No such search drive.
184	B8h	Path environment variable invalid.
192	C0h	No account privileges.
193	C1h	Login denied. No account balance.
193	C1h	No account balance.
194	C2h	Account credit limit exceeded.
194	C2h	Login denied. No credit.
195	C3h	Account too many holds.
197	C5h	Intruder detection lock.
198	C6h	No console operator.
208	D0h	Queue error.
209	D1h	No queue.
210	D2h	No queue server.

Table 2-1 *continued*
Error Code Table

Decimal	Hex	Description
211	D3h	No queue rights.
212	D4h	Queue full.
213	D5h	No queue job.
214	D6h	No job rights.
215	D7h	Password not unique.
215	D7h	Queue servicing.
216	D8h	Password too short.
216	D8h	Queue not active.
217	D9h	Login denied. No connection.
217	D9h	Station not server.
218	DAh	Unauthorized login time.
218	DAh	Queue halted.
219	DBh	Unauthorized login station.
219	DBh	Max queue servers.
220	DCh	Account disabled.
222	DEh	Password has expired. No grace logins remaining.
223	DFh	Password has expired.
232	E8h	Not item property.
232	E8h	Write property to group.
233	E9h	Member already exists.
234	EAh	No such member.
235	EBh	Not group property.
236	ECh	No such segment.

Table 2-1 *continued*
Error Code Table

Decimal	Hex	Description
237	EDh	Property already exists.
238	EEh	Object already exists.
239	EFh	Invalid name.
240	F0h	Wildcard not allowed.
240	F0h	IPX not installed.
241	F1h	Invalid bindery security.
242	F2h	No object read privilege.
243	F3h	No object rename privilege.
244	F4h	No object delete privilege.
245	F5h	No object create privilege.
246	F6h	No property delete privilege.
246	F6h	Not same local drive.
247	F7h	No property create privilege.
247	F7h	Target drive not local.
248	F8h	Already attached to server.
248	F8h	No property write privilege.
248	F8h	Not attached to server.
249	F9h	No free connection slots.
249	F9h	No property read privilege.
250	FAh	No more server slots.
250	FAh	Temporary remap error.
251	FAh	Invalid parameters
251	FAh	No such property.

Table 2-1 *continued*
Error Code Table

Decimal	Hex	Description
251	FAh	Unknown request.
252	FCh	Internet packet request canceled.
252	FCh	Unknown file server.
252	FCh	Message queue full.
252	FCh	No such object.
253	FDh	Bad station number.
253	FDh	Invalid packet length.
253	FDh	Unknown request.
253	FDh	Field already locked.
253	FDh	TTS disabled.
253	FDh	File server copy different networks.
254	FEh	Bindery locked.
254	FEh	Directory locked.
254	FEh	Invalid semaphore name length.
254	FEh	Implicit transaction active.
254	FEh	Packet not deliverable.
254	FEh	Server bindery locked.
254	FEh	Socket table full.
254	FEh	Spool directory error.
254	FEh	Supervisor has disabled login.
254	FEh	Timeout failure.
254	FEh	Transaction ends with records locked.
255	FFh	Bad printer error.

Table 2-1 *continued*
Error Code Table

Decimal	Hex	Description
255	FFh	Bad record offset.
255	FFh	Bindery failure.
255	FFh	Close FCB error.
255	FFh	Explicit transaction active.
255	FFh	Explicit transaction not active.
255	FFh	File extension error.
255	FFh	Filename error.
255	FFh	Hardware failure.
255	FFh	Invalid drive number.
255	FFh	Invalid initial semaphore value.
255	FFh	Invalid semaphore handle.
255	FFh	I/O bound error.
255	FFh	No files found error.
255	FFh	No record found.
255	FFh	No response from server.
255	FFh	No such object or bad password.
255	FFh	Path already exists.
255	FFh	Path not locatable.
255	FFh	Queue full error.
255	FFh	Request not outstanding.
255	FFh	Socket already open.
255	FFh	Socket closed.
255	FFh	Transaction not yet written.

Table 2-1 *continued*
Error Code Table

Decimal	Hex	Description
257	0101h	Invalid connection ID.
2989	0BADh	Unexpected internal condition.
65535	FFFFh	Environment overflow.
65535	FFFFh	No such environment variable.

Trademarks

Novell, Inc. has made every effort to supply trademark information about company names, products, and services mentioned in this manual. The following list of trademarks was derived from various sources.

Novell, NetWare, and the N design are registered trademarks of Novell, Inc.

Certified NetWare Administrator and CNA are collective marks of Novell, Inc.

Certified NetWare Engineer and CNE are collective marks of Novell, Inc.

Certified NetWare Instructor and CNI are collective marks of Novell, Inc.

CompuServe is a registered trademark of CompuServe, Inc.

DR DOS is a registered trademark of Novell, Inc.

ElectroText is a trademark of Novell, Inc.

Hot Fix is a trademark of Novell, Inc.

IBM is a registered trademark of International Business Machines Corporation.

IBM Operating System/2 Local Area Network Server (LAN Server) is a trademark of International Business Machines Corporation.

Internetwork Packet Exchange (IPX) is a trademark of Novell, Inc.

LANalyzer is a registered trademark of Novell, Inc.

Link Support Layer and LSL are trademarks of Novell, Inc.

Macintosh is a registered trademark of Apple Computer, Inc.

Microsoft is a registered trademark of Microsoft Corporation

MS-DOS is a registered trademark of Microsoft Corporation.

Multiple Link Interface Driver and MLID are trademarks of Novell, Inc.

NE/2 is a trademark of Novell, Inc.

NE/2-32 is a trademark of Novell, Inc.

NE1000 is a trademark of Novell, Inc.

NE2000 is a trademark of Novell, Inc.

NetWare Core Protocol and NCP are trademarks of Novell, Inc.

NetWare DOS Requester and NDR are trademarks of Novell, Inc.

NetWare Loadable Module and NLM are trademarks of Novell, Inc.

NetWare Requester is a trademark of Novell, Inc.

Netware Support Encyclopedia is a trademark of Novell, Inc.

NetWire is a service mark of Novell, Inc.

Novell Authorized Reseller is a collective mark of Novell, Inc.

Novell Press is a trademark of Novell, Inc.

Open Data-Link Interface and ODI are trademarks of Novell, Inc.

OS/2 is a registered trademark of International Business Machines Corp.

Packet Burst is a trademark of Novell, Inc.

PS/2 is a registered trademark of International Business Machines Corporation.

Transactional Tracking System and TTS are trademarks of Novell, Inc.

Target Service Agent (TSA) is a trademark of Novell, Inc.

UNIX is a registered trademark of UNIX System Laboratories, Inc.

Virtual Loadable Module and VLM are trademarks of Novell, Inc.

User Comments

Novell would like to hear your comments and suggestions about our manuals. Please write your comments below and send them to us at:

Novell, Inc
Technical Publications
MS C-23-1
122 East 1700 South
Provo, UT 84606
USA

Fax: (801) 429-3002

NetWare v3.12
System Messages
Part # 100-001716-001
July 1993

For technical support issues, contact your local dealer.

Your name and title: ______________________________

Company: ______________________________

Address: ______________________________

____

____

Phone number: ______________________ Fax: ______________________

I use this manual as: ❑ an overview ❑ a tutorial ❑ a reference ❑ a guide ❑ __________

	Excellent	Good	Fair	Poor
Completeness	❑	❑	❑	❑
Readability (style)	❑	❑	❑	❑
Organization/Format	❑	❑	❑	❑
Accuracy	❑	❑	❑	❑
Examples	❑	❑	❑	❑
Illustrations	❑	❑	❑	❑
Usefulness	❑	❑	❑	❑

Please explain any of your above ratings: ______________________________

____

____

____

____

In what ways can this manual be improved? ______________________________

____

____

____

____

You may photocopy this comment page as needed so that others can send in comments also.